PRIVATE SCHOOLS AND THE PUBLIC GOOD

Policy Alternatives for the Eighties

EDWARD McGLYNN GAFFNEY, JR., EDITOR

UNIVERSITY OF NOTRE DAME PRESS
NOTRE DAME   LONDON

Library of Congress Cataloging in Publication Data

Main entry under title:

Private schools and the public good.

Papers presented at a conference held in
Washington, D.C., July 1980.
   1. Private schools — United States — Congresses.
I. Gaffney, Edward McGlynn.
LC49.P74   371'.02'0973   81-7608
ISBN 0-268-01544-9
ISBN 0-268-01545-7 (pbk.)

Contents

PART THREE: CONSTITUTIONAL PERSPECTIVES

Foreword

In July of 1980 in Washington, D.C., the Institute of Public Policy of the University of Notre Dame sponsored a symposium for the purpose of exploring extensively some of the major problems facing nonpublic elementary and secondary education. Recognizing that controversy abounds concerning this highly significant problem in public policy, we attempted to structure the symposium and this volume of essays which emerged from the symposium in such a way as to bring out many facets of this problem as well as to hear from many differing voices.

It is intended that this volume, and the conference which generated it, are to be the first in a series of such discussions and publications under the sponsorship of our Institute. It is our conviction that in an age of very rapidly accelerating change in our social and economic institutions, when government is challenged to alter and adapt its attitudes and programs to deal with radically new problems and new realities, that the institutions of higher education in America (including, specifically, the University of Notre Dame) have a unique opportunity as well as a responsibility, to provide an appropriate forum for the thoughtful and dispassionate discussion of public issues by academicians, practitioners, and policy makers.

We do so for several reasons. First, we believe that policy makers, confronted as they are with a seeming avalanche of complex new problems, would find it useful to have access to the written record of an open, balanced and authoritative discussion of such problems, free of the special pleading and the biased attitudes which presently characterize so much of the dialogue between the public and private sector.

Second, public officials are frequently so immersed in the relentless routine of the governmental process, and are so often compelled to spend their time and energies in crisis management, that they do not often have the opportunity to consider the long range consequences of the decisions which they are forced to make on a daily or hourly basis. Academicians, on the other hand, have the time and resources available for research and for creative thought, but too frequently have no way to cross-communicate effectively with those in government. And thus the larger society is needlessly deprived of an important resource.

Finally, we are convinced that university students, at the undergraduate and graduate level, need the opportunity occasionally to break out of the routine of the lecture hall and the library and to experience at first hand the processes through which public policy is made in a free and democratic society. We even dare to hope that such experiences may lead these students to devote after graduation some reasonable measure of their learning and their talents to the service of the larger community. Those were essentially the reasons for establishing the Institute of Public Policy at Notre Dame, with its three constituent elements: the Center for Civil and Human Rights, the Center for Constitutional Studies, and the White Center of Law and Public Policy.

Our reasons for choosing the topic, "Private Schools and the Public Good: Policy Alternatives for the Eighties," for our first venture stem from a growing concern both about the quality of education in the United States today and about the availability of a good education for all American children, without regard to race, national origin, creed, sex, handicap, family income, or geographic location. My own experiences as Governor of Ohio in the early Seventies, in a state which had its fair share of all of the problems afflicting education today, convinced me that there were two major impediments to dealing successfully with our educational problems. First, there was the propensity of those in government to think in terms of an educational situation which had passed into oblivion 15 or 20 years earlier. In other words, they tended to think in terms that no longer applied to the current situation, and to deal with the problems of an earlier period rather than those of the present or the future.

Second, and even more threatening to any hope of finding a solution to the problems of the Eighties and Nineties in the field of education, was the evident instinct of educators and educational administrators--perhaps understandable in the light of what appeared to be dwindling moral and financial support for education--to divide the educational universe into separate and rival domains and duchies: public schools against private; academic programs versus vocational training; suburbs against central cities; underprivileged children versus the affluent; minorities against majority. That tendency seemed to me then, and seems to me now, to accomplish nothing in terms of advancing the interests of one sector of education in relation to others, but rather to provide ammunition to those who were seeking any and every rationale for curtailing support to education as a whole. Participants in this kind of fratricidal strife were--and are--thus inflicting serious damage on the very enterprise they profess to defend and serve.

Therefore, in this conference and in this volume, we have attempted to provide the opportunity for thoughtful and experienced people to explore freely some of the problems which seriously affect the ability of this nation to provide to all of our young people and all of our children an equal opportunity for genuine human development. Such development is possible only through the benefits of an educational experience which not only transmits the rudimentary intellectual skills required for full participation in our economy and society, but also preserves the fullness of our cultural heritage in all its pluralism and diversity.

We are both reassured and encouraged by the evident quality of the thought and the expression of all those who participated in this first effort, to whom we are profoundly grateful. We are, as well, beholden to Thomas J. and Alberta V. White of St. Louis, whose generous benefactions have supported the activities of the White Center of Law and Public Policy, and have made possible this conference and publication. And we look forward with confidence to the extension of this series of public discussions of public policy.

John J. Gilligan
Chairman
Institute of Public Policy
University of Notre Dame

Preface

Over five million students (11 percent) attend the nation's 20,000 private schools and are taught by a body of dedicated teachers who constitute more than 17 percent of the national total. With the Education Amendments of 1978, Congress created the position of Deputy Commissioner for Nonpublic Education in the Department of Health, Education and Welfare's Office of Education to represent these students and teachers. I was privileged to serve in that post and, subsequently, as Assistant Secretary for Nonpublic Education when the Department of Education was created in May 1980.

The creation of the Department of Education took us from the difficult decade of the Seventies--indeed a bleak ten years for private education, marked by unfavorable court decisions, financial problems, school closings and low morale. In a five year period from 1968 to 1972 private school enrollments decreased by nearly 16 percent. Now, as we begin the Eighties, we can look with optimism to what may be private education's "finest hour."

The issues addressed in this volume have a historical progenitor in the Elementary and Secondary Education Act of 1965, the first piece of federal legislation to provide meaningful and comprehensive educational aid for children. As we wrestle with educational policy alternatives for the 1980s, we should recall that in 1965 Congress made this assistance available to all children in all schools. The genius of the ESEA was that it targeted aid for disadvantaged children, for library development, and for innovation in curriculum development and teaching methods--all national priorities.

One of the basic problems in discussing private elementary and secondary education in the United States in 1980 is the broad spectrum of schools that are included within a descriptive definition, "parochial." This familiar designation describes an historic commitment primarily on the part of two religious bodies, Roman Catholics and Lutherans, to fund and to operate schools as part of their parishes structure. Other private schools are affiliated with religious groups such as Seventh-Day Adventist, Hebrew Day schools, Dutch Reformed (Christian Schools International), Friends and Episcopal. Still other schools provide an alternative to governmentally controlled education without formal affiliation with a religious body, such as Independent schools, Montessori, schools for exceptional children, military and alternative schools.

What also makes this discussion difficult is the recurrent criticism leveled against private education in the United States that it is elitist and racist. The essays of Fr. Greeley and of Fr. Blum in this volume address that charge and ably repute it. The authors point out that over the past decade the minority population in private education has increased significantly. Minority enrollment is 16.5 percent of the total in Catholic schools; 13 percent in Lutheran schools; and 8.6 percent in Independent schools. In inner-city nonpublic schools, minority children are performing well; both they and their parents are satisfied with these schools and are willing to sacrifice in order to attend them. If tempted to look for scapegoats, one might reflect on Dr. Vitullo-Martin's argument that federal policies actually have the effect of discouraging the racial and economic integration of private schools.

It is time we came to grips with the fallacy that public and private schools are dichotomous in the education of America's young. We should begin to speak of these schools in terms of a partnership in which people from different backgrounds and persuasions work for a common goal, the education of future generations. This perspective is more fruitful than endless debates about money and jobs and constitutional prohibitions. It would enable educators from private and public schools to sit down, not as adversaries, but as colleagues willing to learn how they can benefit from each other's experience. The contributions of Dr. Reed, Mrs. Taylor and Mr. Weintraub are good beginnings in this direction. To enter into this discussion in a spirit of mutual respect, however, is but the first step in an essential dialogue concerning the alternatives in educational policy in this decade. It is appropriate that this volume presents not only Mr. Doyle's useful overview of the state of current research on alternative mechanisms of funding education, but also a careful consideration of a number of these proposals by distinguished political leaders like Senators Moynihan and Hollings, and by Dr. Olivas and law professors Coons and Sugarman.

At conferences like the one reported in this volume, the constitutional perspective is a recurrent theme. The case can be made that there is some coherent constitutional doctrine differentiating between permissible programs (such as the transportation of children to school and the provision of mandated services) and arguably impermissible programs (such as tuition tax credits and federal scholarships for children from low-income familes, also known as "baby BEOG's"). Mr. Hammond makes that case in this volume and states the position of the Justice Department in the Carter Administration. It should not be surprising, however, to learn that constitutional scholars are not of one mind on this area of the Supreme Court's work. Professor Scalia, the Justice Department's constitutional lawyer in the Ford Administration, makes the case that the Court's decisions on aid to religiously affiliated education are in a state of "utter chaos and unpredictable change." Litigation on this theme, of course, proceeds on the basis of sharp differences of perceptions of reality, as the comments of Mr. Dershowitz and Mr. Wilson make clear. It is helpful, however, to be reminded by a distinguished constitutional historian like Professor Berns that the Founding Fathers cannot be invoked in favor of the proposition that public support for church-related schools is a genuine problem of constitutional stature. It is, rather, a political question for policy makers.

In Washington in May 1980, at ceremonies commemorating the "birth" of the Department of Education, the Brookings Institution held a seminar at which one of the panelists stated that he believed that aid to private education in the 1980's would be "inevitable." I have no way of knowing what form that aid will take, whether tax credit or deductions, whether grants or loans, or vouchers (and if vouchers, what kind). But I strongly agree that aid to private education would be for the public good and that some form of aid is inevitable if educational pluralism is to be maintained and justice is to be served.

I hope that in future debates on these issues, the essays gathered in this volume will help both to sharpen our perception of the real contribution made to education by nonpublic schools and to foster a sense of partnership among all educators, both public and private, as we work together for our common goal, the education of all of America's children. The accomplishments of private education toward achieving this public goal should be a source of pride to every American.

Edward R. D'Alessio
Executive Vice President
Seton Hall University

Contributors

WALTER BERNS is a Resident Scholar at the American Enterprise Institute for Public Policy Research, Washington, D.C. He is the author of The First Amendment and the Future of American Democracy (Basic Books, 1976), and For Capital Punishment: Crime and the Morality of the Death Penalty (Basic Books, 1979).

VIRGIL C. BLUM, S.J., is the President of the Catholic League for Religious and Civil Rights, Milwaukee, Wisconsin. He is the author of Freedom of Choice in Education (Macmillan, 1958), of Freedom in Education: Federal Aid for All Children (Doubleday, 1965), and of numerous articles concerning nonpublic education.

JOHN E. COONS is a Professor of Law at the University of California at Berkeley School of Law (Boalt Hall). His book, Private Wealth and Public Education (Harvard University Press, 1970) (with William Clune III and Stephen Sugarman) provided the rationale for the Serrano case that initiated the reform of public school financing in the 1970's. With Sugarman, he also wrote Education by Choice: The Case for Family Control (University of California Press, 1978), which provides the rationale for their movement in California for the adoption of an initiative that would provide educational vouchers. Coons is best known for his lilting tenor voice.

EDWARD R. D'ALESSIO is the Executive Vice President of Seton Hall University. He served as Deputy Commissioner for Nonpublic Education in the U.S. Office of Education (HEW) and as the first Assistant Secretary for Nonpublic Education in the newly created Department of Educaton. He also served as Director of the Division of Elementary and Secondary Education of the United States Catholic Conference.

NATHAN Z. DERSHOWITZ is the Director of the Commission on Law and Social Action of the American Jewish Congress. He was a Special Professor at the Hofstra University Law School and has had extensive experience in litigation involving First Amendment issues.

DENIS P. DOYLE is the Director of Planning and Program Coordination, Office of the Assistant Secretary for Educational Research and Improvement, U.S. Department of Education. He has contributed an essay to the volume Parents, Teachers, and Children (Institute for Contemporary Studies, 1977) and has written numerous articles on educational policy for such journals as The New Republic, the Washington Star, the Los Angeles Times, and the London Times Educational Supplement.

EDWARD McGLYNN GAFFNEY, is the Director of the Center for Constitutional Studies and an Associate Professor of Law at Notre Dame Law School. He is the co-author, with Philip R. Moots, of Church and Campus: Legal Issues in Religiously Affiliated Higher Education (University of Notre Dame Press, 1979) and of The Government and the Campus: Federal Regulation of Religiously Affiliated Higher Education (University of Notre Dame Press, 1981).

JOHN J. GILLIGAN is the Chairman of the Institute of Public Policy and holds the Thomas J. and Alberta White Chair at the Notre Dame Law School. He has served as a member of the City Council of Cincinnati, as a member of the Congress of the United States, as Governor of Ohio, and as Director of the Agency for International Development in the U.S. State Department.

ANDREW M. GREELEY is a Senior Study Director in the National Opinion Research Center at the University of Chicago and a Professor of Sociology at the University of Arizona. He is a prolific author whose works include The Education of Catholic Americans (NORC, 1966) (with Peter H. Rossi) and Catholic Scholars in a Declining Church (Sheed and Ward, 1976) (with William C. McCready and Kathleen McCourt).

LARRY A. HAMMOND is a partner in the law firm of Martori, Meyer, Hendricks and Victor in Phoenix, Arizona. He served as Deputy Assistant Attorney General for the Office of Legal Counsel, U.S. Department of Justice, during the Carter Administration.

ERNEST F. HOLLINGS is the junior Senator from South Carolina. He has served in both houses of the legislature of that state, and as its Lieutenant Governor and Governor. He was an early advocate of a single system of public schools in his state to replace the dual system based on race.

ABNER J. MIKVA is a Circuit Judge in the United States Court of Appeals for the District of Columbia Circuit. As a member of Congress from Evanston, Illinois, he served on the House Ways and Means Committee and introduced legislation that would have deferred the payment of federal income tax by taxpayers who finance the education of their children in nonpublic schools.

DANIEL PATRICK MOYNIHAN is the senior Senator from New York. He has served as a cabinet or subcabinet officer to Presidents Kennedy, Johnson, Nixon, and Ford. He is the author of Counting Our Blessings: Reflections on the Future of America (Atlantic-Little, Brown, 1980), and has with Senator Bob Packwood co-authored legislation that would provide an income tax credit to taxpayers who incur educational expenses. He has also introduced legislation that would extend the Basic Educational Opportunity Grant (BEOG) program to elementary and secondary education.

MICHAEL A. OLIVAS is the Director of Research for the National Educational Service Centers, Inc., of the League of United Latin American Citizens. He is the author of The Dilemma of Access (Howard University Press, 1979) and the co-author, with George Brown, Nan Rosen, and Susan Hill, of The Condition of Education for Hispanic Americans (National Center for Education Statistics, 1980).

VINCENT E. REED is the Assistant Secretary for Elementary and Secondary Education in the U.S. Department of Education. He served for six years as Superintendent of Schools in the District of Columbia, and has served as well on the Board of Trustees of Cathedral School and St. Alban's School, private schools in the District.

ANTONIN SCALIA is a Professor of Law at the University of Chicago Law School. He served as the Assistant Attorney General for the Office of Legal Counsel, U.S. Department of Justice, during the Ford Administration.

STEPHEN D. SUGARMAN is a Professor of Law and Assistant Dean at the University of California at Berkeley School of Law (Boalt Hall). His book, Private Wealth and Public Education (Harvard University Press, 1970) (with William Clune III and John E. Coons) provided the rationale for the Serrano case that initiated the reform of public school financing in the 1970's. With Coons, he also wrote Education by Choice: The Case for Family Control (University of California Press, 1978).

BARBARA R. TAYLOR is the principal of St. Thomas Community School in New York City. In 1979 the Coalition to Improve Harlem named her Mother of the Year. She served for over a decade in the public schools of Philadelphia as a teacher, math coordinator, and reading specialist. She also served as a volunteer coordinator of childrens' cultural programs and as a volunteer teacher of dance in Philadelphia, and still enjoys teaching dance as part of her present responsibilities.

THOMAS VITULLO-MARTIN is the Director of Research at Metro-
nomy, Inc., a non-profit research and consulting firm in New
York City concerned with the economic development of cities.
He is the author of <u>Catholic Inner-City Schools: The Future</u>
(USCC, 1979), and of numerous articles on private schools.

FREDERICK J. WEINTRAUB is the Assistant Executive Director for
Governmental Relations of the Council for Exceptional
Children, in Reston, Virginia. With Alan Abeson, Joseph
Ballard, and Martin La Vor, he is the co-author of <u>Public Policy
and the Education of Exceptional Children</u> (CEC, 1976). His
responsibilities at CEC include monitoring the many federal,
state, and local policies that affect the education of
handicapped children, as well as offering the technical
assistance of the Council in the coordination and implementation of those programs.

CHARLES H. WILSON is a partner in the law firm of Williams and
Connolly in Washington, D.C. He served for two years as an
adjunct Professor of Law at the Georgetown University Law
Center, and has had extensive experience in litigation involving
First Amendment issues.

J. SKELLY WRIGHT is the Chief Judge of the United States Court of
Appeals for the District of Columbia Circuit. As a member of
that court since 1962, he has authored several opinions in cases
involving the religion clauses of the First Amendment.

Editorial Overview:
The Public Good of Private Schools
Edward McGlynn Gaffney, Jr.

In The Great School Wars: New York City, 1805-1973, Professor Diane Ravitch of the Teacher's College has described the public schools of New York City as a "battlefield of social change."[1] Her account of the history of schools in New York describes four wars on this peculiar battlefield. The first school war was the early nineteenth century struggle over religion in the public schools. The outcome of this war was the establishment of nonsectarian Protestantism in the public schools and the determination that the more sectarian Catholics should form their own independent parochial schools without public support.[2]

The second school war recounted by Ravitch describes the impact of reform movements in New York that arose in the 1880s and 1890s to respond to the needs of the new immigrants of those decades, largely Jewish and Italian. The focus here is on the rise of professional experts who could assist the Board of Education in evaluating criticism of the "sterile curriculum" and "mechanical methods" of the schools in the late nineteenth century and in divising a new education for the new immigrants.

The third school war, termed by Ravitch a "crusade for efficiency," turned on efforts to divest Tammany Hall of its political control of the school board. Having fought Tammany for decades over issues of efficiency, economy, and honesty, the political reformers of New York could sooner or later be expected to criticize the heavy expenditures of the school system under Tammany rule. As Ravitch puts it:

> [T]hey held that better services could be rendered by intelligent, honest, nonpartisan officials at less cost to the taxpayers. These reformers were appalled that the schools, with more than 20,000 employees, consumed more than 20 percent of the municipal budget without apparent success in their role. They were sure that so large and expensive an operation, while not necessarily corrupt, harbored waste and inefficiency.[3]

The fourth school war described by Ravitch was waged over the presence of racism in New York's public schools. This struggle was triggered at a National Urban League symposium weeks after the Supreme Court's decision in Brown v. Board of Education; at this symposium Dr. Kenneth Clark "charged that the New York City school system was maintaining segregated schools where Negro children received inferior education."[4] According to Ravitch, the discovery of de facto segregation in New York's schools came as a

xvii

profound shock to liberal policy makers, who had thought that the most enlightened policy is achieved by ignoring racial differences. The scandal of inferior education in ghetto schools was but the first shock-wave to rock New York during this fourth school war. In 1961 the city reeled under the revelation that its renowned school system was slipping academically on national test scores; and the credibility of the Board of Education suffered severe damage when a state investigation uncovered "evidence of gross irregularities in the city's school construction funds, involving payoffs, bribes, structural defects in school buildings, and safety hazards."[5] It was in the midst of these difficulties that the battles in the 1960s over integration of the schools, replete with boycotts, reports, demonstrations and counter-demonstrations, were waged. These difficulties were compounded by the growth in teachers' unions at a time of fiscal instability for the city that was to face bankruptcy before the 1970s came to a close.

Although historical determinism has had some distinguished proponents, I am not persuaded that we are bound to repeat our past in an endless cyclical way. The point of giving this resume of Ravitch's brilliant social history of one public school system is not to resuscitate faith in the myth of the eternal return, but to suggest that the four school wars that she recounts contain the principal elements of the large policy questions that still beset not simply the public school system in one city but the educational efforts of the country as a whole in the 1980s, in the nonpublic sector as well as in the public sector. As Ravitch states in her epilogue, "Every important issue remains and recurs."[6]

The essays that appear in this volume suggest that Professor Ravitch's concluding observation remains pertinent in the 1980s. Besides sharing this general theme of recurring difficulties, the very mention of New York provides another point in common between Professor Ravitch's book and the present volume. For example, chapter three, written by the New York based social scientist, Dr. Thomas Vitullo-Martin, charges that federal taxing and educational policies are destructive of the values of racial and ethnic integration in America's inner cities. This essay grew out of his study of the impact of those policies on New York's schools. Chapter four is likewise written by a New Yorker. In it, Ms. Barbara R. Taylor, principal of a highly successful nonpublic school in Harlem, presents in microcosm the more generalized conclusions reached recently by Dr. James S. Coleman in his report on public and nonpublic schools, that stronger academic demands and better student behavior in orderly environments are the key factors expalining why private schools generally produce higher academic achievement than public schools, not who controls them or who goes to them.[7]

Professor Ravitch's story of New York's second and fourth school wars detailed efforts at improving the quality of education for the immigrant underclass and attempts in the past three decades to eliminate the harmful effects of racial segregation. Ms. Taylor's account of her experience in Harlem at the St. Thomas Community School addresses similar concerns in a contemporary perspective.

Two other essays in the first part of this volume--those by Fr. Andrew Greeley and Fr. Virgil Blum--explore the implications for the nation's nonpublic schools contained within New York's second and fourth school wars. Are nonpublic schools "elitist bastions of white supremacy"? Perhaps because of the post-Brown phenomenon of the "private" academies established in some jurisdictions to avoid the Court's ban on publicly supported educational apartheid, some have regarded all nonpublic schools as racist in character. To continue to maintain this position with any degree of seriousness, the proponents of this viewpoint will have to answer the strong empirical evidence to the contrary adduced in chapter one by Fr. Greeley, in chapter two by Fr. Blum, and elsewhere by Dr. Coleman. All three of these researchers have found that private schools are frequently more racially balanced than public schools and that minority students from low-income families achieve higher levels in nonpublic schools than minority students from low-income families in public schools.

Whatever the explanation of these data--and I suspect the debate over the Coleman report has but begun in the spring of 1981[8]--one can hardly continue to suggest that the reason why blacks and Hispanics do better in nonpublic schools than in public schools is the "racist character" of the former. Nor will it suffice, as an editorial writer suggested in the Washington Post on the day that Dr. Coleman formally presented his report, to be content with bald misstatements of economic facts. On the day that Dr. Coleman formally presented his report, the Post editorialized that "Mr. Coleman's comparison of public and private schools amounts to a restatement of the obvious fact that private schools with more money and their own choices of students often get better results than public schools...."[9] As Senator Hollings points out in his contribution to this volume, a tiny fraction of the nonpublic schools such as Exeter, Phillips-Andover, and St. Paul's are well endowed. Perhaps the Post's editorial writer was thinking of these posh and elitist prep schools when he wrote this sentence. He surely was not thinking of church-operated schools that serve low-income and lower-middle income families in urban centers like Washington, New York, Chicago, Detroit, Atlanta, St. Louis, New Orleans, San Francisco, or Los Angeles, with far less money and resources than their counterparts in public education in those cities. To focus for a moment on the largest nonpublic school system in the country, I merely observe Fr. Greeley's finding in chapter one of this volume that the per pupil costs of Catholic schools, which derive only 1 percent of their funding from governmental support, are approximately half those of comparable public schools.[10]

One noteworthy feature of the discussion in part one of this volume is that none of the distinguished black educators who participated in that discussion, including Dr. Vincent Reed, former superintendent of schools in the District of Columbia and currently the Assistant Secretary for Elementary and Secondary Education in the U.S. Department of Education, Ms. Barbara R. Taylor, who served in Philadelphia's public schools for a decade before taking on the challenging role she currently serves at St. Thomas Community School in Harlem, and Dr. Sarah E. Moten of the Institute for the Study of Educational Policy at Howard University, suggest that nonpublic schools are elitist or racist. To the contrary, the discussion focuses on ways in which educators in both public schools and nonpublic schools might learn from one another and might cooperate with one another in enhancing genuine educational freedom for minorities.

It is appropriate that a volume on nonpublic education that appears in the International Year of Disabled Persons should include a comment on that too often forgotten and neglected minority, the handicapped. It is likewise useful that in chapter five Mr. Weintraub not only traces the history of nonpublic education of exceptional children, but also points out serious failures to meet the educational needs of those children.

If the second and fourth of the school wars of new York have certain parallels in part one of this volume, part two provides a point of contact with the third school war in New York, which was waged principally over concerns of efficiency and expense. For the essays in chapters six through twelve of this volume present differing views, often sharply divergent views, over the best ways of broadening educational opportunity. In chapter six, for example, Mr. Doyle points out that there are several different forms of tuition tax credits and several different forms of educational vouchers, and notes that this very variety provides a basis for finding a particular proposal acceptable or unacceptable. Professors Coons and Sugarman, for example, prefer vouchers over tax credits (see chapters nine and ten) but it is likewise clear that they would repudiate a completely nonregulatory model of vouchers such as that proposed by Milton Friedman. In this respect it might be more fruitful to observe the points at which Coons and Sugarman are prepared to support Senator Moynihan (see chapter eleven) and those at which they withdraw their support for his proposals (see chapter ten) than to note the obvious conflict between Senators Moynihan and Hollings (see chapters seven and eight).

Much of the policy debate over a variety of legislative proposals has been premised on the false assumption that the way we finance education in the United States is a zero-sum game, in which giving even a small slice of the budget pie necessarily implies a diminution of the public contribution to public schools. This zero-sum fear appears to be the central argument in Senator Holling's essay in chapter eight, as well as the major premise underlying the existence of an umbrella organization known as the National Coalition to Save Public Education,[11] which has vigorously opposed at least two of the legislative proposals considered in this portion of the volume, tuition tax credits and "baby BEOGs." Although it would be unrealistic to suppose that fears such as those articulated by Senator Hollings and by this coalition can be dissipated by comparative research, one may nonetheless hope that some attention will be paid to Mr. Doyle's observation at the end of chapter six that after the shift in Australian public policy allowing nonpublic schools to participate in public support "there is now a much more broadly based coalition of support for education in general and that the levels of support for education in the public sector alone are higher now than they would have been absent general support for education, both public and private."[12] If Mr. Doyle's observation about Australia can be made applicable in the United States, then the coalition referred to above should not dissolve but expand, by including supporters of nonpublic schools among their number. As Doyle puts it, "rather than viewing private education with suspicion and hostility, supporters of the public school system might gain, both financially and politically, by looking to the private sector for allies in the effort to adopt a strategy of support for education as a whole."[13]

As was suggested above, part two of this volume reports sharp conflicts, even in fundamental approaches to the same legislative proposal (see chapters seven and eight). The contribution of Dr. Olivas in chapter twelve makes clear, moreover, that not all educational scholars are in accord about the benign impact of legislative proposals for funding nonpublic education. Focusing on two such proposals, the Moynihan BEOG proposal and the Coons-Sugarman voucher proposal, Olivas argues from the current operation of the BEOG program at the level of higher education and from research concerning the nonparticipation of the "information-poor" in other federal entitlements such as the food stamp program, that both proposals are fatally flawed in that they would not significantly assist lower income people. The debate between Coons (chapter nine) and Olivas (chapter 12) over adequate provision of information should at least serve to warn legislators of the perils of simplistically nonregulatory proposals such as the Friedman voucher.

The third part of this volume provides the closest parallel to the first New York school war, waged over the establishment of nonsectarian Protestantism in the public schools. As Ravitch suggests, this political resolution of the conflict of the 1840s was no solution at that time from the perspective of the Catholics, who formed their own schools in which they would be free to transmit their religious heritage.[14] In the 1980s, long after the constitutional disestablishment not only of nonsectarian Protestantism but of religion generally, (reflected, for example, in the Regents' Prayer case in 1962,[15] the Bible Reading case in 1963,[16] and the Ten Commandments case in 1981,[17]) America remains sharply divided over the appropriate role of religion in publicly supported education.[18] It is no accident, for example, that the rise and rapid growth of the evangelical Christian schools can be dated after these cases. This phenomenon represents in part a shift of support away from public schools not on the part of Catholics (most of whom, by the way, attend public schools) but by Protestants.

The ongoing debate over religion in the public schools is not reported in detail in this volume, but the parallel and directly related debate in constitutional law over whether it would constitute an impermissible establishment of religion to tolerate public support of some aspects of church-operated nonpublic schools is the central question examined in part three. As Professor Ravitch suggests in her volume:

> The question of separation of church and state continues to be a lively and unsettled dispute. What once appeared to be absolute separation has been gradually abandoned in favor of limited public support for parochial schools. In the 1970s, parochial schools, feeling the pressure of rising costs, renewed their pursuit of greater or even full public subsidy; despite an adverse ruling by the United States Supreme Court in 1973, New York State and several other states continued to search for ways to assist parochial schools.[19]

Nearly a decade after Nyquist, perhaps the only point of agreement among constitutional proponents and opponents of such assistance is that the search for permissible forms of aid continues. As the essays in this part of the volume reflect, conflict rather than consensus prevails as the dominant posture of the participants in this search. There is no agreement among the scholars even on the usefulness of the body of constitutional law that the Supreme Court has constructed in the church-state area since its landmark decision in Everson, authorizing public funds for transportation of children to and from nonpublic schools. The political character of constitutional law is suggested by the fact that two persons who have served in the Office of Legal Counsel in the Justice Department, Larry Hammond and Antonin Scalia, take sharply divergent views as to whether the Court's efforts in this area reflect a coherent body of constitutional principles (chapter thirteen) or the whimsical and constantly changing preferences of the Justices (chapter fourteen).

In chapter fifteen, Nathan Dershowitz, the Director of the Commission on Law and Social Action of the American Jewish Congress, stoutly rejects Scalia's view and supports Hammond in his view that the Supreme Court is coherent and principled. But Dershowitz regards the Justice Department as inconsistent for defending before the courts various acts of Congress similar, in his view, to bills that the Justice Department has found violative of the Establishment Clause. In chapter sixteen, Charles Wilson, an attorney who has successfully represented intervenors in church-state litigation, provides yet another perspective when he faults the lawyers who litigate these kind of cases for failing to do their job of presenting a factual record that illuminates the issues and affords the Court an opportunity to base its decisions rationally on known facts.

The chorus of dissonant voices achieves its full complement in chapter seventeen by Professor Berns, who argues that the Court has badly misunderstood and misstated historical facts in an attempt to justify or explain the decisions it has taken in the church-state area. Berns obviously agrees with Scalia that the Court is badly confused in those results, but perhaps the most intriguing implication of this contribution by a distinguished constitutional historian is that the most significant part of this volume is not the section on constitutional perspectives, but the debate on various legislative proposals reported in part two of the book. For in Berns' view "the question whether church-related schools should be publicly supported in one way or another is a political question, not a constitutional question."[20]

A notable feature of the discussion in this part of the volume is that it reflects the sort of diversity of viewpoints that is reflected in the lead essays and that thus far has been virtually the sole point of agreement among participants in this area of the church-state debate. As Judge Mikva and Judge Wright observe in their comments, this kind of pluralism is itself a strong American value.

One of the telling arguments made by Professors Coons and Sugarman in this volume is that their voucher proposal would provide a structure for protecting educational pluralism.[21] This argument must be evaluated in the light of the suggestion made by the eminent sociologists, Peter L. Berger and Richard John Neuhaus, that the political crisis of confidence that our society is facing has arisen largely because of the diminution of mediating structures that stand between the individual's private life and the large institutions or megastructures of the public sphere. The mediating structures identified by Berger and Neuhaus include the family, organized religion, voluntary associations, the neighborhood, and ethnic and racial subcultures.[22] If, as Dr. Vitullo-Martin suggests in chapter three, the quality of neighborhoods is directly affected by the quality of its schools, both public and nonpublic, then these schools must be added to the list of mediating structures to which greater attention will need to be paid in the 1980's. In this sense, the religious mission and orientation of most of the nonpublic schools in the inner cities might provide a refreshingly new context for the discussion of the relationship between church and state in this country.[23] As an observer of that discussion and sometime participant in it, I hope that this new dimension of societal meaning is pursued vigorously, if only because I have the sense that many of our constitutional discussions of church and state have gotten stuck on the same themes and the same narrow points of view with alarming regularity.

If a new mode of discourse is to be achieved in the discussion of the educational policy choices affecting nonpublic schools in the 1980s, there is a prerequisite that I think must govern the conduct of both proponents and opponents of public assistance for nonpublic schools. That precondition to dialogue is the willingness on both sides of the debate to see the other not in the worst possible light, but in the most favorable possible perspective. Those engaged in church-related nonpublic education, for example, should not take comfort in articles that feature prominently the failure of some of our nation's public schools.[24] They should refrain from doing so if only because rejoicing in the failure of another can be unethical according to the scriptures.[25] Furthermore, such smugness would overlook significant success stories within the public school system recounted, for example, by opponents of public assistance for nonpublic schools such as Senator Hollings.[26] In my view, the better attitude for church-related educators to adopt concerning public schools was articulated by an unlikely source speaking to an unlikely audience, in an address by John Ireland, Archbishop of St. Paul, to the convention of the National Education Association in 1890. In quaint Victorian language, replete with an Irish curse, the Archbishop stated a word of reassurance to public school educators about how he (if not all his co-religionists) regarded the value of American public schools:

> I am a friend and an advocate of the state school....The accusation has gone abroad that Catholics are bent on destroying the state schools. Never was accusation more unfounded....No tax is more legitimate than that which is levied in order to dispel mental darkness, and build up within the nation's bosom intelligent manhood and womanhood....It were idle for me to praise the work of the state school of America in imparting secular instruction. We all recognize its value. It is our pride and our glory. The Republic of the United Stats has solemnly affirmed its resolve that within its borders no clouds of ignorance shall settle upon the minds of the children of its people. In furnishing the means to accomplish this result its generosity knows no limit. The free school of America! Withered be the hand raised in sign of its destruction![27]

Archbishop Ireland's words in 1890 can serve as a salutary reminder to members of his church in the 1980s that little is served in their own interest by launching broadsides on the public school system. One is likewise entitled to hope that some of the less mature supporters of that system will begin to overcome the remarkable self-delusion that public schools have a corner on Americanism, whatever that is. By the same token, the Coalition to Save Public Schools should take no joy in the studies that point to the decline of the nonpublic schools in inner cities.[28] Removing the competition may have been an appropriate goal for pre-Sherman Act moguls, but hardly for contemporary educators.

To suggest the need to move beyond polemic to dialogue might raise hackles in quarters where hostility is regarded as a badge of courage and particularism the sole mode of survival. Taking the view that dialogue is the better path to follow, I would like now to sketch briefly an outline for future conversation concerning the public good of private schools. First, as the Supreme Court made clear as early as 1819 in the Dartmouth College case,[29] and as recently as the Pierce case in 1925,[30] independent schools, including those operated by a religious group, are an essential part of a pluralistic educational policy in this country; indeed as Dr. Lawrence Cremin and others have noted in their accounts of American education, church-operated schools preceded governmentally operated schools in this country by two centuries.[31] Second, as Dr. Coleman, Fr. Greeley, Fr. Blum and others have shown, these schools serve the public purpose no less effectively than do the state schools in preparing students for the public responsibilities of citizenship. Third, the core educational process in these schools fulfills the legitimate requirements set down by state educational authorities. In my opinion, these schools are not immune by virtue of their religious character from reasonable health and safety regulations, nor from the moral obligation and legal duty to judge people on their character rather than on the color of their skin. Fourth, in providing religious instruction as a fundamental part of their educational mission, they offer the opportunity to thousands of American parents to see to it that this dimension of their childrens' lives is not overlooked. To some, of course, this very fact is viewed as a fatal flaw in the argument and brings any program of support of such schools within the prohibition of the First Amendment. I would submit, however, that this part of the argument deserves at least thoughtful response, if not wholehearted support from those who have successfully argued that for a variety of reasons (some historical, some philosophical, some sociological) the religious dimension in the education of children must be restrained in schools operated by the government. If we really believe in pluralism and wish to avoid the appearance of overt hostility to all forms of religious instruction in our society, the coming decade will enable us to translate the typically American value of diversity into public policy. The value of diversity is obviously not served by imposing a sterile uniformity on all modes of education.

These four points are but beginning points in the dialogue that I hope will ensue. That further exploration needs to be done about each of these points should be clear from the ambiguity latent within the fourth point. Coons and Sugarman, who generally support public assistance for nonpublic education, make the commitment to diversity the linchpin of their argument for greater freedom of choice. Mr. Dershowitz, who generally opposes such aid, would nonetheless respect the value of diversity, but he argues that the very prospect of significant governmental assistance to nonpublic schools would constitute a threat to educational pluralism by virtue of the regulation that normally accompanies governmental aid.

It is my firm hope that the dialogue on the public good of private schools undertaken in this volume on a consistently high tone will be pursued throughout the 1980s in a similar spirit of genuine listening and mutual respect. For the time for school wars, I submit, is now behind us.

Professor Ravitch concludes her volume as follows:

> While the language of school wars relates to educational issues, the underlying contest will continue to reflect fundamental value clashes among discordant ethnic, cultural, racial, and religious groups. And this very fact underlines the importance of comity in the politics of education—comity, that basic recognition of differences in values and interests and of the desirability of reconciling those differences peacefully which the school itself aims to teach. The effort to advance comity, in educational affairs and in affairs of the larger society has always been at the heart of public education. Whatever their failings, whatever their accomplishments, the public schools have been and will be inescapably involved in the American search for a viable definition of community.[32]

Ravitch is correct, I think, in suggesting that the school wars were waged in New York not only over educational issues, but also over fundamental value clashes. While one might wish to qualify her somewhat sweeping conclusion that the public schools aimed simply to teach what she calls "comity," I prefer as one trained in nonpublic schools and currently teaching in one to affirm the general thrust of her statement and to add only that the peaceful reconciliation of differences is a value cherished and taught in nonpublic schools as well as public schools and that both nonpublic schools and public schools should be perceived as inescapably involved in the American search for a viable definition of community.

NOTES

1. Diane Ravitch, The Great School Wars, New York City, 1805-1973: A History of the Public Schools as Battlefield of Social Change (New York: Basic Books, 1974).

2. See Vincent P. Lannie, Public Money and Parochial Education: Bishop Hughes, Governor Seward, and the New York School Controversy (Cleveland: Case Western Reserve University Press, 1968); see also Rockne McCarthy, Disestablishment a Second Time: Public Justice for American Schools, to be published in 1982 (Eerdmans Press, Grand Rapids).

3. Ravitch, note 1 supra, p. 191.

4. Ibid., p. 251.

5. Ibid., p. 263.

6. Ibid., p. 401.

7. See Lawrence Feinberg, "Author of Report Says Academic Demands, Behavior Determines Schools' Quality," Washington Post, Apr. 8, 1981, A7, cols. 1-6.

8. See, e.g., Marjorie Hunter, "New Coleman Study is Defended and Criticized by 500 Educators," New York Times, Apr. 8, 1981, p. A 12, cols. 3-4; James. P. Comer, "Coleman's Bad Rport," Ibid., Apr. 19, 1981, Sec. 4, p. 15, Cols. 1-2; Diane Ravitch, "The Way to Make Public Schools Good," Washington Post, Apr. 19, 1981, p. C7, cols. 3-4; and letters to the Editor, ibid., Apr. 24, 1981, p. A 26, cols. 3-4.

9. Editorial, "Public Schools, Private Schools," Washington Post, Apr. 7, 1981, A 16, col. 2 (emphasis supplied).

10. See Tables 7 to 9 accompanying chapter one. See also, Robert Hoyt, "Learning a Lesson from the Catholic Schools," New York Magazine, vol. 10, no. 37 (Sept. 12, 1977), pp. 48-52.

11. Senator Hollings refers to the members of this coalition in chapter eight of this volume; see p. 88 infra. During the debate in 1980 on the Senate floor relating to the Moynihan amendment to extend the BEOG program to elementary and secondary education, Senator Hollings referred to this coalition and read their position paper into the record of the proceedings. 126 Cong. Rec. Sec. 7849-50 (daily ed. June 23, 1980) and Sec. 7971-72 (daily ed. June 24, 1980).

12. P. 78 infra.

13. Ibid.

14. During roughly the same period, there was a similar struggle, with several intersting parallels, over the appropriate role of the crown in financing a national educational system in Ireland. The account of this controversy in this note is taken from Emmet Larkin, The Quarrel among the Roman Catholic Hierarchy over the National System of Education in Ireland, 1838-41 (Cambridge, Mass.: Massachusetts Institute of Technology, 1965).

The first point to be observed about this controversy is that the principal antagonists were not divided along sectarian lines. The debate was not between Catholics and Protestants, but among the Roman Catholic bishops themselves. The Archbishop of Dublin, Daniel Murray, supported the proposal of Lord Stanley in 1831 to set up a system of national schools supported by the crown. Even though the system was nondenominational in principle, Catholics were alloted only two of the seven places on the national governing boards, and the bishops were allowed no final voice in the selection of texts published by the board or in the appointment or dismissal of teachers. Murray served on the national board.

By 1838, however, two of the bishops became sufficiently dissatisfied with the operation of this vast social experiment as to attack it, in the words of William Higgins, bishop of Ardagh, as "likely to undermine the authority of the Catholic Clergy, and ultimately introduce either positive errors or 'Indifferentism.'" (Letter of March 10, 1838, Higgins to Paul Cullen, Rector of the Irish College in Rome). Despite the fact that the great majority of the bishops disagreed with the views expressed by Higgins, John MacHale, Archbishop of Tuam subsequently denounced the national educational system in a series of open letters to the Home Secretary, Lord John Russell (see, e.g., Dublin Evening Post, Feb. 13, Nov. 3,. Nov. 24, 1838). After consulting with his episcopal colleagues, Murray wrote to Cullen: "Dr. MacHale, you will have perceived, is making a violent outcry, in opposition to the sentiments of the great majority of his Episcopal Brethren, against our National System of Education....We are long struggling to obtain public aid, which could be safely applied towards the education of our poor and when obtained he seems desirious to wrest it from us, and throw it back into the hands of those who would employ it against us....As for his pretended hope of procuring a separate grant for the education of the Catholic poor, it is so utterly visionary that no rational person could entertain it for a moment." (Letter of April 18, 1838, Murray to Cullen). Stormy debate ensued between Archbishop Murray and Archbishop MacHale at the national meeting of the bishops in 1839; and the quarrel was furiously and bitterly fought out in the public press over a period of two years.

To quell the controversy, both sides agreed to submit the matter to Rome and each rival submitted a lengthy brief presenting his case respectively for or against the national system. The Roman curia handed the case over to a Dutch Jesuit, Cornelius Van Everbroeck, who produced a 118-page opinion, with a nine-page postscript, more notable for its studied ambiguity than for its clarity of judgement: "The system is neither positively approved nor positively condemned, because in either case the most serious consequences are to be feared." (Archives of the Propaganda Fide, Acta, vol. 203, pp. 419-79). In what persons familiar with the ways of Rome would recognize as fairly typical of her style of governance, the Roman congregation ratified Van Everbroeck's suggestion that a binding decision for either party be avoided, resolving [sic] "that no judgment should be definitely pronounced in this matter and that this kind of education should be left to the prudent discretion and religious conscience of each individual bishop, whereas its success must depend on the vigilant care of the pastors, on the various precautions to be adopted and on the future experience which time will supply." (Circular Letter of Cardinal Fransoni to the four Archbishops of Ireland Concerning National Teaching, Jan. 16, 1841).

A similarly public and stormy controversy over the appropriateness of Catholic participation in the public schools erupted in this country in the 1890s. As with the Irish controversy narrated above, the American controversy featured two bishops, John Ireland, Archbishop of St. Paul, and Bernard McQuaid, Bishop of Rochester,

as the principal antagonists. For an account of this controversy, see
Daniel F. Reilly, The School Controversy (1891-1893) (Washington,
D.C.: Catholic University of America Press, 1943); James H.
Moynihan, The Life of Archbishop John Ireland (New York: Harper,
1953), pp. 79-103; and John Tracy Ellis, The Life of Cardinal Gibbons
(Milwaukee: Bruce, 1952) vol. 1, pp. 653-707.

15. Engel v. Vitale, 370 U.S. 421 (1962).

16. Abington Township School District v. Schempp, 374 U.S. 203
(1963).

17. Stone v. Graham, 599 S.W. 2d 157 (Ky.), rev'd., 449 U.S.__,
101 S.Ct. 192 (1980), rehearing denied, 449 U.S.,__, 101 S.Ct. 904
(1981).

18. See, e.g., William M. Beaney and Edward N. Beiser, "Prayer
and Politics: The Impact of Engel and Schempp on the Political
Process" 13 J. of Pub. L. 475 (1964) reprinted in Theodore L. Becker,
ed. The Impact of Supreme Court Decisions 20-34 (1969). For other
examples of impact studies relating to the Engel and Schempp
decision, see Ellis Katz, "Patterns of Compliance with the Schempp
Decision," 14 J. Pub. L. 396 (1963); Robert H. Birkby, "The Supreme
Court and the Bible: Tennessee Reactions to the Schempp Decision,"
10 Midwest J. of Pol. Sci. 304 (Aug. 1966); Richard M. Johnson, The
Dynamics of Compliance: Supreme Court Decision-Making From a
New Perspective (Evanston: Northwestern University Press, 1967);
Donald R. Reich, "The Impact of Judicial Decision-Making: The
School Prayer Cases," in David H. Everson, ed., The Supreme Court
as Policy Maker: Three Studies on the Impact of Judicial Decisions
(Carbondale, Ill: Southern Illinois University Press 1968) 44-81;
William K. Muir, Prayer in the Public Schools: Law and Attitude
Change (Chicago: University of Chicago Press, 1967); and Kenneth
M. Dolbeare and Phillip E. Hammond, The School Prayer Decisions:
From Court Policy to Local Practice (Chicago: University of
Chicago Press, 1971). For an account of the congressional reaction,
see Beaney and Beiser, supra. And see 125 Cong. Rec. S4128-4131
(daily ed., Apr. 5, 1979) (purporting to limit Supreme Court
jurisdiction over cases involving "voluntary prayer"), and S4138-4152
(daily ed., Apr. 9, 1979) (same); Comment, "Section 1252: A
Jurisdictional Dinosaur," 75 Northwestern U. L. Rev. 175, 176 (1980).

19. Ravitch, note 1 supra, p. 401.

20. Berns, infra, p. 196.

21. See e.g., John E. Coons and Stephen D. Sugarman, "A Case
for Choice," in James S. Coleman, ed., Parents, Teachers and
Children: Prospects for Choice in American Education (San Francisco: Institute for Contemporary Studies, 1977), pp. 129-48. See
also Nathan Glazer, "Public Education and American Pluralism,"
ibid., pp. 85-109; and Gordon Spykman, ed., Society, State, and
Schools: A Case for Structural and Concessional Pluralism (Grand
Rapids: Eerdmans, 1981).

22. Peter L. Berger and Richard John Nenhaus, To Empower
People: The Role of Mediating Structures in Public Policy (Wash-

ington, D.C.: American Enterprise Institute for Public Policy Research, 1977).

23. See, e.g., John Coleman, S.J., "A Theological Link between Religious Liberty and Mediating Structures," in Jay Mechling, ed., Church, State and Public Policy: The New Shape of the Church-State Debate (Washington, D.C.: American Enterprise Institute for Public Policy Research, 1978), pp. 22-48.

24. See, e.g., "Why Public Schools Fail," Newsweek Apr. 20, 1981, pp. 62-73; "Teachers Are in Trouble," ibid., Apr. 27, 1981, pp. 78-84; and "Hope for the Schools," ibid., May 4, 1981, p. 66-72.

25. See, e.g., I Cor. 13:6.

26. See 126 Cong. Rec. S7965-7968 (daily ed. June 24, 1980), citing Lindsy Van Gelder and Peter Freiberg, "Twelve Public Schools That Really Work," New York Magazine, vol. 13, no. 24 (June 16, 1980) pp. 22-29.

27. John Ireland, "State Schools and Parish Schools," in The Church and Modern Society: Lectures and Addresses (St. Paul: Pioneer Press, 1905), vol. 1, pp. 217, 219, 220, 226. See also Timothy H. Morrissey, "A Controversial Reformer: Archbishop John Ireland and His Educational Belief," Notre Dame J. of Ed. 7 (1976), 63-75.

28. See, e.g., Thomas Vitullo-Martin, Catholic Inner-City Schools: The Future (Washington, D.C.: United States Catholic Conference, 1979).

29. Dartmouth College v. Woodward, 4 Wheat. (17 U.S.) 518 (1819).

30. Pierce v. Society of Sisters, 268 U.S. 510 (1925). See Donald P. Kommers and Michael J. Wahoske, eds., Freedom and Education: Pierce v. Society of Sisters Reconsidered (Notre Dame, Ind.: Center for Civil Rights, 1978), and Stephen D. Arons, "The Separation of School and State: Pierce Reconsidered," Harv. Ed. Rev. 46(1976), 76-104.

31. See, e.g., Lawrence A. Cremin, American Education: The Colonial Experience, 1607-1783 (New York: Harper and Row, 1970).

32. Ravitch, note 1 supra, p. 404.

PART ONE
EDUCATIONAL FREEDOM FOR MINORITIES

Introduction

The Hon. Vincent E. Reed

When I was the superintendent of the District of Columbia Public Schools, it was very refreshing and relaxing sometimes to call other superintendents in other large cities and cry about my problems. In turn they would cry about their problems, and we would spend taxpayers' money trying to rejuvenate ourselves by saying that maybe there were some people in the country who have greater problems than we had. In talking to them I found that most of the large school districts in this country, particularly the 50 largest school districts, are having serious financial problems. It has become very apparent to me that education is in trouble from a financial standpoint and that this financial crisis affects public education and private education alike.

Those engaged in private education know all too well about the financial crisis I am referring to. After the passage of Proposition 13 in California, moreover, it should also be clear that public schools will be facing severe shortages in this decade. Let me illustrate this point as graphically as I know how. Last year the State of New Jersey had to take over the financing and operation of an entire school district in that state. Two school districts in Ohio had to be closed down for four or five months last year. Some of the large cities like New York and Cleveland have been on the verge of bankruptcy. And in the District of Columbia we were forced to cut $17 million out of our 1980 budget and $39 million out of our 1981 appropriations. That $39 million represented 1,333 positions. Since June of 1980 we have terminated over 1,300 young people working for our school system. This unfortunate reality came to pass in part because of the seniority clause of the union contract. The teachers who were let go were the younger teachers, teachers who are full of energy and vitality, and teachers who are very bright and very dedicated to the task of educating the children they serve. It is a sad commentary to think that we had to terminate over 1,300 of our younger teachers.

If the financial exigency that we experienced in the District of Columbia is symptomatic of other public school systems and of many areas of private schools, then it seems to make sense that public education and private education get together somehow to maximize scarce resources in order to make sure that quality education remains possible in this country. In order to achieve the goal of quality education for all, the public sector and the private sector need to enter into a new partnership to strengthen one another.

3

There are a lot of things we can do together. The year 1965 now seems like such a long time ago. But I retain vivid memories of cooperative ventures between public and private schools, when I was a high school principal. About ten blocks from the school where I was principal was a Catholic high school. Due to sheer numbers we were able to teach the fifth year languages; and because of a lack of numbers they were not able to afford the fifth year of languages. So we exchanged students. Their students came to the high school where I was and took the fifth year languages; and we went over and involved our youngsters in electronics and some other courses. That experience led me to conclude that some things can be done in a spirit of cooperation to maximize services and facilities. There are a lot of things that can be done along the lines of combined planning for Title I programs, such as joint staff development, student exchanges, and teacher exchanges. There are other kinds of things that can be done in a cooperative way. The whole business of planning for the talented and the gifted can surely be done in a combined manner.

I anticipate, of course, that there will be powerful public pressures opposed to letting children who go to a Catholic school come into a public school and use public funds. But my answer to this objection is that the parents of these children are taxpayers like everyone else, and if they want public education they are entitled to it as well as anybody else. This decision to send their children to a private school entails a freedom of choice protected in our constitutional order. But it does not negate the fact that they are entitled to public education and public services. That is my answer to people who seem only to want to keep the two sets of children separate. My basic feeling is that educators are paid to serve young people and all of us should do that in a combined way so that our young people will be served and will develop no matter where the service comes from.

It is very appropriate that the first set of papers in this volume addresses the needs of minority children in education. Fr. Greeley and Fr. Blum present studies of what is happening with minority children in parochial schools. Dr. Vitullo-Martin has given us a carefully reasoned argument about the ways that federal educational and taxing policies have adversely impacted on inner-city schools. Ms. Taylor provides us with a vivid account of the remarkable success she has had in directing a community school in Harlem. And Dr. Weintraub cautions us against forgetting that handicapped children constitute a minority with unique needs. Each of these papers challenges stereotypes and forces us to rethink the proper relation between public schools and private schools in this country. There is much that each sector can learn from the other. Both need to survive, and neither can neglect the other much longer. I think that these essays challenge us to look forward to a "marriage," so to speak, of public and private schools that would enable them to do some things together without losing their distinct identity, purpose, or mission. If such a marriage of minds and energies can be achieved, the children of America will be the winners.

1. Catholic High Schools and Minority Students

Rev. Andrew M. Greeley

One of the more interesting educational phenomena in the United States in recent years has been the increased enrollment in Catholic secondary schools by black and Hispanic students.[1] Approximately half of the blacks who attend Catholic schools are not themselves Catholic and while more than nine-tenths of the Hispanics in Catholic schools are Catholic, the countries from which Hispanic Americans have come do not have a tradition of Catholic comprehensive education similar to that in the United States. One need only speak to black or Hispanic parents who make the choice of Catholic secondary schools (and primary schools too for that matter) to realize that their choice is based on the assumption that their children will receive better education in the Catholic schools than they will in public schools. Until recently, however, there was no solid evidence to support this "market choice" made by minority parents.[2] But the High School and Beyond study, a longitudinal study of American secondary students, currently being conducted by the National Opinion Research Center for the National Center for Education Statistics under the direction of Professor James S. Coleman, provides data with which the performance of Catholic secondary schools can be analyzed. The sample design of the High School and Beyond study is such that private secondary schools with large black and Hispanic enrollments were oversampled. Thus of the more than 70,000 sophomores and seniors to whom questionnaires were administered, a little more than 7,000 were in Catholic secondary schools and more than 2,000 of these were black or Hispanic. The basic sample design was a national probability sample and the analysis reported in this essay included all the Catholic school students and a random subsample of 7,000 public school students.

Even if the impressions of black and Hispanic parents are correct, and the young people who attend Catholic secondary schools do better academically, it does not necessarily follow that the Catholic schools are responsible for the superior academic outcome. Educational research in recent years has demonstrated that to a considerable extent, outcome is a function of input. Schools which feature young people from well-educated, powerfully-motivated, and affluent families will produce graduates who are very different from schools whose enrollees come from different family backgrounds. To make sure that there is a "school effect," one must first of all hold constant the "family input" variables which might effect the "academic outcome."

6

One must distinguish the background characteristics of a student--familial and personal--from school factors which might also have an influence in academic outcome.[3] In the analysis to be summarized in this essay, the bias was "conservative," that is, in the direction of holding constant all possible background variables before considering the possibility of the school effect.

It is perhaps worth noting what "hold constant" means in this context. The comparisons that are finally made, with the variables at the bottom end of model, are comparisons that are made between Catholic and public school students who have the same family income, the same parental education, the same parental college expectations, the same family learning environment, the same psychological well-being, the same college aspirations when they were in eighth grade, and the same style of using their time.

As Table 1 illustrates, minority students in Catholic schools (and, indeed, white students in Catholic schools) were strikingly different from those in public schools. They were twice as likely (44 versus 22 percent) to report more than five hours of homework a week, and nearly 30 percentage points more likely to say that they were confident that they could graduate from college.

Table 1
ACADEMIC OUTCOME MEASURES
IN CATHOLIC AND PUBLIC HIGH SCHOOLS

	Catholic	Public
A) ACADEMIC PERFORMANCE INDEX		
Z Score		
(Percent of standard deviation from the mean)		
White	25	-01
Black	-44	-91
Hispanic	-23	-77
B) HOMEWORK		
(Percent doing more than 5 hours of homework a week)		
White	42	23
Black	44	22
Hispanic	44	22
C) COLLEGE ASPIRATIONS		
(Percent expect to graduate from college)		
White	64	42
Black	77	48
Hispanic	66	38

Table 2 reports the finding that on standardized achievement tests, prepared for the High School and Beyond study by the Educational Testing Service, Catholic school minority students were half a standard deviation above public school minority students.

Table 2
ACHIEVEMENT TEST SCORES
BY RACE AND TYPE OF SCHOOL ATTENDED
(Z score)

| | Vocabulary | | Reading | |
	Catholic	Public	Catholic	Public
White	32	-05	21	00
Black	-39	-93	-27	-77
Hispanic	-12	-75	-18	-73

| | Math 2 | | Math 2 | |
	Catholic	Public	Catholic	Public
White	25	00	15	-03
Black	-46	-87	-36	-63
Hispanic	-23	-71	-16	-47

| | Science | | Writing | |
	Catholic	Public	Catholic	Public
White	21	12	31	00
Black	-58	-96	-37	-91
Hispanic	-29	-69	-16	-65

| | Civics | | Academic Performance* | |
	Catholic	Public	Catholic	Public
White	23	-04	25	-01
Black	-13	-66	-44	-91
Hispanic	-11	-52	-23	-77

*Reading + Math 1 + Math 2.

As was expected, the young people who went to Catholic secondary schools came from very different backgrounds. Their parents were far more likely to be college educated and have much stronger college aspirations for their children, higher income levels, and were far more likely to provide a learning environment conducive to studying. The young people themselves had strong college aspirations before they came to high school, have much higher personal morale, and have more intellectually-oriented habits with regard to their use of time. It is also true, however, that those who attend Catholic schools give their institutions much higher ratings in terms of the quality of instruction and the interest and competence of the teachers, and describe their schools as both fairer and more effective in their disciplinary programs and having substantially less disciplinary problems. Moreover, both teacher effectiveness and disciplinary environment are not the result merely of the student's background. In part, they are affected by whether a religious order owns the school and a substantial amount of difference remains even after that factor is taken into account. As Tables 3 and 4 illustrate, the differences in disciplinary environment in the Catholic schools are not imaginary. And they are not a function of student characteristics. Rather, they represent a real contribution of the school itself above and beyond the type of student the school recruits.

Table 3
SCHOOL DISCIPLINE INDEX IN
CATHOLIC AND PUBLIC HIGH SCHOOLS

	Catholic	Public
Z score (High Score = low problem)		
White	43	−49
Black	32	−50
Hispanic	58	−58

Table 4
APPROVAL OF SCHOOL'S DISCIPLINE SYSTEM
(Z score)

	Catholic	Public
White	23	−28
Black	24	−20
Hispanic	49	−15

For example, it is theoretically possible that the higher scores on standardized achievement tests of Catholic school minority members, might be the result of family background or school effect or of some combination of both. In fact, when multiple regression equations were constructed to account for the difference in college aspirations of high school students, the background variables account for almost all of the difference. High school students who attend Catholic high schools are more likely to be confident that they will graduate from college because they come from families where there is more education and a greater expectation of college graduation, and because they themselves, before they came to high school, had already planned to go to college. This outcome of Catholic secondary education turns out not to be a real outcome at all, but rather to be an effect of differential input.

The same explanation, however, does not hold for the differences in homework and in academic test scores. About half of the differences between public school and Catholic school minority students can be accounted for by family and personal input variables. The other half of the difference still remains and can only be accounted for when one takes into consideration the disciplinary environment, the quality of instruction, and religious order ownership of the institution. It would appear, then, that the higher academic test scores of Catholic school minority students is in part the result of background, but is also in part the result of a school effect. About one-quarter of a standard deviation on academic tests can be attributed to the school itself above parental input.

It is the nature of such research that one can never exclude any explanation with absolute certainty. Thus it may well be the case that there is a parental input aspect for which we have not accounted in the present research. All that can be said is that before the research began, the assumption would have been in favor of an input explanation of a differential output. Now the burden of probability seems to tilt somewhat in the direction of school effect as a partial explanation for the difference between young minority group members in Catholic and public schools.

Parental choice (either ratifying the choice of the adolescent or constraining it) does make a difference. But all the obvious differences, it would seem, have been taken into account in the present research. There may be more subtle differences, and their possible impact will have to be studied in future research. It is necessary now for those who still insist on a parental input explanation of the success of Catholic schools to specify precisely what the family factor is that may be responsible for this apparent success.

One may push the present analysis a bit further by asking whether there is some structural dimension of Catholic secondary schools not likely to be the object of parental choice which when varied produces a variant in the apparent Catholic school effect. It was my suspicion in the beginning of the present research that the Catholic school academic effect would in part be especially in the smaller schools where there could be more personal attention. Since size of school was not likely to be something the minority parents would take into consideration (he or she or they would most likely choose the school that was reasonably close regardless of size), it seemed reasonable to ask whether it was indeed a variation of Catholic school effect that varied with school size.

The finding went in the opposite direction of what I had anticipated. It was precisely in the largest schools (schools with more than 500 students) that this Catholic school effect was most noticeable, a difference of two-thirds of a standard deviation between Catholic and public school students. In other words, school size does not affect the academic achievements of those who attend public schools, but it does affect academic achievement of those who attend Catholic schools. Even in the small schools, the Catholic school students did better academically, but they did strikingly better academically in schools with more than 500 students. And indeed the amount of the difference between public and Catholic schools that must be accounted for by variables other than family background increases drastically in larger schools so that two-fifths of a standard deviation in the difference of achievement scores remains after the background factors have all been taken into account. And this very substantial difference diminishes to statistical insignificance when disciplinary effectiveness, quality of instruction, and religious order ownership are taken into account. The facts that the outcome varies with school size and that the relative effectiveness of the school impact also varies with school size and that school size is not likely to be an object of parental choice—all enhance the probability that we are dealing with an authentic school effect and not merely a choice or family input effect.

The likelihood that there is an authentic school effect is enhanced by the fact that there is only a small correlation between parental social class background and academic achievement in the Catholic schools. Indeed by the time students are seniors, the difference between the academic achievement of those from college educated families and non college educated families is practically non existent. This phenomenon is true for whites, blacks and Hispanics. The success of the Catholic schools is not among those who come from affluent and well educated black and Hispanic families but among precisely the opposite—from the less affluent and non college educated.

Presumably the phenomenon is "ethnic"; the Catholic secondary schools were established between 1900 and 1960 to facilitate the upward mobility of the immigrant poor. Somehow they learned how to eliminate social class disadvantages among those immigrant poor. They continue to do so, though now a different clientele is being served than those for whom the schools were originally founded. Ironically half the white Catholics in Catholic schools come from college educated families—from families whose own upward mobility was facilitated by these schools a generation ago. For such young people Catholic schools do not make a great deal of academic difference (indeed if the school is small and diocesan owned, it is likely to produce lower achievement scores than the public schools among its white Catholic college family clientele).

The success of the Catholic secondary school in eliminating the social class impact on educational achievement means that they in fact do what the public schools claimed at one time to do, but in fact do not do now—provide an equality of educational opportunity independent of the social class of parents. The Catholic schools seem, in fact, to be the real "common" schools.

Obviously more research is needed to confirm the findings reported in the present essay. It would, however, be appropriate to note that in most other "input/output" research, scholars would speak with considerable confidence if they had data such as those analyzed in the present essay.

But is it not true, as some critics of the present research have judged, that black students are more likely to be in all-black schools if they attend public schools and therefore the real effect of Catholic schools is one of racial integration? In fact, this assumption proves not to be the case. As can be seen in Table 5, a black young person attending a Catholic secondary school is just as likely as a black young person attending a public secondary school to be in an all-black school—and is as likely also to be in a racially-integrated school.

Table 5
RACIAL INTEGRATION (AS DESCRIBED BY BLACK STUDENTS)
(Percent)

	Catholic	Public
Few blacks	30	29
Half blacks	21	28
Most blacks	32	24
All blacks	17	19
	100%	100%

Moreover, as Table 6 illustrates, there is no correlation in academic performance and racial integration for those who attend public schools. But there is one for those who attend Catholic schools. Catholic schools achieve superior academic results at all levels of integration but especially where the black young person is in a school where most of the students are white. In other words, racial integration does indeed have an academic effect, but only in Catholic schools; this enhances the power of the Catholic school effect. Thus, even when the racial integration factor is taken into account, the phenomenon of differential effects for minority young people who attend Catholic schools persists.

Table 6
ACADEMIC PERFORMANCE FOR BLACKS
BY RACIAL INTEGRATION
(Z Score)

	Catholic	Public
Few blacks	-01	-83
Half blacks	-39	-78
Most blacks	-47	-72
All blacks	-52	-70

Those black and Hispanic parents who choose Catholic schools, then, apparently do receive an academic payoff for their choice over and above that which they themselves contribute. In their own economic and motivational resoures, the "product" they buy is a bargain. As Table 7 illustrates, average tuition at Catholic schools is around $850 a year (no different for schools with substantial numbers of minority students), less than half that of "other" private schools, and less than a third of that of elite private schools.

Table 7
TUITION AT PRIVATE SCHOOLS

	Mean	STD
Catholic	$ 857	$ 278
Black Catholic	839	196
Hispanic Catholic	855	162
Elite private	2,713	936
Other private	1,928	1,212

Furthermore, as Table 8 illustrates, the per pupil cost of Catholic schools is not much in excess of the tuition. And as Table 9 illustrates, of the approximately $1,000 per year per pupil cost, more than three-quarters is accounted for in tuition; 9 percent comes from fund raising (bingo, raffles, etc.); 11 percent more comes from subsidies (presumably from parishes or dioceses); and only 1 percent comes from government help.

Table 8
PER PUPIL COST FOR VARIOUS SCHOOLS

	Mean	STD
Public	$1,807	$ 689
Public alternative	2,218	677
Ordinary Catholic	1,097	374
Catholic black	1,139	489
Catholic hispanic	962	210
Elite private	3,598	2,503
Other private	1,508	1,583

Table 9
FUNDING OF CATHOLIC SCHOOLS
(Percent)

	Ordinary	Minority
Tuition	74	79
Fund raising	9	7
Subsidy	11	9
Endowment	2	0
Other	3	4
Government	1	1
	100	100

Per pupil cost in Catholic schools is approximately half of that in public schools. About $200 of the $1,000 per year difference in per pupil cost can be attributed to the fact that Catholic schools pay their teachers less ($8,000 a year for a beginner with an A.B. as opposed to $10,000 in public schools), have a higher student/faculty ratio (18 students per faculty member as opposed to 13), and are slightly less likely to have M.A.s or Ph.D.s (45 percent versus 50 percent). The rest of the difference, however, cannot be explained by data presently available to us. In other words, Catholic schools do a better educational job for minority young people (and all young people for that matter) and they do so for $1,000 a year less, $790 a year less even when you take into account lower salaries, larger classrooms, and less teacher training. One might perhaps forgive public school administrators if they are wondering where the Catholic school administrators purchased the mirrors with which they work these miracles.

Neither the research project, of which this article is a synopsis, nor the article itself will take a stand on public policy questions, particularly concerning federal aid to Catholic secondary schools. One could make an argument from the present analysis that such aid ought to be increased because the Catholic secondary schools apprently do such an effective job in educating minority children. Or one might also argue that intervention of government through its assistance in the work of Catholic secondary schools might impede their effectiveness. At the present time I am content merely to note that with only 1 percent of their budget covered by government assistance, Catholic secondary schools do very well indeed.

The High School and Beyond research on Catholic secondary schools is by no means finished. The project will continue for four more years and, God and funding agencies willing, the Catholic school phase of the project will also continue. At a later stage the impact of Catholic primary schools on minority students will also be considered. It is by no means impossible, for example, that some of the impact reported here of Catholic secondary schools will turn out to be a function of the fact that many of the young people who attend secondary Catholic schools have also gone to Catholic parochial schools for their grammar school years. Moreover, an attempt will be made to specify more thoroughly what it is about the classroom experience in Catholic schools that seems to be so successful.

Finally, both in future phases of the High School and Beyond project, and hopefully in other research enterprises, family background characteristics must be studied more rigorously to diminish the likelihood that the effects reported in the present project are not, in fact, the parental choice effect masking as school effect.

Even more difficult than explaining the Catholic school impact, however, is explaining why this impact has not hitherto been studied. The phenomenon of enthusiasm for Catholic schools among black and Hispanic parents is well known. Yet no agency private or public has been willing to fund research on the subject. Indeed, one project was rejected by the National Institute of Education (while Patricia Graham was director) on the ground that it would tend to "redound to the advantages of those schools"—certainly a curious criterion for a presumably scholarly government agency to utilize.

Six percent of the minority students in the country attend Catholic secondary schools. Approximately 10 percent of the minority children are in Catholic primary schools. The achievements of the students who attend such schools are dramatic and the costs of such achievements are remarkably low. How could educational scholars and scholarly funding agencies continue to ignore such a fascinating educational laboratory? Very likely they will continue to ignore the achievements of Catholic schools and the problem of why they do so will continue to be at best inexplicable.

Furthermore, Catholic agencies should be far more willing to fund research on Catholic schools. At one time long ago it seemed that Catholic institutions did not want to research Catholic schools for fear they would be found effective.[4] It almost seems that there is a crisis of confidence and of identity that has plagued Catholic education for many years. Those who wish to continue this crisis of confidence will find no consolation in the data analyzed in the present project.

NOTES

1. The data summarized in this report were collected by the National Opinion Research Center under contract with the National Center for Education Statistics. The analysis was funded by grants from the Ford Foundation and the Spencer Foundation. I am grateful to the members of the High School and Beyond team for their cooperation, especially to James Coleman, Carol Stocking, Fansayde Calloway, and Lawrence Dornacker. Comments from other NORC colleagues were very helpful--Robert Michael, Norman

Bradburn, William McCready. Data processing assistance at NORC was provided by Donald Tom, and typing by Mary Kotechi and Chris Lonn. University of Arizona assistance was available from Michael Hout and Dolores Vura of the Department of Sociology, and Daniel Bailey of the Computer Center.

2. The word "minority" is used to stand for the words "black" and "Hispanic." No special ideological meaning is attached to the word.

3. The model used to explain differences in standardized achievement test scores focused on family characteristics, student characteristics, and school characteristics. The family characteristics used in this model were: father absent, income, parental education, parental aspirations for student's college attendance, family learning environment (specific place to study, daily newspaper, encyclopedia, typewriter, more than 50 books, a room of one's own, pocket calculator), family monitoring of homework. Student characteristics were: psychological well-being, college aspirations in Grade 8, hours of television watched per week, use of time (high on reading for pleasure, reading the newspaper, talking with mother or father about personal experiences, low on visiting with friends at local gathering place, going out on dates, driving around, talking with friends on telephone, thinking or daydreaming alone). School characteristics were: owned by a religious order, student rating of teachers (quality of instruction and interest in students), discipline problems (truancy, skip class, talk back to teacher, refuse to obey instructions, get in fights with each other, attack or threaten teachers.)

4. An additional reason for this result may be the unwillingness of Catholicism in the United States either to recognize that good research costs money or to pay for high quality products.

2. Why Inner-City Families Send Their Children to Private Schools: An Empirical Study

Rev. Virgil C. Blum, S.J.

Inner-city private education is truly a great educational phenomenon in America today. It is in fact the Catholic Church's greatest apostolate to the poor of every religious belief. Low-income minority families, discriminated against by state and federal legislatures, by state and federal courts, make tremendous financial sacrifices to send their children to inner-city private schools.

Several years ago the Catholic League for Religious and Civil Rights initiated a study to ascertain who these families are and why they make the sacrifices entailed in sending their children to private schools. The study was made in 64 randomly selected inner-city schools in eight cities: Los Angeles, New Orleans, Chicago, Milwaukee, Detroit, New York, Newark and Washington, D.C. The 55 responding elementary schools serve a total enrollment of 15,312, of whom at least 70 percent are members of racial minorities.

The elementary schools, which have an average enrollment of 278 children, are heavily dependent on lay teachers, with only 30 percent of their teachers being religious men and women. The schools operate under open admissions policies. The expulsion of children is rare, but sometimes students are advised to transfer to a school where more adequate counselling is available.

The Catholic League study examines the attitudes of about 4,000 elementary school parents, 339 teachers and 55 principals who responded to our survey. The information provided by the parents reveals who they are (their religion and ethnicity, their economic status, their educational level, their family structure), their perceptions of inner-city schools and, most importantly, their perceptions of the kind of education their children are receiving in inner-city private schools.

Although nine of ten inner-city private schools are Catholic or ex-parochial schools, almost one-third of the families with children in these schools are Protestant, and 2 percent have no religious affiliation. Of the Protestants, 21 percent are Baptists, 4 percent are Methodist and 6 percent are members of other Protestant denominations. Of the black families, 53 percent are Protestant and 44 percent Catholic. Of the Hispanic families, 98 percent are Catholic and 2 percent Protestant. Of the white families, 92 percent are Catholic and 6 percent Protestant. Of the Orientals, 82 percent are Catholic, and 6 percent Protestant. The remainder have no religious affiliation.

17

The deep commitment of minority families to inner-city private education is clearly demonstrated by the sacrifices entailed in their choice of inner-city private schools. Fifteen percent of the responding families report annual incomes of less than $5,000; another 35 percent report incomes of from $5,000 to $10,000; 22 percent report incomes of from $10,000 to $15,000; 14 percent report incomes from $15,000 to $20,000; and another 14 percent report incomes over $20,000.

It is noteworthy that 72 percent of families with children in inner-city private schools report annual incomes of less than $15,000. This constitutes an over-representation of low income families, since only 36 percent of all U.S. families have incomes of less than $15,000. More remarkable still is the fact that 50 percent of inner-city private school families live on less than $10,000 a year, in contrast to 27 percent of all U.S. families. All but 14 percent of the respondents are members of families whose annual income was below the median income of U.S. families, which was just under $20,000 in 1978.

It should be noted that of the 15 percent of all inner-city private school families with an annual income of less than $5,000, 35 percent are unemployed and receiving welfare payments. Of the 35 percent of the families with an annual income between $5,000 and $10,000, 4 percent are unemployed and on welfare.

In comparison with all U.S. adults, a smaller proportion of inner-city private school parents has dropped out of school before completing the eighth grade. On the high school level, there is no discernible difference in the educational attainment of the two groups. On the college level, inner-city private school parents are slightly better educated than all U.S. adults. Twenty-two percent have completed from one to three years of college, as compared with 13 percent of all U.S. adults. Fifteen percent graduated from college or had some professional or graduate education, which is equal to the percentage for all U.S. adults. It should be noted, however, that all elementary school parents today are better educated than all U.S. adults.

Blacks, Hispanics, whites and Orientals differ to a remarkable degree in educational levels. While 44 percent of the blacks and 52 percent of the Orientals were educated beyond the high school level, only 23 percent of the whites and 18 percent of the Hispanics were educated to that level.

In looking at the family structures of children in inner-city private schools, we find that 60 percent are two-parent families with both mother and father present; 35 percent are one-parent families with only the mother present; 1 percent are one-parent families with only the father present; and 4 percent are being raised by one or both grandparents. Why do these minority parents send their children at great personal sacrifice to inner-city private schools? Why do they pay an average tuition of $390 a year, when, down the street at a government school the taxpayer will spend approximately $2,500 a year for their child's education?

The greatest degradation of poverty is the unavailability of choice. Most poor parents in America are suffering that degradation. In the education of their children they have no choice of religious and moral values, no choice of educational environment, no choice of dedicated and committed teachers, no choice of personal involvement in the education of their children. The state through its truancy laws forcibly compels parents to send their children to schools, but monopolizes the resources so that only the government schools get significant public assistance. The net result is that parental rights remain only theoretical for most poor people.

Why, then, do some of these poor and powerless parents send their children to inner-city private schools in old delapidated buildings, to schools with totally inadequate facilities and equipment, to schools with teachers grossly underpaid, and in which they themselves are expected to contribute labor and services? In our Catholic League study, minority parents answered that question in a voice that was virtually unanimous. They send their children to inner-city private schools because they want a better education, a quality education for their children. By quality education, they mean an education that includes religious and moral values, an education with rules and discipline, an education that treats their children with respect, an education provided by teachers and staff who care about their children and their image, and impress on them high levels of expectation, an education to which they themselves contribute labor and services, an education that makes their children so interested in learning that they discuss school at the dinner table.

This sort of quality education is what parents get for their children, for example, at St. Leo in Milwaukee, of which we have much firsthand knowledge. St. Leo closed as a Catholic school in 1970, became the Leo Community School, declined to 70 students, and went bankrupt. Under the leadership of associate pastors Fathers Robert Schneider and Thomas LeMieux, St. Leo reopened in 1977 with 280 students, and with a waiting list of some 500 hopeful families. Ninety-eight percent of the students at St. Leo are black, and 90 percent are Protestant; 85 percent qualified for free meals under the government-funded breakfast and hot lunch programs.

Families with children at St. Leo found what they wanted: quality education, as demonstrated by the performance of transfer students in the Iowa Test of Basic Skills and other standardized tests, which were administered both at the beginning and end of the school year. Fourth-graders entered the school scholastically at an average of two years below grade level. Tests at the end of the year indicated that the children had progressed to within three months of their expected reading level and four months of their expected levels in math and study skills. The sixth graders came to the school more than two years behind on the average, yet they finished the year only nine months back. The seventh graders lagged two-and-a-half to three years back, yet within ten months, they were performing at a level only one year below the expected achievement level for seventh graders.

Like St. Leo, most inner-city private schools live a precarious existence. About 30 percent of their teachers are religious women and men receiving very low salaries. It is these teachers who, because of years of experience in the schools, are the administrators and provide the stability and continuity so essential to a school. Most lay teachers, especially male teachers, cannot long continue at a salary that is only half of what they could get at a local public school. Many lay teachers do in fact transfer to public schools or take other employment, thus leaving the burden of administration and continuity in the hands of a dwindling number of religious women and men, many of whom are rapidly reaching an age when they will be forced to retire.

Nonetheless, many highly qualified lay teachers do continue in inner-city private schools at great sacrifice because of their care for minority students, their feeling of achievement and personal satisfaction in serving the educational needs of the underclass, their expectations of success, and their sense of community with minority parents who contribute labor and services to make the school a success. This is job satisfaction.

In looking at the teachers' training and experience, we find a number of factors that contribute to the quality education sought by inner-city parents.

First, teachers in private inner-city schools have credentials virtually identical to those of teachers in public schools. About 90 percent of the teachers we surveyed have either bachelor's or master's degrees (71 percent BA or BS, 19 percent MA or MS), and 10 percent reported that they have "other" degrees; nearly all the teachers are state certified or could be if they were so requested.

Second, the teachers' experience in the classroom shows a healthy balance between veterans (those with 10 or more years), those at a middle level (five to 10 years experience), and newcomers (those with less than five years). In fact the two ends of the scale, those under five years and those over 10 years, account for 83 percent of the teachers, while the remaining 17 percent fit the middle-level of five to 10 years. It can be assumed that the blend of vigor and idealism associated with freshly trained teachers, when combined with the maturity and wisdom of the veterans, produces a healthy educational environment. This seems to be the case, for when the teachers were asked in an open-ended question why they taught in their particular school, they ranked "harmonious working relationships with administration, faculty, parents and students" as the second most important reason; the reason drawing the most responses was "to provide religious education."

There is a caveat, however, that must be noted here. We find that of the 30 percent of all private school teachers who are members of religious communities, three-fourths are veteran educators, while only one-fourth of the lay teachers (27 percent) fit the veteran category. In fact, over half of the lay teachers (56 percent) have less than five years of teaching experience, and over one fourth of them (27 percent) are in their first year of teaching. So, while the blend of young and old does contribute to quality educational experiences for minority children, our study shows that the stable cores of the teaching staffs are teachers who are members of religious communities, and it is the lay teachers who supply the new faces, fresh ideas, and the idealism of youth. It also shows that single lay teachers are more likely to be in the category of least experience.

Dr. Thomas Vitullo-Martin, in his 1979 study of inner-city Catholic schools commissioned by the United States Catholic Conference,* has indicated that there is a strong likelihood that many inner-city Catholic schools will disappear because "the church appears to have reached its organizational limits for their support." Using data provided by the National Catholic Educational Association, he argues that during the 1967-73 period Catholic urban schools declined at a 10 percent rate, while Catholic inner-city schools declined at a 20 percent rate. But when he takes into account various problems in definition of 'urban' and 'inner city,' he presents an adjusted percentage which shows that inner-city Catholic schools closed at a five times faster rate than did urban Catholic schools--from a 1967 high of 1,490 schools to a 1973 low of 1,052.

Dr. Vitullo-Martin's dreary forecast appears to be corroborated by Catholic League data. A major finding of our study is the emphasis it places on the precarious future of inner-city private schools. In the Catholic school system as a whole, Catholic inner-city schools have the highest tuition rates; that is, parents least able to pay must pay the most. Vitullo-Martin underscores this reality when he says that tuition payments for inner-city parents frequently amount to as much as 10 percent of the average family income.

When we look at who teaches in these schools, we sense the problems that loom with regard to the schools' ability to survive. We have said that 30 percent are nuns or brothers, that 75 percent of them have had more than 10 years of teaching experience and only 11 percent have taught less than five years. So age becomes an important factor. An additional factor is that fewer and fewer men and women are entering religious life; and of those within the declining ranks of religious orders or societies, many are leaving or have left the teaching profession. Today there are less than half as many teaching religious as there were a decade ago. So the sources

---

*Editor's Note: See Thomas Vitullo-Martin, Catholic Inner-City Schools: The Future (Washington, D.C.: United States Catholic Conference, 1979).

for such highly committed individuals who draw subsistence pay are drying up. And on the basis of the ability to offer financial incentives to attract and retain top-level lay faculty, it appears that the schools are in a bind. Of all the teachers we questioned, nearly one-third had annual salaries in 1977-78 of less than $5,500 (80 percent religious) and only 13 percent had salaries of more than $9,500. When looking only at the salaries of lay teachers, we find that 41 percent fit the range of $5,500 to $7,999, and 30 percent are in the $8,000 to $9,500 range.

The low salary of lay teachers is clearly a problem. It is especially evident when compared with salaries of public elementary teachers. In inner-city private schools the average annual salary in 1977-78 was about half that of public school teachers, $7,654 compared with public school teachers' annual average of $14,617. The problem is made more acute by the fact that the teachers in the inner-city private schools generally have the credentials to move into the public schools.

In looking more closely at the salaries of the lay teachers, we see that a greater reliance is placed on single lay teachers who are beginning their careers—75 percent of them earn less than $8,000 and the average annual salary is $6,423. Although the salaries of married teachers are better, they still do not offer much of an incentive; the salaries of two-thirds of the married teachers cluster in the $5,500 to $9,499 income bracket.

In trying to explain how lay teachers can work for such low salaries, we hypothesized that their income from teaching was supplemental, that it was not the sole means of support. The hypothesis did not hold up. We found that 70 percent of the lay teachers depended upon their teaching income as their sole or primary means of support.

What all this means is that these inner-city private schools, although offering sorely needed quality education for poor minority children and although seen by parents who use them as being the "only" hope they have for a decent future for their children, will be forced to close their doors because the church has apparently reached its limits of support, and because poor parents cannot stretch their few dollars any further.

That prospect of the continued closing of inner-city private schools is all the more painful when one senses the meaning that such a loss has on the lives of the children in these schools, on the dreams of parents who are already making incredible sacrifices to better the lot their offspring inherit, on the missionary-like lives of principals and teachers in these schools, indeed, on the very quality of life in the neighborhoods of America's inner cities. But there is a more terrible loss, it seems to me, and that loss is an intangible as far as the statistics of our study are concerned. It is the loss of a unique spirit of joy and hope that permeates the atmosphere in these schools, an atmosphere that draws parents to a personal involvement in their children's education, and that binds teachers, parents and children together in a spirit of family-like regard. It is that loss of belonging to and living in a community that is most painful. In our study of teachers we call that spirit job satisfaction and mobility, and we find that for most teachers it is the reason that low salaries can be tolerated. But it is naive to think that there is not a financial breaking point, that these schools can continue without additional sources of revenue.

It has been said that the greatest degradation of poverty is the unavailability of choice. The poor are virtually powerless to make choices in the education of their children. But self-sacrificing teachers and self-sacrificing parents, working in close cooperation, do develop a sense of "powerfulness" that makes choice of a private school possible, translates into job satisfaction, and creates the very conditions of quality education in inner-city private schools. In the midst of adversity, this parent-teacher relationship creates a sense of pride in minority students and their parents—a precondition of the better education minority parents want for their children. Such job satisfaction does not provide adequate financial support for a growing family, but it does explain, at least in part, why so many highly qualified lay teachers persevere in their jobs in inner-city private schools.

From 1972 to 1977 black and Hispanic enrollment in inner-city private schools decreased by 9 and 11 percent, respectively. Even while the number of minority children in these schools decreases, state and federal policies, and a host of economic, technological, social and legal pressures combine to induce middle-income parents to leave the inner city for the suburbs, thus eroding further the basis of parish support of inner-city parochial schools. Left largely with pensioners and poor families, a substan- tial percentage of whom are Protestant and therefore non-contributors to the parish Church, inner-city parish schools will find it increasingly difficult to meet operating costs.

Is higher tuition the answer? Before adopting this alternative, one must recall that our study indicates that 50 percent of inner-city private school families have an annual income of less than $10,000, and that 36 percent of the families are single-parent. What potential do they have for paying sharply high tuition charges? Very limited, to say the least.

Most families with children in inner-city private schools are making great sacrifices to pay tuition out of meager incomes. How much more can they sacrifice to provide quality education for their children? In view of the precarious conditions of most inner-city private schools, the answer to that question may well determine whether these schools will survive to serve inner-city minorities.

Minority parents rightly feel that they have been discriminated against because of their color or ethnicity. They have been denied equal rights in virtually every phase of human existence. Although the battle for civil rights for minorities in the 1960s has changed much of that, the right of meaningful educational choice for minorities is still to be won. State and federal tax policies have severely damaged the inner cities, thus leaving minority families with government schools that provide inferior education. Moreover, governments have persistently denied education tax funds to parents who choose high quality private schools for their children's education.

In defense of their fundamental rights in education, minority parents are today beginning to protest this denial of education tax funds. In our inner city study, minority parents gave virtual unanimous support to government programs that would provide public funds for the education of their children in the schools of their choice.

3. How Federal Policies Discourage the Racial and Economic Integration of Private Schools

Thomas Vitullo-Martin

For more than a decade private schools have been voluntarily increasing their enrollment of black and Hispanic students. Minority families are seeking to register their children in private schools, although the federal and state governments have offered no incentives to private schools to accept minority students. On the contrary, despite the federal authorities' concern for the potential segregating effect of private schools, the government has pursued taxation and program policies that make the enrollment of minorities in private schools more difficult.

MINORITY ENROLLMENTS: PROBLEMS

Even without such governmental policies, private schools have trouble enrolling minorities. Each of the two largest private systems--Catholic and Lutheran--is operated by a church whose membership is only about 2 percent black. To enroll black students, these church-operated schools--which account for about 75 percent of all private school enrollments--would have had to change traditional policies of orienting education services to members of their own religion.

Table 1

PERCENTAGE CHANGE IN BLACK ENROLLMENTS IN
PRIVATE SCHOOLS, 1969-1979

Level	Percentage Black, 1969		Percentage Black, 1979	
	School-aged Population	Private Schools	School-Aged Population	Private Schools
Elementary	14%	4%	15%	8%
Secondary	12%	5%	15%	7%

Source: Bureau of Census, Current Population Reports, "Population Characteristics," Series P-20, No. 355, Issued August, 1980.

In 1969 only 4 percent of private elementary school students were black, but by 1979 8 percent were black. If black students had been proportionately divided between public and private schools,

25

these schools would have been 14 percent black in 1969 and 15 percent black in 1979, matching the proportion of blacks in the elementary-school-aged population. Private schools fell short of these goals, but made remarkable progress in closing the distance by almost doubling the proportion of blacks in their schools in the decade.

In any event, perfect distribution of minorities in private schools is an inappropriately high standard. First, private schools are not evenly distributed throughout the country, but are concentrated in cities, especially cities in the Northeast and Midwest. Minorities, on the other hand, are still concentrated in the rural areas of the South and the Southwest. While 55 percent of all minority students lived in the South and West in 1977, these regions enrolled only 35 percent of private school students. Hence, for private schools to enroll a perfect proportion of minority students, they would have to enroll higher proportions of minorities than are living in their drawing areas.

Second, because no public subsidies exist for private schools, they must charge tuition or raise revenues from contributors. Most private schools do both. In the past decade, inflation and institutional changes in the major private system aggravated the difficulty of increasing minority enrollment, because minorities as a group had disproportionately low incomes throughout the decade. Catholic schools raised the average elementary school tuition 350 percent, from $54 to $187, between 1969 and 1979. Schools serving racial minorities raised tuition faster and to higher levels because they lacked the parish membership necessary to provide the kind of subsidies that permitted parish schools their traditionally low tuitions. Catholic parish schools serving minorities have average tuition and fees closer to $450; Lutherans report similar tuition increases.

Minorities, it would seem, should be increasingly priced out of the private schools, not enrolling in record numbers. Pricing mechanisms are not abolutely effective in blocking attendance of lower-income students at private schools. Minorities are increasing enrollments because of the efforts of the private schools and because minority parents are willing to spend a greater portion of their income on education--for private school tuition--than the average family. Public policies have in no way aided the movement. To the contrary, these policies have impeded the movement.

National statistics on the family income of students in private schools show that students from lower-income families do not have as much access to private schools as those from middle-income and upper-income families. These national statistics are not as revealing as they might seem, for the reason I have already mentioned: a disproportionate percentage of lower-income students and minorities live in the rural South, where there are fewer private schools.

Are minorities priced out in areas where private schools are relatively evenly available to all? In the Northeast, private schools account for 20 percent of all schools; and, because they tend to be smaller than public schools, they account for 14 percent of all students. The statistics show both that the use of private schools is surprisingly evenly distributed among all income categories, and that poorer students are priced out of the schools to some extent. Students from median-income families are almost half-again as likely to attend private schools, and students from wealthier almost twice as likely to do so.

Table 2
K-12 ENROLLMENT IN NORTHEASTERN PRIVATE SCHOOLS,
BY FAMILY INCOME, 1975

Family Income	Total Enrollment (in 1,000s)	Private School Enrollment (in 1,000s)	% of Families in Private Schools	% of Private School Enrollment
Under $5,000	842	58	7%	4%
$ 5 - 9,999	1,862	189	10%	12%
$10 - 14,999	2,235	259	12%	17%
$15 - 19,999	2,214	329	15%	22%
$20 - 29,999	2,529	431	17%	28%
$30,000 or more	1,220	253	21%	17%
TOTALS	10,902	1,519	14%	100%

Source: Survey of Income and Education, 1976: Bureau of Census Special Tabulation, Congressional Record, May 20, 1978, May 20, 1978, pp. S4156-S4162.

Private schools serving large numbers of lower-income students are typically sponsored by parishes or congregations, which spread the cost of providing education across their local church membership. In the past, many churches were able to eliminate tuition entirely and subsidize the school from church contributions.

But in the past fifteen years, as neighborhoods have changed, parishes--especially inner-city parishes--have found non-church members enrolling their children in the parish school, but not becoming members of the parish church. These parishes have not been able to maintain their level of subsidy of their schools, which have had to increase tuitions. In the private school systems serving the largest portions of lower-income students, the highest tuition burdens in the system are in the lowest-income areas. Tuition costs here can range from 10 percent to 20 percent of family income for the lowest-income families. Despite this trend, minority enrollments have increased in the private schools serving lower-income families. As we will see, however, federal policies have made financing schools serving lower-income families more difficult and have discouraged, rather than encouraged, the integration of these schools.

MINORITY ENROLLMENTS: THE RECORD
OF THE PRIVATE SYSTEMS

The racial enrollment statistics I have used so far (Table 1) vastly understate the actual minority enrollments in private schools by leaving out Hispanics and recent European immigrants. Because of the way the census data has been collected, it is not possible to discuss the enrollments of Hispanics or Eastern European immigrants simultaneously with those of blacks and other racial minorities.

We can get a better idea of total minority enrollments in private schools by looking at the statistics collected by the private system. Unfortunately, no system reports any information on European or other immigrant minority enrollments.

Between 1970 and 1979, Catholic elementary schools increased their minority enrollments from 11 percent to almost 20 percent, and Catholic secondary schools went from 8 percent to almost 15 percent minority. Catholic elementary schools have an 8.4 percent Hispanic-surnamed population. The total is undercounted because it does not fully reflect dramatic increases in Hispanic enrollments in several Eastern seaboard cities.

In the West, Catholic schools often enroll higher percentages of minorities than the public systems. In California, for example, minorities made up 44 percent of Catholic school enrollments, but only 41 percent of public enrollments.

The Lutheran Church-Missouri Synod, has reported comparably high concentrations of minorities in its schools. In 1978, its elementary schools were 12.5 percent minority (most of them non-Lutheran) and its high schools were 16.3 percent minority (14 percent black), a slightly higher proportion of blacks than in the high school population nationally.

Table 3
CATHOLIC SCHOOL ENROLLMENT, BY ETHNICITY

Elementary	1970-71		1979-80	
	Number	%	Number	%
American Indian	18,023	.5	7,600	.3
Black American	171,991	5.1	195,600	8.5
Asian American	18,240	.5	44,700	2.0
Spanish-surnamed	177,917	5.3	193,000	8.4
All others	2,969,307	88.6	1,852,100	80.8
	3,355,478	100%	2,293,000	100%

Secondary				
American Indian	2,438	.2	2,400	.3
Black American	37,447	3.7	53,400	6.3
Asian American	5,219	.5	12,200	1.4
Spanish-surnamed	38,643	3.8	55,500	6.6
All others	924,341	91.8	722,500	85.4
	1,008,088	100%	846,000	100%

Source: National Catholic Education Association Data Bank.

The growing importance of private schools to minorities is most dramatically evident in the statistics for selected private systems serving cities with large minority populations. In several Catholic systems, the portion of the schools within the central city boundaries are approaching or have surpassed 50 percent minority enrollments. For example, in New York City, the elementary schools of the Archdiocese of New York (serving the Bronx, Manhattan and Staten Island) are 53.2 percent minority and the high schools 33 percent minority. The percentages would be higher were it not for the effect of near-white Staten Island. The archdiocese's Manhattan elementary schools, for example, were 79.1 percent minority. The Brooklyn diocesan schools, which serve Brooklyn and Queens, have lower proportions of minorities (as do those boroughs), but their elementary minority have been increasing and have reached 34 percent--18 percent Hispanic and 16 percent black. And minority enrollments have increased in absolute numbers even though the Catholic system has closed 28 schools since 1972.

Table 4
ETHNIC ENROLLMENTS IN NEW YORK CITY CATHOLIC SCHOOLS, 1979-80

	Elementary		Secondary	
American Indian	75	.1	19	.1
Asiatic	2,601	4.0	507	1.8
Black (non-Hispanic)	11,392	17.5	3,035	10.5
Hispanic	20,506	31.6	5,802	20.0
White (non-Hispanic)	30,406	46.8	19,630	67.7
TOTALS	64,980	100%	28,998	100%

Source: Unpublished tabulations, Archdiocese of New York City Catholic Schools.

The Catholic schools of Chicago have experienced similar concentrations of minority students. Chicago's Catholic Elementary schools are now 46.4 percent minority, and secondary schools are 30.5 percent minority.

Table 5
ETHNIC ENROLLMENTS IN CHICAGO CATHOLIC SCHOOLS, 1979-80

	Elementary		Secondary	
American Indian	64	.1	59	.2
Asiatic	2,584	3.2	481	1.4
Black (non-Hispanic)	22,469	27.5	5,888	16.9
Hispanic	12,723	15.6	4,175	12.0
White (non-Hispanic)	43,772	53.6	24,189	69.5
TOTALS	81,612	100%	34,792	100%

Source: Unpublished tabulations, Archdiocese of Chicago Catholic Schools.

The San Francisco Catholic elementary schools are 61.2 percent minority and 20 percent non-Catholic; the secondary schools, 43.3 percent minority.

Table 6
ETHNIC ENROLLMENTS IN SAN FRANCISCO CATHOLIC
SCHOOLS, 1979-80

	Elementary		Secondary	
American Indian	42	.3	27	.4
Asiatic	3,640	26.2	998	14.4
Black (non-Hispanic)	1,440	10.4	506	7.3
Hispanic	3,015	21.7	1,282	18.5
Other non-white	361	2.6	187	2.7
White (non-Hispanic)	5,390	38.8	3,929	56.7
TOTALS	13,888	100%	6,929	100%

Source: Unpublished tabulations, Archdiocese of San Francisco
Catholic Schools.

The Catholic secondary school statistics in these cities show lower minority enrollments for several reasons. First, secondary schools increase their minority enrollments gradually, several years after the minority students' initial enrollment in elementary schools, as these students move up the grade levels of the system. Second, tuitions at the secondary schools in these cities average at least twice the elementary school tuitions, but can be as much as five times as great. Tuitions in New York City, for example, average $800. Third, and most interesting for those concerned with racial integration, private schools have established a reputation for superior performance that attracts white students back to schools, even those in racially changing neighborhoods. For instance, Cardinal Hayes High School which serves the South Bronx--a heavily Hispanic and black area of New York--has maintained a relatively stable 18 percent white enrollment for several years. In 1979, the school attracted 245 white students from areas as distant as middle-income and upper-middle-income Riverdale, Bronxville and Pelham Bay. It is not surprising that a school with a reputation for quality can hold or attract at least some white students, since that theory is the basis for magnet schools desegregation plans. At least in some instances, it is the private school's success at holding white students and remaining integrated that keeps down the percentage of minority students attending.
This is an important observation. Private schools as well as public schools can help a city to maintain an integrated population because they can hold racially mixed communities together. In a study of out-migrations from Seattle neighborhoods, Joseph Harris found that in neighborhoods under racial pressure, 36 percent of the public school families left for the suburbs during a three-year period, compared to only 6 percent of the Catholic school families.

FEDERAL OBSTACLES TO PRIVATE SCHOOL INTEGRATION

The movement of minorities into private schools should lay to rest the belief that these schools are elitist and racial havens. Whatever they may have been once, they are not that now. No thanks to federal policies. While federal officials bemoan the impact of private schools on racial integration, the net effect of federal intervention has been to exacerbate their racial and economic isolation. Furthermore, it seems clear that the private schools are being chosen by minorities—especially those who are not members of the church operating the schools—because of the quality of the education available. The federal government has pursued a program of improving the educational opportunities available to minority children as a means of preventing the formation or perpetuation of a racial or ethnically based underclass. The federal government ought not to ignore for ideological reasons what many parents regard as the best education available to their children.

Integration Aid Programs

The federal government bears a special burden for the racial segregation of private schools in Southern states whose segregation laws were forced on private schools by the 1907 Berea College case. Southern laws required private schools to segregate. Although private school systems in the South did not fall within the jurisdiction of Brown, most of them voluntarily desegregated. Many private systems—Lafayette, Louisiana; Mobile, Alabama; St. Louis, Missouri—desegregated on their own initiative, and before their companion public school systems obeyed court orders.

Having authorized the states to force integrated private schools to segregate, the federal government bears a special obligation to aid private schools' integration through programs assisting them in financing the enrollment of minority students. Since the First Amendment was not deemed to constitute a barrier shielding private, church-operated schools from the imposition of segregation upon them in the era of Jim Crow and the notorious "Black Codes," it is perverse to argue now that the First Amendment's prohibition against a governmental establishment of religion credibly prohibits the federal government from acting to repair the damage caused to these schools by state actions enforced by judgments in federal courts.

The posture of the federal Department of Education in 1980, however, shows an extraordinary indifference to the integration problems of private schools. Despite the concern expressed by numerous officials in that Department that private schools cause desegregation problems, the Department currently neither manages nor advocates any programs that would aid or encourage private schools to integrate. The Department provides direct assistance to public schools through its regional race and sex desegregation assistance centers and through the Emergency School Assistance Act (ESAA). The desegregation assistance centers provide schools with technical assistance to handle problems of civil rights compliance, and ESAA provides federal funds to public school districts that are under court orders to desegregate or that are adopting voluntary plans to overcome the problems of segregation.

Federal laws mandate that private school students be served in these programs with services equivalent to those given public school students. The Department of Education's implementing regulations (called EDGAR, an acronym for Education Department General Administrative Regulations) spell out this requirement in considerable detail. EDGAR states that federally funded services shall be given to private school students by the "subgrantee" (typically the public school system), in the amounts consistent with their number and need; that the private school students be selected for receiving services on the same basis as the public school students; that they receive the same services where their needs are the same and different services where their specific needs differ. However, the regulation likewise provides:

> (a) A subgrantee may not use program funds to finance the existing level of instruction in a private school or to otherwise benefit the private school; (b) The subgrantee shall use program funds to meet the specific needs of students enrolled in private schools rather than--
> (1) The needs of a private school; or
> (2) The general needs of the students enrolled in a private school.

These regulations were principally designed to meet the major problems of the Title I program authorized under the Elementary and Secondary Education Act (ESEA), a program that disburses services to students to overcome reading and other academic problems.

ESAA grants and technical assistance are to help school systems integrate. The programs incidentally may provide services to students, but only in the context of a plan that relates services to the problems of segregation or to desegregation efforts. Only public schools can apply for the ESAA funds, and under current regulations, only public schools can receive federally funded technical assistance for desegregation. But the public school must include private school students in any services it develops to overcome racial imbalance.

So far as I have been able to determine, ESAA-funded services have not been used to help private schools eliminate what they determine to be their integration problems. The services must be selected to meet the public school problems. In fact, one could interpret EDGAR to prohibit any effort to remedy private school segregation problems directly, since any federal funds used in the effort would be serving the "needs of the private school," and this is prohibited. This leads to absurd situations in which the planning for the integration of private schools can be federally assisted only when public schools claim that the private schools must develop such plans for the success of the public school program.

The Department of Education has not systematically monitored the ESAA program to ensure that private school students are appropriately served. So we can describe how the program is being carried out only on the basis of reports from various public and private school officials. They all suggest that there is widespread participation of private school students in ESAA programs, that the students receive services analogous to the Title I services, but that the schools themselves receive no assistance in helping them define, confront, or remedy problems they may have with segregation or with multi-racial student communities. And it appears that even this limited amount of assistance was eliminated in the last year of the Carter administration.

ESAA regulations were strengthened in 1978 (effective 1980), to require clearer connections between federal assistance and desegregation efforts. As a consequence the Department of Education refused to renew grants to a number of public districts, either totally or in the private school components of their proposals, because these districts failed to tie their private school efforts to desegregation plans. This is a kind of Catch-22, since any genuinely effective desegregation effort must be concerned with schools as entities, and not simply with students as individuals needing help. But most federal officials interpret EDGAR and the ESAA program regulations to prohibit any direct aid or assistance which would serve directly the needs of private schools as entities. The only way out under existing regulations is for public schools to take responsibility, in their federal proposals, for private school integration; but this makes public schools responsible for something that only private schools can accomplish.

This tightening of regulations has proven costly to private schools and to the racial integration ESAA has attempted to foster. In the summer of 1980, for example, a large number of private schools that had been receiving ESAA funded services for students were eliminated from the program without warning. Again, no tally is available of the number eliminated, but there are many examples. In California, for instance, the private schools of San Diego, San Bernardino, San Jose, Stockton, and San Francisco were all eliminated from the ESAA program. For some systems the loss was considerable. San Diego private schools, with their large Hispanic enrollments, lost $350,000 worth of educational assistance because the public school proposal was judged inadequate. In practice, this means that a school like John F. Kennedy Memorial School (Catholic) in San Francisco will no longer receive programs in intercultural relations for its diverse student enrollment, which is approximately one-third Hispanic, one-third white, and one-third black and Asiatic.

More serious still, because it is self-defeating, is the failure of the Department of Education to deliver any technical assistance to private schools (so far as I have been able to determine) despite the fact that court-ordered plans to desegregate public schools in several communities (Boston, Cleveland, Los Angeles, Houston) have embroiled private schools in desegregation conflicts. The federally funded desegragation assistance centers (which received $55 million in fiscal year 1981) act as troubleshooters for the local schools moving through desegregation plans. But these centers recognize no responsibility for helping private schools plan the best possible strategy for aiding the desegregation process, even though private school cooperation is manifestly necessary to the success of any public school plan, and despite the fact that private schools are indirectly affected by the court orders or by public school efforts. The private schools are affected indirectly, first, by becoming subject to at least the threat of "white flight," a threat that will increase in magnitude as the federal government ties suburban and central districts together in its desegregation cases. Second, they are affected, at least potentially, by their remaining as neighborhood schools (and therefore more likely of a single race) after the public schools have become more integrated regional schools. They get a reputation for segregating that they do not actively earn.

The private schools are also directly important to any successful efforts to integrate education, because—especially in the country's largest cities—they educate a large portion of the students. Over 25 percent of New York City's students, 40 percent of Boston's, and 50 percent of Albany's students are enrolled in private schools. The point is not "if only all these students were in the public schools, public schools would be integrated." That reasoning ignores both the extent of minority presence in urban private schools (which is greater in private schools than in public schools in a number of cities) and the pattern of mobility of white students in urban areas, which has been to leave city public schools not for city private schools, but for suburban public schools. The point is that it is irresponsible and unrealistic to aid the integration efforts only of public schools and to ignore the impact of nonpublic schools on desegregation efforts.

The regulations guiding the applications of ESAA and the technical desegregation assistance to private schools need to be reinterpreted. The programs are designed to encourage voluntary desegregation efforts, and so fit well the needs of private schools which, ultimately, can only encourage and not order desegregation efforts on their parents and students. But, as applied, they provide no help to private schools whatsoever. It is important that public and private schools coordinate their planning and efforts in confronting segregation problems to the extent possible, but the present approach of handing the entire problem, responsibility and resources over to the public school, does not encourage cooperation or solutions. EDGAR need not present the insurmountable obstacle many believe it is. It, after all, only prohibits the use of federal funds "for the benefit of the private schools." It is reasonable to argue that assistance specifically designed to aid the private schools integrate is not aid for what is on their own private agenda, but aid for a public purpose, to encourage them to adopt as their own the public goal of integration. Neither ESAA aid nor the technical desegregation assistance, when given to private schools, would turn public money over to private purposes.

The implications of my argument are that the federal government should directly aid private schools to integrate, and to coordinate their efforts with public schools in the face of court-ordered desegregation plans. In fairness, however, I must acknowledge that there is one way in which things are better as they are. Private schools are not currently subject to any of the federal regulations public schools must follow as a result of accepting federal money. Private schools may well be drawn into the same morass of rules, and these would be even worse for them because the rules have already been worked out to fit the characteristics of public systems, without regard for the distinct character of private schools. Put another way, it is increasingly difficult for the federal government to offer any pure incentive programs, because all come freighted with a growing burden of regulations.

FEDERAL DISINCENTIVES TO INTEGRATION

There is a way out. The federal government has in its control an effective incentive system which does not enmesh private institutions (or at least has not so far) in the labyrinth of regulations guiding public schools: the tax system. Unfortunately, however, the tax system has become—so far as the integration of education is concerned—a perverse incentive. Through its policies governing tax deductions, the federal government heavily subsidizes public schools in exclusive suburban districts, and it heavily penalizes middle-income and wealthier families that decide to use the integrated city private schools. Most amazingly, it strongly penalizes private schools that attempt to integrate their enrollment by offering scholarships to lower-income and minority students. The remainder of this essay examines in detail how the federal government provides these subsidies and penalties.

First, the entire operating expense of local government—including local schools—is raised by state and local taxes and is deductible from personal income subject to federal taxation. Second, this deduction is, in effect, a federal subsidy of local expenditures. Third, in places where the average family income is relatively high, the average tax bracket is higher; consequently, the value of the average deduction is greater. Fourth, as a result, affluent suburbs receive a far greater per capita subsidy from the federal government than do central cities, and this federal aid covers a far greater proportion of all local expenditures in these wealthy areas. Fifth, public school aid through the tax system far exceeds direct programmatic aid that the federal government gives to support education.

In 1980, state and local governments raised over $100 billion to support the operations of their public schools. The federal government refunds a portion of this tax burden to state and local taxpayers--at least to those whose incomes are high enough to permit them to itemize deductions on their federal income tax returns. By deducting state and local school taxes, taxpayers reduce their federal tax obligation. In effect, the federal government takes on some of the burden of paying for local schools (and for other local services). The system of tax deductions for local school expenses amounts to a transfer payment from the federal government to the local school district via the income tax system. The higher the median income of a school district's residents, the higher their median tax bracket, the more valuable the tax deduction to them, and the greater the amount of the federal reimbursement of the local school budget.

An exact calculation of the cost of this program to the federal government is impossible because public school systems do not generally report data on the income range of the population they serve. I believe that a cost estimate of $30 billion is in the ball park. This is four times the total of the federal education budget (about $7 billion in FY 1981), which makes the tax refund device a much more important federal program in aid of education than its program of direct grants. Unfortunately, although the program of direct grants is modestly skewed to aid lower income areas, the tax refund program is heavily skewed in favor of the wealthiest communities.

The net effect of federal intervention in education is to subsidize the wealthiest families in the most economically and racially segregated schools far more than the families using the poorer and predominantly minority schools in central cities. For example, Pocantico Hills, a Westchester County suburb of New York City, operates only elementary schools and spent $10,000 per pupil in 1979-80, compared with New York City's approximately $2,700 per pupil for its elementary schools. The median income in Pocantico Hills was twice that of New York City in 1970 and the difference has probably increased since then.

The IRS does not report income tax data for communities, so we are forced to make some assumptions about the tax brackets of the average taxpayers in New York City and Pocantico Hills in order to estimate the comparative value of federal aid to these cities through deductions of local taxes that support their schools. And in calculating the value of aid through the tax system to public schools, we must first determine the portion of per pupil expenditure in the school system raised through taxes at the local and state levels, because only this portion of the school bill becomes a deduction from the income tax obligations of the school district's residents. Federal aid to the district is not paid for out of local taxes and, therefore, is not a deduction from federal tax obligations. To calculate the actual federal tax aid to a district, we must subtract the value of federal educational assistance to the local public school district from its per pupil expenditure.

Next, we must determine the average tax bracket of the school district's residents, since the value of the deduction of local school taxes varies according to the taxpayer's bracket. For example, if a taxpayer is in the 25 percent bracket, an increase in local school taxes of $1,000 means a reduction of federal taxes by a little more than $250. The taxpayer has to come up with 75 percent of the new taxes because the federal government, in effect, shares the cost of the taxation by lowering its own tax bill. If the taxpayer falls into the 50 percent bracket, his or her federal taxes are reduced by a little more than $500.

State and local income taxes follow the federal regulations on these deductions, so the amount of local school taxes paid for through tax deductions is correspondingly greater. For those in the 50 percent tax bracket who live in New York State and work in New York City, the deduction is worth almost 70 percent of the local tax obligation. In other words, when a local government increases taxes by $1,000, these high-bracket taxpayers effectively pay only $300 in additional taxes. The other $700 that comes to the local system is, in effect, a transfer payment from local, state, and federal governments to the taxpayer's school system.

For New York City, whose population is at about the national average tax bracket, and Pocantico Hills, the amount of aid through these tax benefits can be reasonably estimated by multiplying the median tax bracket for the community by each school district's per pupil expenditure, less federal programmatic aid (since federal aid is not raised by local or state taxes and is not therefore a deduction on federal income tax obligation.) For our two systems, we find the following results.

For New York City.

Aid to the city from the federal government through the tax system alone equals about $464 in 1979. When the total value per pupil of federal programmatic aid is added, the total approaches $800. These amounts are calculated first by establishing the tax bracket for the median income in the city. In 1975, the last year for which census figures are available, median income was $13,459, placing the average resident at the 16 percent tax bracket. Because of the effects of inflation, both median income and tax bracket have increased since that date, so these calculations are conservative. Next we establish the total expenditure for schools, less the federal contribution, per pupil. In 1979, this amounted to approximately

$3.2 billion total, less $.3 billion federal aid, serving approximately 1 million students, for a per pupil expenditure from local and state funds (and therefore deductible from federal tax obligations) of $2,900. At the 15 percent tax bracket, the federal government rebates--or pays--$464 of this bill.

Unfortunately for New York, the city does not actually receive the benefits of this subsidy through the tax system. The IRS estimates that close to 90 percent of New York City residents take the standard deduction (form 1040A) in which they do not itemize local taxes as a deduction, and do not receive any federal tax break from increases in local taxes. Thus the residents of the city get almost none of the tax system aid that we have described here. Virtually all federal benefits to the city come from the federal programmatic aid.

For Pocantico Hills.

Aid to the district through the federal and state tax systems amount to almost $7,500 per pupil. There is virtually no increase due to federal programmatic aid, since the district is too wealthy to be eligible for most federal aid programs. For Pocantico Hills, the amounts are caluculated by establishing that the median family income in 1975 (based upon an extrapolation from the 1970 census) was approximately $50,000, and the combined federal state and local income tax bracket was 75 percent. The system's per pupil expenditure--based upon gross expenditures of $3.6 million, less federal aid of $800, serving the needs of 360 students--equals approximately $10,000 each. At the 75 percent tax bracket, this amounts to a federal and state transfer payment to the local schools of about $7,500. The federal portion of this would be about $5,000 per pupil. Of course, few wealthy families actually pay taxes at the 75 percent rate (which is the rate "on the last dollars earned", not on total income); but the reason they do not is because of tax deductions like those for these exclusive schools. Through the tax system, Pocantico Hills receives at least 10 times more aid per pupil from the federal government than does New York City. After crediting New York City with the programmatic aid it receives from the federal government, we find that Washington still gives Pocantico Hills almost seven times more aid per pupil than New York. So Pocantico Hills is quite attractive to anyone who can afford to move into its district, including the wealthiest families leaving the city.

TAX DISINCENTIVES FOR USING PRIVATE SCHOOLS

Upper income New Yorkers are most likely to enroll their children in religiously affiliated or independent private schools, schools that charge high tuitions because they are not supported by a church, foundation, or other outside source. Tuitions range from $2,000 per year to $6,000, with an average charge of about $3,000. In addition, parents must pay for school bus transportation and other services normally borne by local governments or public school systems. The present tax system effectively doubles and triples these costs.

The amount of the penalty the tax system imposes varies according to the federal, state and local income tax brackets into which the family's income falls. Representative federal tax brackets in 1980 for a married couple filing jointly are shown in Table 7.

Table 7
REPRESENTATIVE FEDERAL INCOME TAX BRACKETS FOR
SELECTED PERSONAL INCOMES, 1980

Taxable Income (in thousands)	Tax Bracket
$ 8-12	22%
16-20	28
24-28	36
32-36	42
40-44	48
52-64	53
76-88	58
100-120	62
140-160	66
180-200	69

As a rule, state and city taxes average one-third of federal taxes for New York. For the sake of clarity, let us take an extreme example, that of a family with a very high income. The line of argument, however, applies to all tax levels. A New York City family with a taxable income of $45,000 is in the 50 percent federal tax bracket. In addition, it is at approximately the 17 percent state and local bracket. After paying taxes ($14,700 federal and $4,500 state and local) the family has $24,800 remaining to pay non-deductible living expenses such as food, clothing, rent, and tuition to private schools. Tuition and expenses related to education for two children in private schools in the city would average about $8,000 per year, approximately one-third of the family's after-tax income, leaving it with $16,800 for other expenses. Clearly, using private schools requires a deep commitment to living in the city, since nearby public schools in the suburbs often have a reputation for comparable or better quality.

If expenses for education were deductible, as they would be if they were simply business expenses or religious contributions, the impact on the family would be quite different. A $8,000 deduction from a taxable income of $45,000 would bring the family income down two tax brackets. It would pay $10,800 federal and $4,200 state and local taxes on its $37,000 taxable income. After all taxes and education expenses were paid, the family would be left with $22,000 or $5,200 more than it has today, without the tax deduction, for other expenses. If educational expenses were tax deductible, the cost of private education to this family would be cut by 65 percent.

Consider once again, but from a different angle, the present situation in which educational expenses cannot be deducted. How much must the upper-income family earn in order to pay $8,000 per year in private education expenses? In its tax bracket, it would have to earn $24,000 in order to cover the $8,000 private-school expenditure (assuming the $24,000 income is "earned income" and subject to a maximum federal tax of 50 percent and corresponding maximum state taxes). The federal, state, and local governments would be taking $2 for every $1 the family spent to educate its children in private school.

Our examples have substantially understated the economic incentives for the family to move from the city. The commitment to a private school is not a one-year commitment, but stretches out over 12 to 15 years of nursery, elementary, and high school. Tax consultants estimate the out-of-pocket expenses of a family using only private schools to be in the range of $40,000 to $60,000 per child, or $120,000 to $180,000 of pretax, earned income--if the education expenses cannot be deducted. If a family with two children remained in the city, the family would have to spend $250,000 to $333,000 of its earnings for education in private schools.

At present, the alternatives are remarkably attractive. The same family could move to an exclusive suburban school district and invest in a home--a capital investment--the money it would have spent on private schools in the city. The home investment would produce tax deductions that allow the family to shelter a substantial portion of the $250,000 to $333,000 it has available to invest over the 15 years or so its children are in tuition-free public schools. Moreover, the family's suburban home will probably appreciate in value in that time.

In the suburb, the family can enroll both children in public schools, paying only the taxes on its property. Property taxes are a function of local tax rates and of the assessed value of the property and so cannot readily be projected. Let us assume that the family pays $3,000 per year in property taxes. Of this, 60 percent to 80 percent would be assignable to the costs of the public schools, or about $2,400 for both children. This amount would be deductible from the family's taxable income, lowering its tax bracket and saving it about $1,600 in taxes. Thus, the real cost to the family of the suburban public school education would be about $800, or $400 per child.

In summary, under the present tax system, the family must spend $24,000 of its gross income to remain in the city and use private schools, or $800 of gross income (which is the additional tax obligation the family must meet in the suburbs after federal deductions are accounted for) in the suburban public system. I observed above that the statistics describing the enrollment in private schools by family income show that lower-income families are priced out of private schools as a consequence of their economic circumstances (see Table 2). The tax deduction laws exacerbate the difficulties that lower-income families experience in paying private school tuition because they effectively increase the amount of money the family must earn in order to pay it. Thus, the tax policy reduces the number of minorities able to pay private school tuition and encourages the segregation of the system. Existing policies also tend to discourage the use of private schools by upper-income parents since the effective cost of education in a private school for these families is several times the nominal tuition.

This might suggest, on balance, that the tax system has a benign influence on the tendency of wealthy families to separate their children from poorer or minority children. However, that inference is not correct because the typical alternative for a high-income family is not the heterogeneous urban public school, but the homogeneous, elite public school. Because the income statistics on public school enrollments have not been available on a district-by-district, much less a school-by-school basis, the extent of economic and racial isolation that exists within public schools has been hidden. In private schools, as we have seen, some efforts are made to integrate the student population both racially and economically. Hence, the existing tax system encourages upper-income families to place their children in racially and economically isolated suburban public schools. The effect is also to limit the number of lower-income children in private schools. However, the system has a stronger discouraging effect on upper-income families, and therefore tends to make private schools more economically integrated, statistically speaking, than they would be if only market forces operated.

We cannot simply assume, however, that private schools would let market forces change their socio-economic mix of students. Lower-income students in private schools are subsidized by the school or by a sponsor. They are present in private schools because the schools have adopted policies that oppose market forces. The existing tax system takes a neutral or hostile position toward these policies. The IRS has proposed changes in tax regulations--now being argued in court--to make the policy even more hostile.

The two principal types of subsidy to low-income students in private schools are (1) subsidy to the school organization as a whole, which permits a lowering or elimination of tuition; and (2) subsidy to individual families or students in the form of scholarship aid. Some schools follow both policies. Typically, scholarship aid is funded from a school's general revenues, including tuition income. Existing tax regulations prohibit the deduction of any portion of the tuition payment, even the portion supporting the scholarships of lower-income and minority students. Thus, existing tax regulations make it more difficult for private schools to offer scholarships when the scholarship expenses are paid by tuition. Frequently private schools are subsidized by churches, and this subsidy enables them to enroll lower-income and minority students with only minimal scholarship aid. The churches, in turn, are supported by contributions from parishioners, including parents. These contributions are the church's version of the local taxes supporting the public schools. The IRS has recently proposed rules that deny parents the deductions of contributions to churches if they enroll their children in a church school subsidized by the parish on the ground that these contributions are a form of tuition. The proposal would make the church subsidy even more difficult. If the change were enforced, it would tend to limit the practice of parish subsidy to schools and the ability of schools to maintain tuitions low enough to enroll children of the poor.

I am not proposing that we should remove the effects of taxation in shaping public and private schools, but we should observe the kinds of schools that are being shaped by existing policies. Current taxation policy (1) provides far more aid to the wealthy than to the poor; (2) encourages the segregation not only of metro-politan areas, but of both urban and suburban public and private schools; (3) further discourages lower-income children from attending private schools; and (4) makes it harder for the private schools to offer scholarships. Taxation has integrating and seg-regating effects, which should be controlled to advance the national ideal of racially and economically integrated schools. The pursuit of this goal in both public and private schools would not entail great cost, but it would provide an important benefit for American society.

4. The St. Thomas Community School: A Harlem Success Story

Barbara R. Taylor

St. Thomas Community School, located in the middle of Harlem, is an example of freedom of choice in education. Our experience at this school over the past decade shows what can happen when you do have that freedom of choice. St. Thomas Community School provides an example of what educational freedom is doing for a group of people who are determined that their children shall have quality education. Ours is a school which strives to be a place where children, parents and staff work together, confident that the school is theirs to mold into a kind of school where growth for all is possible and where all will want to grow.

It serves children of kindergarten through eighth grade. The underlying philosophy of STCS is to provide each child with the opportunities to realize his potential in order to participate fully in life. Therefore, the staff of the school must believe that every child can learn, whatever his background, parental culture or ethnic origin, and they must hold themselves accountable individually and collectively for the progress of the children.

St. Thomas Community School was formerly a Catholic school, but by 1968 the surrounding area was 98 percent non-Catholic. The school was located within a ten-block radius of seven public schools where children were reading and functioning two grades below level in mathematics and reading. The parents of these children had average yearly incomes of about $7000, but they wanted the same quality education for their children that the affluent could readily provide. Out of these needs grew the concept of a community school, a school where policy and direction would be governed by parents, where students would be admitted on a first come, first served basis regardless of religious affiliation or academic rank as long as the services of the school could help the individual child, and a school that would serve as a center of resources for the people and the community.

Approval was secured from the Roman Catholic Archdiocese of New York for a three-year experimental program as a community school, operating from September 1968 through August 1971, during which time the Archdiocese subsidized the program. An evaluation of that experiment by an Archdiocesan educational team in the final year of the program gave the school an overall rating of eight on a scale from one to nine. An evaluation by public school superintendents gave the school a rating of nine. Despite this high evaluation of our work, in March of 1971 the Archdiocese informed the school they could no longer provide major financial support for the school.

By this time, however, the parents had formed a completely autonomous parent association. They had become the policy makers; they had endorsed their own principal and teachers and had assumed volunteer and paid positions in the school. They had also received a grant of $21,000 from the Urban Coalition to set up their own office, staffed by a coordinator and two clerical workers, to organize the parents to run their school effectively. The staff had updated the curriculum. Emphasis was on educating children as individuals. The achievement scores had improved; and, most importantly, the children were enjoying school and showing respect for the regulations they had a part in framing.

Inspired by the success of the experimental years and determined to continue along these lines, the parents now initiated their own fund-raising program. In addition to paying tuition and book fees, the parents raised $90,000 for the school year 1971-1972. During the following school year, the parents leased the school building from the parish, and the administration applied for a charter from the New York State Board of Regents. It had been anticipated that the 1972-73 budget could be met through a combination of state aid, foundation support, and parent fundraising. However, state aid was declared unconstitutional in the Nyquist case.* Foundation support was withheld pending receipt of our charter. The parents did raise $76,500 by January, and they sought to establish the school as a distributor of household products and cosmetics. It was thought that this proposed business venture would not only serve as a means for parents to pay their school bills but would also provide personal funds for the family. Welfare families, we thought, could be encouraged to use the business as a means of gradually removing themselves from the welfare rolls. Unfortunately, we soon discovered that this type of business venture was disallowed because it was considered pyramiding.

On January 25, 1973, St. Thomas Community School, Incorporated, was approved by the New York Board of Regents for a charter as an independent school with full academic accreditation. We could then qualify for grants from foundations and corporations.

The parents of the school have accepted the responsibility of policy makers. Since the staff is chosen by the parents, the parents have a great deal of confidence in the staff and they respect the abilities of the administration and the teaching staff to fulfull their respective roles. The executive board consists of fifteen members, twelve of which must be filled by parents and three of which are reserved for community people who do not have to have children in the school. This board meets biweekly with representatives of

---

*Editor's Note: See Committee for Public Education and Religious Liberty v. Nyquist, 413 U.S. 756 (1973).

the student council and the principal. Officers meet alone biweekly and once a month with parent leaders. The parent leaders are representatives of parents of each class in the school, and the general assembly of parents meets once a month. The parents have grown in their understanding of their role as co-teachers and models. They realize that much of the learning of their children stems from the contact with them and that the major job of the school is not discipline alone, but education with discipline.

Some paid positions, such as teachers, teacher aids, and clerical workers, are now being filled by parents. The parents also work as volunteers in classrooms, the play street or in the office. The school has taken on the responsibility of assisting parents in these roles as models and co-teachers by making these jobs available for them and by making sure they are involved in the jobs of volunteer work in this school. When this is not possible, they are expected to demonstrate their interests and their commitments by participation in special projects such as repairs for the school, sharing experiences, or printing.

As the financial backbone of the school, parents have engaged in fund-raising events that run the gamut from sale of homecooked dinners and pastry to raffling off a car. More recently, a benefit game between NBC TV and WBLS radio was arranged by the parents, who have received a commitment from these teams to make this an annual affair. Families receive direct credit to their personal accounts for fund-raising efforts. For example, on a $5 ticket $1 may be used for the cost of the affair and $4 would be credited to the family so that a person selling ten tickets might have $40 of credit directly to their account.

As for the staff, salaries for all staff members are far below the norm for the jobs they are doing, since money to bring their salaries more closely into line with those in the public sector has just not been available. This is a further indication of the commitment of the staff. All teachers are well qualified and certified. In brief, any one of the staff could be employed elsewhere and command a much better salary. Teachers are told when being considered for placement that teaching in STCS is not a nine to three job. They are made aware that in-service training, workshops, team meetings, and curriculum meetings will be going on. It is made clear that their sponsorship of extracurricular activity is appreciated and really expected.

The students have a student council. Elected members from grades three through eight form that council and meet with their teacher sponsor once a month. The students have created their own guidelines in the form of a handbook compiled with the aid of parents and staff. They also have the power of equal representation with parents and staff whenever there is a question of whether a student's presence is detrimental to the school.

It is the aim of our program to foster and encourage self-discipline based on love and respect for self as well as for others.

The example of parents and staff must necessarily play an important part in the realization of this aim if children are going to have a chance of achieving it.

Our curriculum is complete in that it meets the New York State requirements. Parent members and students have all been involved in making the curriculum meaningful without sacrificing quality.

Standards are not lowered because the school is a predominantly black school in the so-called "ghetto." All students are accepted where they are, and complete respect is shown for whatever experiences they bring with them to the school. The staff, however, seeks to build upon those past experiences, and to provide new experiences so that the students can realize their potential and participate fully in life.

Grades seven and eight are departmentalized. Individualization throughout the school is accomplished by the use of parent aid, the buddy system, tapes and headsets, reading machines, film strips, and similar educational tools. We use some open classroom methods as well as traditional classroom methods, according to the needs of the particular group. I think that flexibility is important because we have discovered that some children can't take open classroom.

In standardized testing our first, second, and third grades have consistently tested a grade above level in the April test phase each year. All other grades are consistently on level or above level.

Our children take the Cooperative Exam for High School Placement and also the Special Exam for the Specialized High School and qualify for the best high schools, such as Stoderson, the Bronx High School of Science, and Brooklyn Tech, Music and Art. The majority of our students are now going on to college.

We have a complete set of extracurricular activities, including basketball, softball, and dance. I am particularly proud of the dance group since I teach dance.

We have recently been approached by a group of concerned parents to open a satellite of St. Thomas in the South Bronx of New York or to assist the group in establishing their own school. We are planning with this group now. With them we are considering having a six-day school. The six-day activities would be activities to help the school remain self-sufficient while helping to minimize the cost to families of the school, by operating such things as a thrift shop and a buying club, with the hope of expanding that buying club into a food co-op.

St. Thomas Community School has been alive since 1968 and it has been independent from the Archdiocese of New York since 1972. Because we have survived for over a decade as a community school, we feel strongly that our experience is evidence of the viability of alternative schools. The academic performance of our students is certainly proof that ordinary minority students can achieve and readily excel if the proper ingredients are well mixed.

We consider those ingredients to be _parents_ who are involved, a staff who must be concerned, dedicated and accountable, and students who are motivated by the involvement of their parents and the concern of the staff.

In short, St. Thomas Community School represents an alternative school system that is predicated on love, enthusiasm, interest, concern, flexibility, and involvement. We feel that children are our most valuable treasure. They are the future of all of us. Surely they must be allowed to reach their full potential. If the ultimate goal of education is to prepare these children for their legacy, then to me our duty is clear. We must support every effort that makes this possible.

5. Nonpublic Schools and the Education of the Handicapped

Frederick J. Weintraub

The relationship between the public and private sector in education of the handicapped has had a very long and complicated history. In 1972 a study was done of New York State's programs of financial support for private schools for handicapped children. The authors concluded, "At a time when considerable debate is taking place, nationally, over some sort of voucher plan for educational services, it is interesting to note that for handicapped children vouchers had been an accomplished fact for some time." I would like to address here the history of the relationship between the public sector and the private sector in education of exceptional children, its present status, and some of the problems and issues of the coming years.

The history of special efforts for the education of the handicapped begins in the nineteenth century with famous names like Horace Mann and Samuel Howe (then members of the Massachusetts State Board of Education) and Henry Barnard from the Connecticut State Board of Education. In 1817, Barnard and the Reverend Thomas Hopkins Gallaudet established the American School for Education and Instruction of the Deaf and Dumb (now known as the American School for the Deaf) in Hartford, Connecticut.* Fifteen years later, the Perkins Institute for the Blind and the Massachusetts School for Idiotic and Feebleminded Youth (now known as the Fernald School) was set up in Massachusetts. While these residential schools received support from the state legislature and other sources, they were governed and operated as private schools. In 1848, 1851, and 1852, the legislatures of Massachusetts, New York and Pennsylvania appropriated funds to private schools for the education of mentally retarded

---

*Editor's Note: The son of Thomas Hopkins Gallaudet, Edward Miner Gallaudet, founded the federally supported National Deaf-Mutes College in Washington, D.C., in 1864, and served as its first president. In 1894, its name was changed to Gallaudet College; and even after passage of the Vocational Rehabilitation Act of 1973, which was meant in part to open up federally funded educational resources to the hearing impaired, Gallaudet College remains an important resource for providing a liberal education for deaf persons and for training persons to work with and for the hearing-impaired.

children. Many of the state schools for the handicapped, as well as many local public schools, began as private schools, and some still remain privately governed.

A look at the long history of education of the handicapped in this country discloses a number of significant aspects of public policy. First, very early in the nation's history private schools were recognized as a legitimate vehicle to meet public responsibility or public desire. There were handicapped children that the public education system did not wish to educate. Thus, because there was no public alternative, private schools were established with public support.

Second, these schools were frequently established by parent associations. For example, associations for retarded citizens had a long history of establishing and operating schools for their children as well as for other groups. Professionals, both in their private capacity as individual citizens and in their corporate identity on boards of clinics, hospitals and universities, also established schools for handicapped children.

Third, the traditional proprietary schools were established by entrepreneurs. It should be noted that the use of the word "school" includes schools of high quality, as well as a wide range of facilities that call themselves schools and that in many states are recognized as such, but would not meet any level of reasonable standard. It has also included two types of church-operated schools: the traditional parochial schools, such as the schools operated by the Archdiocese of New York, which has had a long history of running education programs for handicapped children, and the special schools, operated by various religious orders, specifically established to serve handicapped children.

As these schools became public-private or private-public schools, the line between public and private became very hazy, especially as more and more public money was used to support such schools. For many of the schools, the original idea was that they were a temporary phenomenon designed to meet the failure of the public education system and had as a primary purpose to get the public education system to meet its responsibility, at which point such schools intended to go out of business. For example, some schools were operated by parents who at the same time were fighting with the public schools to start the program in the hope that these schools would then go out of business.

Many of the professionally established schools were created for the same purpose; that is, to prove that a group of children could be educated, and to demonstrate to the public schools how it could be done. In many instances the public schools learned the lesson and have since established similar programs. Many of the private schools, however, then decided to stay in business and to compete with the public schools.

A look at state funding of private schools reveals basically five different approaches. One is the straight sum approach, according to which a tuition grant of x amount of money is given for every mentally retarded child, or every emotionally disturbed child, or blind child, or otherwise exceptional child that is placed in a certain school. That sum of money did not necessarily equal the amount of the tuition, and it was expected that parents would pay the additional cost or it would be raised through some charitable means. The second approach was called "education cost only" financing; the state and/or local school district would pay to the private school or to the parent a sum of money equal to what the average cost of education was in that school district. If the average cost of education was $500 and the tuition cost was $3000, then the state and school district paid $500; the difference had to be paid by the parents. Third, some states operated under a sliding scale system where parents were required to submit their tax records and demonstrate their amount of income and the amount that the state and the school district would pay would be adjusted accordingly. The fourth method, total payment of all costs of placing exceptional children in private schools, has been adopted by only one or two states. Under the fifth approach, educational costs are shared by the school district and other public agencies; for example, Mental Health or Public Health agencies might contribute to the cost of residential treatment and other services.

Not only did the state and local governments historically have a role in the financing and placement of children in private schools for the handicapped, but the federal government also had a major role. Parents of handicapped children have long been entitled to a federal income tax deduction for the cost of placement of those children in private schools. The rationale for the deduction is that the placement was being made for medical reasons.

A second major federal program commenced in 1965 under Public Law 89-313, better known as Part B of Title I of the Elementary and Secondary Education Act, that provides aid to state-supported schools and institutions. This was a program primarily designed to assist children who were in state institutions for the retarded or state schools for the deaf and the blind. Under the provisions of this statute, however, a private school that was receiving state aid was treated as a state-supported school and institution. The state gave federal project grants to the private schools and continues to do so.

A third federal program is in the Department of Defense. Known by the acronym CHAMPUS, the Civilian Health and Medical Program for the Uniformed Services provides support for handicapped children of military personnel. In the case of an overseas assignment where it was inconvenient to take a handicapped child, if a doctor agreed to placement in a private school the child was sent to a private school and the cost was totally paid for by the Department of Defense. Many private schools for the handicapped in this country historically were heavily supported through CHAMPUS funds.

Research, model, and development programs funded by the Office of Special Education have also directly benefited private schools engaged in education of the handicapped. In fact, this federal program was one of the first that consistently permitted private schools as well as private associations and research firms to participate in its research and demonstration activities, mainly because of the historical relationship between the private and the public sector in terms of education of handicapped children.

Universities have used private schools for the training of teachers. For example, Lexington School for the Deaf in New York City, which is a private school that is publicly funded, is the training base for teachers of the deaf for Columbia University. Federally supported private schools constitute a unique phenomenon in the history of the education of the handicapped. Gallaudet College, for example, is federally supported and yet a private school. The model Secondary School for the Deaf in Washington, D.C., is technically a private school financed by the federal government. The Kendall School, an elementary school for the deaf also in Washington, D.C., is another example.

This history has been traced up through 1977. Although I am unable to obtain an exact figure, I estimate that in 1977 approximately a billion dollars of public funds (federal, state and local) were being spent in private education for the education of handicapped children. One consequence of this financial fact that many private schools for the handicapped are 80, 90 or even 100 percent publicly funded is that the whole question of what a private school is has to be raised seriously. The question is: When is it private and when is it not private? Is it a private board that makes a school private, or is it private funding?

The right to education movement (the PARC case, the Mills case,* as well as other cases in which the courts have found the issue of assuring or guaranteeing all handicapped children the right to an education) also dealt with this unique phenomenon of the relationship between the public and the private sector in this regard. In the PARC case in Pennsylvania, which was the first of the right to education cases, the private schools for handicapped children in the State of Pennsylvania filed a countersuit after the court had ruled that handicapped children in fact had a right to an education. Their suit said that establishing the right to an education for handicapped children was contrary to the interests of private enterprise. The court did not agree. The question that the courts had to wrestle with was the fact that parents were in fact being re-

---

*Editor's Note: See Pennsylvania Assn. for Retarded Children (PARC) v. Commonwealth of Pennsylvania, 334 F. Supp. 1257 (E.D.Pa. 1971), 343 F. Supp. 279 (E.D.Pa. 1972); and Mills v. Bd. of Ed., 348 F. Supp. 866 (D.D.C. 1972).

required to pay part of the cost of private education when that education was provided as a means of meeting public responsibility. In the Kruse case the constitutionality of that situation was raised before the Supreme Court, and the result was a clear, resounding "No."* The result was that public schools that had historically used private schools as an escape but at a minor cost for them, suddenly were found to be responsible for total costs. This began a process that in the last five or six years has become a constant call to re-examine the ambiguous historical relationships between the government and private schools that developed in the education of the handicapped.

Public Law 94-142, the Education of All Handicapped Children Act, institutionalized the policy of free appropriate public education for all handicapped children. Even where such education is provided through a private means, it must be at no cost. "At no cost" does not mean at no cost to the public school system; it means it shall not be paid for by the parents. In other words, other means can be utilized. A whole set of other questions relating to standards has also been raised by the Act. Not only must the parents not be charged, but the standards and criteria utilized in the education of the child must meet the public standards and criteria. Thus, if a public agency places a child in a private school, then that private school must meet the public standards and criteria such as those articulated in the Individualized Education Program (IEP). The IEP is what determines the placement in the private school. This means that the public school is not only setting the rate or the contractual relationships and the standards, but is also setting the criteria governing what will happen to that child in that private school.

There also is the question of long-term responsibility. Historically, placement of children in private schools by a public agency meant out of sight, out of mind. The child was placed and not thought of again. An annual review of that placement is now required to determine whether it continues to be the appropriate vehicle for providing services.

There are some other issues that will need to be discussed in the future regarding the relationship between private schools and public schools in providing special education for handicapped children. One issue concerns the question of whether private schools are continuing or are willing to continue to play a shifting role in terms of the population that they serve, or whether they are now in a situation of being static and, therefore, in competition with the public schools for the children. Again, historically most of the private schools were established as a stop-gap measure at a point in history until the public schools assumed the responsibility. Many of

---

*Editor's Note: See Kruse v. Campbell, 431 F.Supp. 180 (E.D.Va.) vacated and remanded, 434 U.S. 808 (1977).

those schools moved on to serve the more severely handicapped children that the public schools could not serve. The serious policy question is: Are the private schools really interested in continuing to play a shifting role in educating handicapped children? If the answer is no, then a whole new set of relationships needs to be examined in the future.

Another issue is the serious question of licensing of private schools. One of the major placers of handicapped children in private schools is not the public education system, but the judicial system. The worst possible thing that can happen to a person in this country is to be a handicapped child who is a ward of the court. In this country there is a massive interstate commerce of handicapped children. Private schools—using the word "school" in loose terms—are literally buying up children. There are thousands of cases of children being shipped from Illinois to Texas to places that the agencies in the State of Illinois have never visited and have never seen. Some are private homes in which there are no certified personnel. In some of these instances children have been forced to live outside and have been physically abused. There are schools, financed heavily by CHAMPUS, that have stayed open because of federal support despite state efforts to close them for inhumane treatment. These are all private "schools," existing under public funds but with no public accountability. In education of the handicapped we are beyond the question of public support of private schools. The questions we now face are: When is a school private or public? What standards should be required and how should they be enforced?

A third serious problem worthy of investigation is the relationship between private schools and persons in private individual practice. There are private psychologists doing evaluations of children being served in the public system. Those private psychologists also happen to have some relationship to a private school, either as an employee or as a board member. And it just so happens that many of their evaluations of exceptional children conclude with the recommendation that these children be placed in the private schools with which the professionals are affiliated. There are questions of conflict of interest that need to be examined. A final problem that needs to be studied is the growing tendency by courts and welfare agencies to place exceptional children in private schools and send the bill to the public schools.

In summary, as the issue of public support of private education continues to be examined, proponents and opponents and policy makers may find value in examining the strengths and weaknesses of a long history of experience in education of handicapped children. Since the education of the handicapped has never been the subject of a comprehensive study, perhaps the first thing that educational policy makers should promote is such a study. It would not only shed light on a long history of efforts by both private schools and public schools to serve handicapped children, but would also serve to remind us that handicapped children constitute a minority in need of all the genuine help that they can get.

Discussion

DR. REED: In response to Mr. Weintraub's presentation, I would like to say that in the District of Columbia there is no doubt as to who is paying for special education for handicapped children. The public schools are paying for it. As a result of the Mills case under Judge Waddy, a decree was handed down several years ago that the D.C. public schools had to educate all youngsters regardless of need, with no consideration for budgetary constraints or anything else. As a result of that decision, during the last school year, we spent $23 million in special education. Three million dollars went to private schools for educating 643 students. Some of the bills went as high as $78,000 and $79,000 per child for their education.

Our biggest fight here has been that we feel the city should bear some of that expense because not all of that cost was directly related to education. Some of the cost was for room and board and other kinds of things that we felt the city's social services should be paying for. We had to take the mayor to court to try to get the city to pay their part of the expenses, because we are reaching a point now where we are spending $23 million for 9,000 students, the number of students we have in all of our special education programs. It is almost impossible to create within the system the capability of dealing with all the special needs of all handicapped children. Sometimes it is far cheaper to farm that out to private institutions.

The other problem we have is that we find that so many parents unfortunately want to abandon these children and get rid of them and put them into institutions so they no longer have to be bothered with them. We had four cases last Christmas where parents refused to let youngsters come into the home as they came back for Christmas vacation.

A third problem is that the D.C. school system is predominantly black, and there are some white parents who are willing to have their youngsters in private institutions and labeled special education as long as they don't have to go to black schools with black children.

As Mr. Weintraub has reminded us, the education of handicapped children is a serious problem. But I can tell you that when I was in court last year, I felt like crying when the judge made me look as though I were the big ogre who didn't want to pay for the education of these youngsters, when all I was saying to him was I want the city to pay their part of it. Financing special education is a far more complex situation than meets the eye, but these youngsters have to be serviced; and I am very concerned because three private schools where we had young people last year were closed by State officials because of negative evaluations. Too many of these institutions perform custodial care and made no serious educational efforts whatever. They put children in pens, and that is about all they do to them for a very large, lucrative fee.

DR. VITULLO-MARTIN: Let me leap in with two questions for Ms. Taylor. Did you find any public policies of the City of New York or the state or the federal government that aided you in starting your school or keeping it operating? And do you find that your school in any way damages the public schools in the area where it is located?

MS. TAYLOR: No, I do not find that it damages them. In fact, I have a very good working relationship with the public schools in the area. We have even used some of their facilities and they come to us for help too. I am on the Education Committee of Planning Board 10, so that I have a good working relationship with the public school system. We can learn from each other, and I don't think that one negates the other in any sense of the word. I think that some of the things that we have been doing have made some of the public schools in the area more alert. Certainly they have access to much more equipment and materials than we have, but all of this has just created healthy competition.

DR. REED: I think we should work together, Ms. Taylor. I have always said, "Thank God for private schools." I don't know what I would do if the private schools sent all their children back to us. I think there are some young people who cannot fit into the public school setup. In order for these children to be fully developed, they need smaller classrooms and the kind of instruction offered in private schools. I happen to think that this kind of diversity is healthy, so I have no problem with working very closely with private schools, and I think we should encourage that spirit of cooperation across the country.

DR. SARAH MOTEN, INSTITUTE FOR THE STUDY OF EDUCATIONAL POLICY, HOWARD UNIVERSITY: Having had a lot of experience in the public school system, I guess that is where my heart is. But I was fascinated by your presentation, Ms. Taylor, and I would like to ask whether you have had any problems with the local government trying to impose any of their policies on your particular school situation. I would also like to know whether you have been able to look at the adjustment of your graduates at the high school level, and whether there is any plan to follow these students through the twelfth grade, for example, to see what the attrition rate is or what the dropout rate is, or to evaluate the on-going success of your program.

MS. TAYLOR: In answer to your second question, I can state that we have made plans to evaluate our work. I do have some statistics available concerning what our children are doing and where they are going after they leave St. Thomas. We do not find that the children have difficulty adjusting when they go into high school after they have left our program. They qualify for the best high schools and go on to college.

In response to your first question, we have not had any trouble, as far as policy is concerned, with the local school board. They have been very cooperative, and there really have been no problems. Perhaps this is because our school is not the traditional kind of private school. Our school is a place where poor people who want to work hard can give their children the same thing that more affluent people give their children. The kind of children who come to our school are not from the upper middle class families. Their parents are poor people, many of whom are on welfare; and they really struggle and make an effort to keep our school alive. Most of the children at St. Thomas are so-called "ghetto" children; so when they really want an eduction, they can adjust when they go into high school.

I am an old public school educator. I taught in public schools for many years in Philadelphia before I came to New York, so I sympathize with the public school. I also welcome the kind of opportunity I have at St. Thomas because I am not held back by some of the red tape that you get in public school. At St. Thomas Community School I have freedom to work, to experiment, and to evaluate.

MRS. MAE DUGAN, CITIZENS FOR EDUCATIONAL FREEDOM (ST. LOUIS, MO., CHAPTER): Citizens for Educational Freedom is an organization that was founded 21 years ago. We have our national headquarters here in Washington, D.C., and the main thrust of our organization is to protect and defend parents' rights in education. As I listened to the panelists, I noted there was one area and one factor in the discussion of education that was ignored, although it was floating around like a ghost, and that is, the choice of the parents concerning what is best for their children. The right of parents to direct and control the education of their own children, including the choice of a school, the choice of a kind of education, whether it is private, public, god-centered or what have you, is a human right. It is listed in the United Nations Declaration of Universal Human Rights.* In my opinion, public policy in the United

---

*Editor's Note: Article 26 of the International Declaration of Human Rights, adopted by the General Assembly of the United Nations on December 10, 1948, provides: "1. Everyone has the right to education. Education shall be free, at least in the elementary and fundamental stages. Elementary education shall be compulsory. Technical and professional education shall be made generally

States today should recognize this basic human right of parents. If it fails to effectuate this right (for example, by denying tax benefits or by denying a fair share of education for handicapped children in private schools), then the government risks being perceived as violating a very fundamental human right.

DR. JOSEPH SKEHAN, PRESIDENT, NATIONAL ASSOCIATION OF THE LAITY: I was delighted to hear about the St. Thomas Community School in New York, Ms. Taylor. Do you know how many schools there are throughout the country which were sponsored in any way by a diocese and then moved on to a communal, self-governing kind of arrangement?

MS. TAYLOR: I know of a few community schools that developed out of parochial schools. Unfortunately, those in New York have folded. I don't know of another one in New York. There was an experiment up in Boston that did pretty well for a while.*

DR. VITULLO-MARTIN: There are some community schools in Chicago, in Milwaukee, and in Kansas City. The basic problem with inner-city Catholic schools is that they are primarily supported by the parishes. There is very little money that comes from a diocese to elementary schools. To begin with, the diocese gets its money from the parish, so there is very little redistribution. And in the inner city, when there is a very large black population, very few are Catholics or active members of the parish. When this is the case, the parish does not provide much socialized support for the cost of education, so the costs of the school gets thrown onto tuition and generally the tuition is pulled or pushed out of the range of the parents. In short, the financial problems for inner-city Catholic schools

---

available and higher education shall be equally accessible to all on the basis of merit.

2. Education shall be directed to the full development of the human personality and to the strengthening of respect for human rights and fundamental freedoms. It shall promote understanding, tolerance and friendship among all nations, racial or religious groups, and shall further the activities of the United Nations for the maintenance of peace.

3. Parents have a prior right to choose the kind of education that shall be given to their children." 3 U.N. GAOR, I, at 71; U.N. Doc. A/810.

*Editor's Note: For an account of the Highland Park Free School that was established in Roxbury, a predominantly black section of Boston, after the Archdiocese of Boston closed its parochial school, see Charles Lawrence, "Free Schools: Public and Private and Black and White," Inequality in Education 4(1970) 8-12.

are very difficult and very serious.

There is a second problem dealing with governance. When a Catholic church supports a Catholic school, a sizeable group meets on Sundays. This fact creates an informal government arrangement where there is a system of trust that builds up between parents and the people who run the school. They know everybody by their first names. But when there are non-Catholics in large numbers in those schools, they aren't part of the parish. The priests and nuns who are the administrators of the parish, and even the lay administrators, have a harder time knowing those families. There is not the same level of trust built up. The non-Catholics tend to treat the schools as simply another version, but a much better version, of a public school. In this sense there can be significant problems of governance.

DR. EUGENE LINSE, CITIZENS FOR EDUCATIONAL FREEDOM (ST. PAUL, MN., CHAPTER): My question concerns the recommendations that Dr. Vitullo-Martin might have in reversing what he has suggested as the trend involving governmental hostility toward nonpublic education. Although in our state we have had relatively good relationships between public and nonpublic schools, most recently there has been a development in which the Department of Education and the Board of Education have been separated from the Board for Teaching. The Board for Teaching will now certify teachers in all schools in the state. The Board has now set up some new regulations which say that no teacher can be certified to teach in any school in the state unless the practice teaching that has been done by that student is done exclusively in a public school. Somehow it doesn't really make sense to me to require practice teaching in public schools for teachers who are going to teach in nonpublic schools. That is to me another illustration of this kind of conflict, but I would welcome any recommendations that you might have to reverse the trend.

DR. VITULLO-MARTIN: I think that many of these problems are best settled at the state level, because I would expect that the people in Minnesota will not tolerate for very long the sort of regulation that you have referred to. A uniform rule established in Washington about these things might help a few states, but it would damage a lot of others because there is such a variety of practices out there. So my general bias would be to leave these things at the state level and have the states work them out themselves.

My attitude towards public and private schools is a community-centered attitude. Schools are a resource for the community in which they exist, and the schools within a neighborhood tend to work together. Generally they are not at each other's throats. They tend to share students and facilities; and people in the public schools often do whatever they can for the nonpublics without telling the downtown offices. In my view, that is a reasonable attitude towards education. The idea that helping a private school is somehow going to hurt a public school is a very bureaucratic view of things. In reality, if you build up the resources of one set of schools in a community, that should spill over and build up the resources for the other set as well. Education isn't a zero sum game in which if one side wins the other side loses. A neighborhood gets a reputation for having good schools; that reputation helps both public and nonpublic schools in the neighborhood. If a neighborhood gets a reputation for having lousy schools, it hurts both schools in the neighborhood. In my view, the notion that public and private schools should be at each other's throats doesn't aid education in the least.

MR. WEINTRAUB: I appreciate the concept of parental choice, but this assumes that a choice does in fact exist. As I relate to the question for handicapped children, parents historically did not choose the private sector over the public sector as a matter of choice; it was simply the only way to get an education for their children. One cannot simply presume that all the Catholic schools throughout the country, that St. Alban's School in D.C., that Lutheran schools and all of the other parochial schools are now ready and willing to open their arms to handicapped children. I think from the vantage point of handicapped children, there seems to me to be a lot of questions about whether there is really any meaningful choice, and if so what those choices are and how they become operative.

MRS. MARILYN LUNDY, PRESIDENT, CITIZENS FOR EDUCATIONAL FREEDOM: I would like to call attention to semantics that have been used here. We have been talking about public and private schools as if the public schools are the only ones that serve the public need and the private schools are something off on the side. We should really be talking about government operated schools and nongovernment operated schools, because all of these schools, whether private or public, are serving the public need. Our contention is that when government makes education compulsory and taxes everybody for it, that is fine, but it must distribute those taxes in such a way that the parent's primary and constitutionally guaranteed right is not hindered in making that educational choice. Through our distribution of educational tax dollars, we are making quality education a privilege dependent upon wealth or dependent upon the ability to find a religious or civic group to subsidize it. CEF feels that is basically wrong; it is a violation of human rights; it is a violation of civil rights; and it is a violation of religious freedom. So our whole contention is that we believe there should be a change in the distribution of tax dollars.

In addition to my CEF hat, I wear another hat by virtue of working many years in the delivery of social services in the inner city of Detroit. I see the crying need and desire of the inner-city people to determine their own destiny, to determine their children's education. I see a great desire among minority people in Detroit for a voucher or a refundable tax credit or whatever. Yet I sometimes see their leaders opposing these sorts of proposals. In light of this, I would like to ask the panelists whether you think that the minorities would really appreciate and make use of an educational voucher or some comparable system of financing education.

DR. VITULLO-MARTIN: One reform in educational financing that has been proposed is to do away with all tax deductions that deal with education, so that everyone would start on an even plane and with relatively equal advantages. This proposal could have an enormous redistributive effect sending monies back to the central cities. But there is a serious difficulty with this proposal. Doing away with deductions doesn't change the circumstances of people whose incomes are under $5000 or $6000 very much. They don't pay a lot of taxes, and if they are on welfare they don't have any taxable income. So this proposal would not enhance the educational choice of poor people. The fact is that they don't have any meaningful choice, because they can't afford the alternatives that may or may not be available. Hence the refundability provision in the tuition tax credit proposals is of major importance for poor people, because it would equalize the benefits of tax deductions. This proposal would, I think, make a great deal of difference to people in the inner city.

I had worked with the Corps Community School, which was a Catholic school in the South Bronx that did fail financially. We had come up with the proposal that the public school system of the City of New York give scholarships of $500 per pupil to the students atending this school. For purposes of state aid, these students would be counted as students supported by the public system of the City of New York. At that time, state aid to the New York City Public Schools was $800 per pupil, so the city's public school system could have made $300 in the transaction. Furthermore, there was no religious problem in this particular case because the Core Community School was a community school and there was no genuine First Amendment issue. And that is true, by the way, for an increasing number of inner-city schools.

One reason why Ms. Taylor's school, for instance, can be as successful as it is, is that parents have such a great need for the education and such a great difficulty in providing it. In other words, one reason why there is such wonderful parent cooperation in the fundraising activities of St. Thomas Community School is that there isn't any other choice for the parents. Hence, people come together and work very hard to guarantee the success of the whole affair.

The economic proposals may have the ironic effect of diminishing parental involvement. If educational funds go directly to the school, which would probably be the worst possible way of doing it, or if people are provided with the purchasing power at no cost to themselves, the demand for their contribution of their own efforts may thereby be diminished. It would probably not be eliminated, for people do work for schools even when they have a lot of money, but I think that it would be lessened, especially among poor people who have many more demands on their time and many more difficulties to confront.

MS. TAYLOR: I disagree with that. When we do get small grants from foundations, that only encourages them; and the people put the money to sensible use. When you are continually fighting for things you believe in, after a while you do wear out. Fund raising can be wearisome; you can get exhausted and think that you cannot do this anymore. Then along comes a grant of $20,000 or $30,000, and it gives you renewed energy. You cannot exist completely on your own unless the parents are really able to pay the full cost of education, and our parents are not able to do this.

MR. WEINTRAUB: I think that is right. I would just like to reemphasize the point I was trying to make before. I appreciate the notion of freedom of choice; I personally believe in it. I just want to make sure there is a choice. It is very difficult to talk to a Catholic parent of a severely retarded kid who believes strongly in Catholic education and who has at some expense sent every other child in that family to a Catholic school that their retarded child can't go to a Catholic school because he is retarded. And it is very difficult to deal with the parents of Hassidic Jewish children in New York City, where religion and culture and education are so inextricably bound together, that their child can't go to the yeshivas or can't even stay at home to read the prayers and engage in other religious observances with the family, but must be shipped off to the state school for the deaf. What I am saying is that for a large group of children there still to this day does not exist freedom of choice. When the day comes that the private system is willing to talk about providing freedom of choice for handicapped children, then I think the parents of handicapped children who have fought long and hard to get into the public sector would become more interested in talking about a more generalized notion of partnership between the public and private sectors.

SISTER ANN DURST, STUDENT, GEORGETOWN UNIVERSITY LAW CENTER: I am presently a law student, but I have been an administrator in nonpublic education, and I would like to respond to Mr. Weintraub because I believe he has raised a very important question or perhaps given me a very important insight. We are talking here about nonpublic education, but I believe more fundamentally we are talking about the education of children. Because we are always concerned with the realities of the finances sometimes we do not ask the right question. I think his question is well put. Are there choices out there? I would be interested to know whether or not nonpublic education would be willing to offer that choice to the handicapped or exceptional children. I think the question is well made or well put, because what we are really talking about is fundamental public policy. The primary question we are asking is whether or not the people of this country are interested in creating meaningful educational choices. How we finance that does seem to be a secondary question. Having been a former college president, I know what fundraising is all about. But as critical as the financial question is, I think the prior question really is the policy question of confronting the lack of educational freedom of choice for so many people in our country.

RABBI BERNARD GOLDENBERG, NATIONAL SOCIETY FOR HEBREW DAY SCHOOLS: My comment is addressed to Mr. Weintraub. I would like perhaps to jog your understanding a little bit more, Mr. Weintraub. Our families in the areas you mentioned--the closely knit groups you mentioned--are large families of eight to ten or eleven or twelve children. They are perfectly willing to sacrifice to preserve their religion, their culture, and their language. I do not think there has ever been a subconscious feeling, let alone a serious conviction among Jews that the government or anyone else should pick up the tab for that. But many of us believe that the guidance and the education which the deaf or the handicapped need is a legitimate activity for the government to be involved in. And I want to state for the record that anytime we have been able, we have been willing to provide educational choice for any member of a Hassidic or a non-Hassidic family, provided we have the funds. But so much of the budget for these poor, large families goes for their religious education and/or secular education in regular parochial schools. So how can we provide that choice if there is no government funding for the secular endeavor of guidance and education of the handicapped? Precisely what did you want us to do?

MR. WEINTRAUB: What I am saying is that a Hassidic deaf child, a child who wants to go to school and study the Torah and who wants to learn Hebrew, does not really have that choice, but his brothers and sisters do have that choice. That is the concern I am raising. Now I don't want to get into a debate with you on the use of funds. I agree that there is not enough money, but there has also never been a priority in the use of money that would suggest that that choice should even be there. What I am saying is that if we are going to make a presumption that choice does exist, then we had better examine that presumption. If it is our desire to make choice exist, then there may be a number of changes that will have to occur within both private and public policy to assure that the choices exist in fact. The issue I have raised in relationship to Hassidic children could be applied to any of the other groups that I have discussed.

DR. JOSEPH McELLIGOTT, MEMBER, NATIONAL ADVISORY COUNCIL ON THE EDUCATION OF DISADVANTAGED CHILDREN: I serve on the staff of the California Catholic Conference, and would like to report that the minority student population of the Catholic elementary and secondary schools in our state is currently 44 percent, as compared to 41 percent minority student population in the public schools.

I would also like to say that the report on the St. Thomas Community School sounds much like many of our schools. People sacrifice to go to our inner-city schools. One of the things that they really should not be forced to sacrifice are some of the federally funded services that Congress has provided for them, particularly in the Education Amendments of 1978. Although Congress has called for strengthening the participation in some of these programs by children who attend private and parochial schools, ever since the creation of the new Department of Education there has been an erosion of this kind of participation. For example, our youngsters are being removed from the receipt of services under the Emergency School Aid Act. We see no follow-through in the Follow-Through Program coming from the Department of Education. We see our youngsters being ignored under bilingual programs. And we are ignored when we appeal to the Department for our share of the funds authorized in the Education of All Handicapped Children Act of 1975.

It also occurs to us that the new Office of the Assistant Secretary for Nonpublic Education is an office that has not really been able to do anything at this time. In short, since the creation of the Department of Education, the promise made in the Education Amendments of 1978 that federal assistance would flow to minority youngsters in our inner-city schools is not being realized.

DR. AL H. SENSKE, EXECUTIVE DIRECTOR, BOARD OF PARISH EDUCATION, LUTHERAN CHURCH-MISSOURI SYNOD*: I am concerned about the fact that parents are losing their choice in the cities because even though nationally the number of Lutheran schools has grown, the number of pupils and the number of schools in the cities are going down. If we look at a map of Chicago from 1965 and plot our Lutheran schools there, and compare it to a map of 1980, half the dots are gone. My concern is not so much that we are losing the schools, as that parents in that city no longer have our schools as one of their choices. Let me state this concern differently, and I hope without pretense or arrogance or hostility to the public school system in my city. I would simply like to say that I agree with Congressman Gephardt, who has said on occasion that if

---

*Editor's Note: Dr. Senske served as Assistant Secretary for Nonpublic Education in the U.S. Department of Education during the Carter Administration.

there were no Catholic and Lutheran schools in the city of St. Louis, that city would be more of a disaster than it is. I wonder if we have the hard facts, the research, the reports that can really verify that, so that we can say to our country that by keeping private schools open, no matter what denomination or what kind of schools they are, we are really helping the cities and really giving people a choice.

DR. VITULLO-MARTIN: My response is that I think the research certainly could be done, and I have been trying to do some of it, but it has not been done. Research that would satisfy the academic community, however, is very difficult to do. At one level it makes common sense when you see private schools in a city being reasonably integrated and you see public schools being segregated and public schools in the suburbs being segregated, that the nonpublic schools are of benefit to the integration of the cities and that they help to hold them together. But the actual research has not yet been done. I think it should be done.

By the way, St. Louis is a particularly interesting problem. The student population in the public schools is, I think, nearly 80 percent black. And the public school system is under a court-ordered desegregation plan. The areas of St. Louis that are still integrated, or at least that help to integrate the city, are neighborhoods that are still vital. They are served by private schools, some of which are all white and some of which are integrated. The important thing that must be faced is that these neighborhoods are served by private schools. The public policy to integrate the public schools is going to affect all these neighborhoods in their own structures, and it is going to affect the private schools in St. Louis. The likely effect on the private schools is to encourage greater de facto segregation in these schools. They will be either racial havens, as everybody has always feared; or, more likely, their neighborhoods will be disrupted and there will be an acceleration of the movement of the people from their stable neighborhoods out of the city. So the net result of the civil rights effort to desegregate the public schools may be to increase the segregation of the private schools and within a relatively short time to increase the segregation of the public schools as well, as James Coleman and some others have maintained.

My concern is that in St. Louis there is no public effort to help the private schools deal in their own voluntary way with the impact that public policies are going to have on the private schools. There are no funds, no support staff, and no public commitment of any sort to foster desegregation in these schools or to insure that they assist in the process of relieving racial tensions and increasing neighborhood stability.

PART TWO

LEGISLATIVE PROPOSALS FOR BROADENING EDUCATIONAL OPPORTUNITY

Introduction
The Hon. Abner J. Mikva

I am very pleased to make a few comments on the papers gathered in this section of the volume. First, I consider the theme explored in this volume to be one of the most timely topics imaginable. I do not know whether there will be significant public aid for private education in the eighties, but I am sure that public policy affecting the nonpublic schools will continue to be a lively public policy issue. This is the case because we are basically a pluralistic nation. The pluralism of this country is not an accident. It is an aspect of our society that is cherished and that we must preserve.

Throughout my legislative career I maintained that proposals to help private education should not be assumed to be hurting the public school system or to be diminishing our commitment to a free public education for all. Now that I am on the federal bench it would be improper for me to endorse or recommend any of the specific legislative proposals discussed in these essays. But it would be no breach of judicial ethics for me to state that I still think that in many of the big cities of this country, educational pluralism may be the only salvation of the public school system. For without some kind of a model of a good private system, the whole concept of quality education in the public schools in the inner city may go down the drain. And that would be a tragedy that would benefit nobody.

Our educational system has had such a profound effect upon the country that it is impossible to cost out all the benefits. No one can put a dollar figure on the value of avoiding the type of rigid class structure which has afflicted so many other nations. And no one can measure the obvious contributions that a low cost and accessible educational system has made to the United States' enjoyment of the highest standard of living in the world over the last forty years. Finally, no one can compute the effect of an education system that has kept our society vital and creative when others have slipped into stagnancy.

One of the strengths of the essays in this section of the volume is that they subject various legislative proposals for broadening educational opportunity to close and careful scrutiny. Mr. Doyle's essay is a helpful overview of a broad variety of these proposals, and it serves as a reminder that we have something to learn from the educational policies that have developed in other English-speaking countries such as the mother country, England, our neighbor to the north, Canada, and even outposts of the Commonwealth such as Australia and New Zealand. Professors Coons and Sugarman would obviously prefer their own proposal of an educational voucher over the proposal of a tuition tax credit, but it is helpful to have their reasoned statement of why they do so. And their essay on federal scholarships for elementary and secondary school students from low-income families represents the first serious policy analysis of the "baby BEOG" proposal that I am aware of.

Another virtue of this sampling of thought on educational policy is that it is balanced and fair. Senator Moynihan, who has sponsored legislation for both tuition tax credits and "baby BEOG's" contributes a thoughtful and provocative essay that is countered by the contribution of Senator Hollings, who has often taken the lead in opposing his colleague's proposals on the floor of the Senate. And the Coons-Sugarman voucher proposal is subjected to the critical analysis of Dr. Olivas, who suggests that "information inequities" would keep the voucher plan from being of much use for "the disadvantaged and information-poor."

I might be allowed to observe wistfully that no one was found to champion the proposal for deferral of taxes that I put forward when serving in Congress, a proposal that regretably languished in the House Ways and Means Committee in 1978.* In any event, I think that the following chapters represent a valuable contribution to the ongoing discussion of one of the most pressing public questions facing our society, the question of how we structure and preserve freedom of educational choice in an open society.

---

*Editor's Note: Judge Mikva's proposal, H.R. 1961, (95th Cong., 1st Sess.) would have allowed a taxpayer to defer a portion of his income tax based on the expenses incurred in connection with the education of the taxpayer, his spouse or any dependent at an institution of higher education or a vocational school. It was defeated by one vote in the House Ways and Means Committee, the deciding vote being cast by the Chairman of the committee who voted to break a tie. For a brief discussion of this proposal, see Tuiton Tax Relief Bills, Hearings before the Subcommittee on Taxation and Debt Management Generally of the Committee on Finance, United States Senate, 95th Cong., 2nd Sess. 401-408 (1978).

6. Public Funding and Private Schooling: The State of Descriptive and Analytic Research

Denis P. Doyle

No volume assessing the public good of private schools would be complete without facing the question of public funding of private schooling. I use the term "schooling" deliberately to try to draw the distinction between the funding of private schools and the enterprise of schooling for which children themselves might be funded.

In an examination of this issue, there are three central questions, two research questions, and one policy question. Although the policy question is most important, other essays in this volume address this question directly, so I focus here primarily on the research issues. The first research question is descriptive, and deals with the scope and extent of existing funding arrangements for private schools both at home and abroad. The second research question is analytic, dealing with the implications of those funding arrangements, at two levels. The first level involves understanding why various kinds of children and families patronize private schools by appropriate descriptive categories; and the second involves a dispassionate assessment of the relative impact of the various funding mechanisms that could be designed and put in place. It is especially important to attempt to identify the effects of different funding systems on both private and public schools.

The policy question is whether or not public funds should be used to support private education, in what amount, and by what device. This question can be informed and illuminated by research, and will itself suggest research lines of inquiry, but it cannot be answered by research because it addresses the fundamental issues of education in a free society, religious divisiveness, socio-economic isolation, of racial integration, equity, and excellence. And for private school supporters it raises what is perhaps the most important issue of all, the extent to which government control might follow public funding.

Two assumptions underly my views on this matter. One is that it is not a foregone conclusion that aid to private schools is either good or bad; it is genuinely an open question and one best suited to political debate in public forums. Second, because researchers should

---

*This essay was prepared while Mr. Doyle was a Federal Executive Fellow at the Brookings Institution. The views presented in this essay are made in a personal capacity and do not reflect the official position of the Department of Education or of the Brookings Institution.

disclose their biases, I can state that my guiding principle in this area is that public policy is best served by an analysis strategy which emphasizes a no-loss/no-gain orientation. The issue before both the researcher and the policy maker is neither to diminish nor strengthen one sector of the educational enterprise at the expense of the other, but to develop public policies which will encourage a vigorous and healthy educational enterprise in both sectors.

In a certain sense, it is unfortunate that the issue of religion clouds this debate because the economic, public policy and other social issues surrounding it would be more easily and more rationally discussed if religion were not a factor. But it is impossible to avoid religion. I say this more as an assertion of fact than of value because the numbers are overwhelming. Well over 90 percent of private school children attend religiously affiliated schools. In the public policy realm, at least, nonpublic schools and religiously affiliated schools are virtually synonymous. It simply makes no sense to think of aid schemes that would provide funds for that tiny fraction of exclusively secular private schools. The aid schemes that have been debated, discussed and enacted, both in this country and abroad, fall into four very broad categories, two of which, it would appear, are patently unconstitutional. The first involves direct transfer payments to institutions, either for operating expenditures or capital expenditures.

Programs of this kind are very common abroad. They exist in the U.K. and Canada, the Netherlands, Australia, Belgium and Ireland. Australia is extraordinarily interesting because it is a federal system with a written constitution similar to ours in one very important respect. It includes language, virtually verbatim, from our First Amendment.* And using this language, Australia funds private schools, which comprise about 30 percent of that nation's student body. They have simply interpreted their constitutional provision in precisely the opposite way that ours has been interpreted, at least since the <u>Everson</u> case in 1947. The Australians reason that so long as all religions are treated equally, the state remains neutral. As interesting as the Australian experience is, it is probably not relevant to the U.S. because of the strong tendency in the Supreme Court to prohibit institutional aid for private religiously affiliated elementary and secondary schools.

The second major form of aid is direct transfer payments to institutions on behalf of individuals. Typically this is cast as a capitation formula. Although this approach is used less frequently in

---

*Editor's Note: Section 116 of the Australian Constitution provides: "The Commonwealth shall not make any law for establishing any religion, or for imposing any religious observance, or for prohibiting the free exercise of any religion, and no religious test shall be required as a qualification for any office or public trust under the Commonwealth."

other countries, it is progressively more and more common in our country in the public sector largely because it is one of the principal features of the school finance reform movement of the past two decades. In fact, the movement toward capitation formula funding in the public sector may have some long term implications for the private sector. But in the short run, it would seem that this policy option is not likely to be found constitutional.

But there are two other ways to make transfer payments to provide for schooling which might be constitutional. Those would provide benefits to individuals rather than institutions. Direct transfer payments to individuals include such things as vouchers, entitlements or scholarships, and those mechanisms are widely used abroad and on a much smaller scale here at home. The State of Vermont, for instance, is divided into school districts, as most states are, but in Vermont only two-thirds of the districts actually run schools. The other third have resident children but pay tuition for them to be educated in non-district schools, both public and private. There is in fact a continuous history of this tradition throughout New England. Vermont is the last surviving example of consequence, but it has existed in Massachusetts, Connecticut, and Maine. There are still a half-dozen surviving public academies, privately managed schools which serve local townships at public expense but retain their private character.

There remains another set of transfer payment arrangements which enjoy the highest likelihood of enactment politically: they are indirect transfer payments, which include subsidized loans, tax deductions or tax credits. As it happens, Australia also uses tax deductions, but is shifting decisively to direct transfer payments to institutions. But this does provide a model of a system which, to date, is only speculative in our country.

I would like to be able to report that research, either comparative or domestic, will help to resolve the question of aid to private schools, but the truth is that research in the field of private education is very slender indeed. The good news, however, is that we are beginning to develop a body of knowledge which is quite promising. Descriptive data is now available on a fairly consistent basis, and its quality is improving. We are beginning to know who goes to private schools by gender, by ethnicity, by race and, to a lesser extent, by income, and that information is being steadily improved. But to underscore the newness of even the descriptive data, one example should suffice. The Condition of Education for 1979, published by the National Center for Educational Statistics, predicted a slow, gradual decline in public school enrollments through 1984 and a leveling off of private school enrollments through 1984 extending at a steady state until the end of their projections in 1986. The 1980 Condition of Education, however, contains revised estimates which are quite remarkable. It shows a more rapid decline in the public sector than had been projected in 1979 with a slower recovery after 1984, and it shows what can only be described as a dramatic increase in private school enrollments through 1989, as far as the authors of the report care to predict. Between 1979 and 1980 NCES has revised its projections from no growth to an estimate of a twelve percent increase in private school enrollments in the near future. Such refined projections are essential if we are to inform the debate about private schools.

In addition to descriptive data, we also have some analytic information from an education demonstration project that was conducted by the Federal Government. That was the Alum Rock Tuition Voucher Program. The results from that experiment are interesting, even fascinating to some academics, but they tell us only a limited amount that is useful in the way of formulating public policy because of the idiosyncratic nature of both the community in which the demonstration occurred and the demonstration itself. It was a hot house demonstration which has produced some marvelous anecdotes, but it does not permit drawing broad generalizations.

We are, then, heavily reliant on comparative information from other countries, as limited as that may be. One study of special interest is currently under way in British Columbia, jointly supported by the National Institute of Education and the provincial government. It is aptly characterized as a naturally occurring voucher experiment. The provincial government has made available $500 per child in existing private schools. While new private schools are not permitted to share in public funding, this program presents a fascinating opportunity to study the effects of a transfer payment system in a society very much like our own. Professor Donald Erickson, Director of the Center of Research on Private Education at the University of San Francisco, is the principal investigator.

There is an undercurrent running beneath any discussion of private schooling that research findings can and do address, and that is the myth suggesting it is an elitist, racist enterprise. The evidence at hand does not support such findings. To the contrary, we know that private school children in a statistical profile look very much like public school children. In a recent publication by the Bureau of the Census, for example, Susanne Bianchi concludes that, controlling for socio-economic factors, the fact of being white increases the probability of private school attendance by only one percent. This is probably the strongest evidence we have to date suggesting that race or ethnicity is not the key variable in private school attendance. In addition, we know that there was a massive decline in Catholic school enrollment in the Seventies, that the decline is leveling in the Eighties, but that there has been an extraordinary increase in Catholic school minority enrollments over the same period, with a 12 percent increase in minority enrollments. In those jurisdictions for which there is good evidence, we also know that the public school-private school comparison is very favorable to private schools. For example, the 1978-1979 student enrollment figures indicated that Catholic schools in California were 41 percent minority and the public schools only 37 percent minority.*

Unfortunately, the most interesting question is the hardest one to answer; do private schools skim by intellectual or academic ability? There is almost no evidence in this area at all, but by happy coincidence, Australia helps with the answer. An Australian researcher who is now a senior official in the Australian government, in earning his doctorate at the University of Chicago, examined that very question. He found that, "compared, I.Q. tests for Chicago parochial school and public school students show parochial students testing lower than public school students." While it may be odd to draw any solace from such a finding, it does suggest that the major private school provider is not skimming the more academically able students.

I mention these issues not to suggest that the evidence is conclusive, but to bring into question the myth that private education is a bastion of white privilege and exclusivity. The research under way by people like Erickson, Coleman, Greeley, and Vitullo-Martin will continue and it will be expanded upon by other scholars. It will certainly help to clear the air. In addition, the availability of improved data will make it easier to answer these questions intelligently and will help us move forward as the issue of aid to nonpublic schools remains on the public agenda.

If even descriptive research in the field of private education is in its infancy, the question of analyzing the probably impact of alternate funding plans is still more difficult to address. But it is not impossible, because the public sector itself exhibits examples of each of the four options discussed earlier. As I have indicated, capitation formulas for public schools is one of the key events of the seventies that will probably continue in the eighties. There are also important forms of indirect aid through the tax systems, described in some detail by Vitullo-Martin.

There is, then, enough evidence from the public sector to give us some general idea about the implications of structurally similar funding schemes in the private sector. It is accurate as a generalization to observe that the more direct the funding relationship, the more behavior at the school level is constrained, and the less direct, the greater the autonomy of the school. Working across the spectrum from institutional funding to tax credits, it is safe to predict that tax credits would be the least obtrusive, and that

---

*Editor's Note: Sources: California Executive Council for Nonpublic Schools; California State Department of Education; and National Association of Independent Schools (NAIS), as cited in Thomas Vitullo-Martin, "New York City's Interest in Reform of Tax Treatment of School Expenses," City Almanac Vol. 13, No. 4 (Dec. 1978), p. 8.

direct funding schemes would be the most obtrusive in terms of government control of education.

The issue may be moot, however, because of the Supreme Court's apparent foreclosure of the possibility of direct funding. The irony will not be lost on private school supporters, for it suggests those schemes most likely to be found constitutional are those least subject to close public regulation and scrutiny.

I have deliberately postponed discussing a fifth scheme, which, while intriguing, has not yet been seriously discussed as an alternative, and that would be to simply cash out the federal education budget altogether. That would be, as Chris Cross has described it, a megavoucher program. Although such a plan is politically inconceivable, conceptually it permits a whole new approach to the legal question of public support of private schooling. If all children were provided federal entitlements, for either private or public school, the issue of a suspect class of children would not arise. Since 90 percent of American children attend public schools, the benefits flowing to the 10 percent who received entitlements which they could negotiate at private schools would be incidental to the larger program.

The issues of transfer payments for children is of special interest today because the age group of six to eighteen is now surrounded by them. At the level of higher education, the government has deliberately decided as a matter of public policy to provide aid to individuals rather than to institutions. Children under 15 who are in day care, and whose parents work are also eligible for day care tax credits. The Internal Revenue Service has even ruled that the day care tax credit may be claimed for children who attend fee-charging kindergartens. It may be that the IRS knows more about the educational effects of kindergarten than do educators, but it is somehow anomalous to permit the credit for kindergarten and not other grades.

If I have avoided addressing the strengths and weaknesses of the various proposals that have been advanced for aid to private school, the reason is that the strengths and weaknesses are not intrinsic to tax credits or vouchers or tax deductions or direct or indirect transfer payments. Rather, the strengths and weaknesses are a reflection of the public policy decisions incorporated in the mechanisms employed; the mechanism themselves simply reflect other public policy decisions and values.

Vouchers serve to illustrate this point. They have had a very uneven history because there is no single voucher system. In Vermont, vouchers are noncontroversial. They are successful, they are workable, and they have been in place for well over a century. They are neither racist or elitist.

A pernicious variant of vouchers, however, followed Brown v. Board of Education. Several states attempted to frustrate court-ordered racial integration by using educational vouchers to permit white children to attend private school at public expense.

Such a scheme was patently unconstitutional and was struck down by the court.*

A third voucher scheme was supported by the U.S. Office of Economic Opportunity and led to the Alum Rock demonstration program. At least in attenuated form it was a test of the voucher plan developed by Christopher Jencks. This scheme was very carefully and self-consciously designed to increase racial integration, and to serve low income children generally. It provided significant financial incentives for poor children, and it is not surprising that it achieved its limited objectives.

A fourth, still theoretical voucher model has been developed by Jack Coons and Steve Sugarman, of the University of California. Their principal purpose is to encourage racial integration. Certainly other models can be conceptualized that do that and do it successfully.

In sum, vouchers, like tax credits or scholarships and loans, can be designed to serve a variety of social purposes. They can increase or decrease social class and racial isolation, they can encourage centralization or decentralization, they can lead to greater or lesser state control of private schooling. But these outcomes are a function of the model selected. In short, the task of model design follows public policy. It cannot and should not lead to it.

In addition to broad policy questions of equity, access and excellence are the more prosaic questions of administrative flexibility, feasibility and expense. They are always important in debating public issues, and I think it is clear that vouchers or other transfer payment programs for private schooling would be no more clumsy or awkward or expensive than the existing arrangements we have for reimbursing public schools. Tax credits or tax deductions clearly offer an extraordinarily straightforward, simple, and inexpensive way of making support available.

Two final observations are in order. Just as not all voucher systems are alike, so also not all tax credit proposals are alike. Like the Laffer curve, in which the extremes of no tax or one hundred percent tax produces no revenue, the extremes of tax credits are similarly dysfunctional. But the extremes of tax credit possiblilities are worth briefly examining, because the range of monies that might be made available to families provides an exaggerated example of probable behavior. The existing system of very modest support does not influence student or institutional behavior significantly, except perhaps as a modest stimulus to the philanthropic impulses of the already well to do. At the other end of the scale, a total tax credit, which would permit the family to enjoy 100 percent tax relief for every dollar spent for tuition and fees could have extraordinary effects. It would act as a very strong incentive for families to move

---

*Editor's Note: See Griffin v. Bd. of Supervisors of Prince Edward County, 377 U.S. 218 (1964).

into the private sector.

The issue, then, is as old as the political process, for it requires finding that nearly magical balance point in which the tax credit is large enough to help private school parents, but is not so large as to work to the disadvantage of existing public schools. I don't know what that point is. I don't know if anybody knows what that point is and I doubt that research can do more than dimly illuminate it. But it is certain that the best way to find that point is to thrash it out in public debate and public forums. It is a political problem; one that may be informed by research, but one for which there is no research "answer."

One other point deserves a final comment. The conventional wisdom in much of the public and private sector holds that a major change in the way we finance education—adding private schools to the public expense ledger—is essentially a zero sum game. I would argue that, at least on the basis of comparative research, that is clearly not the case. The zero sum fear is based on a false assumption that the education pie is finite, and that even a small slice for private education will diminish public education.

There are two dimensions to this problem, one economic and one political. In the world of economics, tax credits are not solely reimbursement for private expenditures that meet social objectives, they are themselves a stimulus to encourage private investment. This dimension of tax credits would be as true of education as other forms of investment. Tax credits, then, could be expected to increase aggregate investment, public and private, in education. In this light, they are a positive growth strategy for the education enterprise as a whole, one that might be particularly welcome in a period of decreasing rates of growth.

The other dimension, the political one, may be even more important, for the old conditions of support for public education are today on very shaky ground. But rather than viewing private education with suspicion and hostility, supporters of the public school system might gain, both financially and politically, by looking to the private sector for allies in the effort to adopt a strategy of support for education as a whole. The crucial question, of course, is whether or not the gains that private schools would enjoy would be offset by losses in the public sector. While we cannot answer the question definitely, the strongest evidence comes from Australia, where one third of the students are enrolled in private schools supported by public funds. Every indication suggests that there is now a much more broadly-based coalition of support for education in general and that the levels of support for education in the public sector alone are higher now than they would have been absent general support for education generally, both public and private.

7. What the Congress Can Do When the Court Is Wrong

The Hon. Daniel Patrick Moynihan

I would like to make three simple points concerning various legislative proposals to fund aspects of nonpublic education. First, when taking up any subject for serious reflection, I have retained from my years in academe the practice of asking what the state of the subject is in the other industrial democracies, to what degree the subject is a generalized condition of this sort of social arrangement, and to what degree it is particular with us. To my knowledge, ours is the only industrial democracy in the world that does not routinely provide aid to nonpublic schools as part of its educational system. This is a problem unique to the United States. That fact alone says something, I think.

My second point is that the origin of this policy choice lies not in the intention of the framers of the First Amendment in the First Congress, as Walter Berns and Michael Malbin and others have shown, but in the Catholic-Protestant antagonisms of the 19th century. That is well known and amply documented, although it is surprising how much it has had to be rediscovered. It should suffice here to recall that in 1875 President Grant was thinking of running for a third term and needed an issue. For some now obscure reason, he chose the tension between Catholics and Protestants as his principal issue, and made his choice public in an address to the Army of the Tennessee, in Des Moines, Iowa. Out of that came the Blaine Amendments. The Republican Party platform of 1876 took this issue as a central feature. And then we had a whole generation in which the Blaine Amendment was voted on repeatedly in Congress. It passed in one house or the other, never both, but a version of it was adopted in New York and in several western states as part of the state constitutions.

My third point is that when one reflects seriously on the quality of education provided in many of our urban centers, one is entitled to the judgment that the Supreme Court has been simply wrong in repeatedly telling state legislatures that they may not, consistently with the First and Fourteenth Amendments, provide a variety of forms of aid to elementary and secondary schools that are operated by a church or religious body. I offer just a former professor's judgment that the Supreme Court is simply wrong in this. This is not unprecedented. To the contrary, there has not been a period in our national life in which the Supreme Court has not, in fact, been wrong about a major issue of the time. When I say that the Court has been wrong, I do not mean wrong in the sense that I think it wrong, but wrong in the sense that the Court itself later said, "We were wrong." For example, the Court was plainly wrong in Dred

Scott. The Court held in Plessy that separate but equal facilities were constitutional. After Brown v. Board of Education the Court now holds they are not. The Court held in Lochner that labor legislation was a violation of the Fourteenth Amendment. After Adkins the Court no longer holds that. In 1979 the Court ruled in the Gannett case that the public does not have an independent constitutional right of access to a pretrial judicial proceeding. A year later only Justice Rehnquist could be found to support the vitality of Gannett and the Court ruled 7-1 in the Richmond Newspapers case that the trial of a criminal case must be open to the public. Courts, then, can be wrong. Even the Supreme Court.

I would maintain that the Court has been egregiously wrong in much of the reasoning it has employed in defense of its decisions concerning public aid for nonpublic education. For example, the Court was reduced to saying in Tilton that a federal statute that provided aid to a Catholic college was constitutional, but that similarly direct subventions to Catholic high school would be unconstitutional, because of a presumably well known difference in religious impressionability as between college freshmen and high school seniors. If you'll say that, you'll say anything. It was not an academically defensible statement. No respectable psychologist would say it, and I regret that the Court chose to say it, for saying it is so does not make it so. It would have been more honest and straightforward if the Court merely said that it did not want to overrule the Congress in its determination of educational policy.

Many other cases in this area are similarly embarrassing and confused. So poorly reasoned are the cases that one federal appellate judge, Joseph F. Weis, was led to ask recently in an opinion dealing with the New Jersey tuition tax deduction: "Where does this regime of judicial hostility to these schools arise from?" Acknowledging that the Nyquist decision bound the Court of Appeals, the judge nevertheless stated his opinion that the Nyquist decision was itself erroneous.

I have argued elsewhere the case that this judicial hostility to nonpublic schools does not derive from the Establishment Clause of the First Amendment, but from the Supreme Court's erroneous interpretation of that constitutional provision.* In that essay I likewise suggested that it was difficult to avoid the judgment that Justice Blackmun's dissent in the Gannett case was right and that the majority of the Court was wrong. Once such a judgment is posited, serious policy makers must face the question, "What do you do when the Supreme Court is wrong?" I think that the public response to Gannett provides us with an answer to this question. Heated debate began promptly. Some of the Justices, including the

---

*Editor's Note: See Daniel Patrick Moynihan, Counting Our Blessings: Reflections on the Future of America, (Boston: Atlantic-Little, Brown, 1980) pp. 162-190.

Chief Justice, got into the act of clarifying their position and of half-apologizing for it in speeches off the bench. Legislation was contemplated. And litigation ensued. Even before remedial legislation was enacted, the Court had already begun the process of confining its Gannett rule in Richmond Newspapers. It may be too early to claim that the Court has vindicated the prediction I offered when Gannett was announced, but it is timely to recall that prediction:

> In the end the Court either will reverse itself, or set forth rules for the closure of courts so narrow and restricted in their application that the controversy will go away. It may be hoped that it does not require a generation for this to come about.

I repeat these words here not to crow about the Court proving me right, a rare event to be sure, but simply to emphasize that public policy makers who are clearly persuaded that the Court is wrong have a duty to engage in debate, to propose remedial legislation, and to correct an erroneous decision.

The debate should, in part, focus on the meaning of the Establishment Clause and the early history of state aid to church-related schools. I am persuaded that dispassionate scholars like Nathan Glazer, Mark DeWolfe Howe, Walter Berns and Michael Malbin have adequately demonstrated that the Court's reading of that history is simply wrong. But I do not repeat their arguments here because I think that the public debate should likewise be focused on contemporary aspects of educational policy. Among those, racial justice in education remains a central issue. The alleged elitism of the private schools is a pseudo-issue. Access to public resources on an equitable basis is probably the principal issue.

The concern about racial justice in our educational policies is central because we cannot afford to compromise or delay the promise of quality education for all Americans held out in Brown v. Board Of Education. But it would be wholly gratuitous to assert that nonpublic educators as a class are less concerned about racial integration in their schools than their counterparts in the public schools. Dr. James Coleman and Father Andrew Greeley have completed solid empirical studies that should lay to rest the silly contention that Catholic schools are elitist and racist in character. All too often, however, one hears the view that nonpublic schools are "bastions of white privilege and exclusivity." One doesn't have to be much of a political scientist to recognize that those words are politically loaded and are used to evoke certain symbols. I have been involved with the question of public support for nonpublic education for over two decades. When I came to Washington with President Kennedy, one of the principal arguments against providing aid to the parochial schools was that they were bad schools. Letting children remain in them, it was thought, would confine them to a life of educational disadvantage; the sooner they were closed down, the more access these children would have to equal education. In only two decades' time, these schools have turned from being inferior to being schools of such quality that opponents of aid for these schools now argue that if everybody had the slightest opportunity to enter them, there would be no public school system left.

This remarkable misuse of language has emerged in Congressional debates on two proposals that I have sponsored in recent years, the tuition tax credit proposal considered in the 95th Congress and the "baby BEOG" proposal considered in the 96th Congress. The people who have advocated this kind of financial support for nonpublic education were beaten badly in the 95th Congress, then very badly in the 96th. The tuition tax credit was defeated in 1978 in the Senate by a vote of 56 to 41. That was a large bill which would have cost about five billion dollars; it would have been a real transfer of money in education and in the society. In 1980, we proposed a much smaller program, to give elementary and secondary children from low-income families access to Basic Educational Opportunity Grants. This would have cost about a hundred and twenty million dollars a year, which is not a large sum in terms of education appropriations. We lost 71 to 24.

We were beaten in no small part because of the implacable opposition of the Carter Administration, and much more importantly, that of all the major educational organizations of the country, most of which are involved in progressive political causes. The National Coalition to Save Public Education was formed over tuition tax credits and put the matter rather strongly. It said: "Aid to nonpublic schools carries with it the danger that public funds will be used to support sectarian purposes or ideological viewpoints, in violation of the Constitution and American principles." When someone on the Right stands up and says something is un-American, what does one normally hear from progressive institutions? They protest, do they not? In the old days champions of civil liberties would have said, "That's shocking. It's like McCarthyism." The President of Notre Dame would undoubtedly have been very upset and sensed a threat to our liberties. But these schools are called un-American and no one says a word. An inflammatory charge which in another context would produce a reaction of outrage here produces no reaction whatever.

The Secretary of Education, Shirley Hufstedler, voiced her opposition to my proposal as follows: "We are also concerned this proposal could have an adverse impact on the public school system." The reasoning here was that to the extent that they reduced the cost of alternative, private schools, BEOGs for elementary and secondary students could provide an incentive for students to leave the public schools, possibly eroding local support for the public schools. In response to the argument that there was not much money involved in my BEOG proposal, our principal opponent in the debate on the Senate floor put it this way: "Let us say if there was one million dollars or one dollar, we would have to oppose this for exactly what it is. That is, an attempt to destroy public education, to discriminate against minorities and the disadvantaged, and to totally abandon the needy in America." Not a word of public protest about this slander on Catholic schools was heard from Notre Dame.

I can readily understand it if a colleague of mine were to stand up in the Senate and say, "I think this is a bad bill, and I don't think that we should do this. I think we should have one system of schools and not two or three or four." But we should not be expected to stand by idly when people attack the nonpublic schools recklessly and irresponsibly. These schools are good schools. They have been there a long time, longer in fact than the public schools, and they provide a useful service in our society. They shouldn't be called un-American and they shouldn't be called "bastions of white privilege and exclusivity." It must be remembered that for six generations the Catholic schools have educated the children of the rural proletariat that landed in Manhattan. As Nathan Glazer and I tried to show in Beyond the Melting Pot, they were not thought to be "bastions of white privilege and exclusivity" until quite recently.*

Although Coleman and Greeley have shown that this characterization of parochial schools as racist and elitist is simply untrue, one has the impression that it has become fashionable to think that it is true. Perhaps this is because the people who most successfully control the media and who manage our symbols of progress have it all over the people who advocate proposals for broadening educational opportunity. Consider, for example, the views of the Washington Post and the New York Times, the two central organs of judgment in these matters. About tuition tax credits, the Washington Post said: "The bill threatens to do incalculable damage to the country's public schools." And the Times said: "The bill would encourage the dismantling of public education." These are very strong words and very threatening language. But no effective response was made by anyone who said, "You can't say that sort of thing without having me disagree with you." What is perhaps most regrettable about the editorial posture of the Times and the Post is that these influential shapers of public opinion have accepted the definition of this issue when public education is understandably anxious about its future. What previously was simply an adjunct school system has emerged as possibly an alternative school system, and that has roused deep anxieties and extraordinary fears.

---

*Editor's Note: See Nathan Glazer and Daniel Patrick Moynihan, Beyond the Melting Pot: The Negroes, Puerto Ricans, Jews, Italians and Irish of New York City (Cambridge, Mass.: M.I.T. Press, 2nd ed. 1970).

Those anxieties and fears, I regret, now appear to be the basis for remarkable distortions of reality. For example, in the late 1960s, educational vouchers were generally regarded as a progressive proposal. All liberal faculty members would wish to be associated with it. Good foundations would support it. But with the space of a decade this proposal has somehow been transformed into a "bastion of white privilege and exclusivity."

Sometimes it takes a long time to overcome that kind of opposition in national politics. As a political scientist, I would not think that the Court would change its views on the Establishment Clause and church-related schools within this century. Although I am willing to be proved wrong on this one, I do not think that the prospect of change in this area is enhanced by the abandonment of pluralism and choice as liberal ideas and liberal values. It has, however, become increasingly clear that public funding of nonpublic schools will be advocated with vigor by persons on the political Right. As the issue becomes more and more a conservative cause, it will, I suppose, become less and less a liberal one. If that happens, it will present immense problems for a person such as myself who was deeply involved in this issue long before it was either conservative or liberal. And if it prevails only as a conservative cause, it will have been a great failure of American liberalism not to have seen the essentially liberal nature of this pluralist proposition.

8. The Case against Tuition Tax Credits

The Hon. Ernest F. Hollings

In August of 1978, on the floor of the U.S. Senate, public education ran head-on into the Packwood-Moynihan tuition tax credit scheme. In my opinion, the future of American education hinged on the outcome of this confrontation. Careful study convinced me that this proposal would turn our nation's education policy on its head, benefit the few at the expense of many, proliferate substandard segregation academies, add a sea of red ink to the federal deficit, violate the clear meaning of the First Amendment to the Constitution, and destroy the diversity and genius of our system of public education. Fortunately, my Senate colleagues agreed with me and defeated the inclusion of tuition tax credits for elemenetary and secondary education by a vote of 56 to 41.

My colleague from New York proposed tax credits for private elementary and secondary education upon the assumption that the government has an equal duty to both public and private schools, and he charges that "the federal government has systematically organized its activities in ways that contribute to the decay of nonpublic education."

Let us be clear at the outset that the duty is not equal. The government's duty to the public is to provide public schools. The duty of the government toward private schools is to leave them alone. This is fundamental. Now comes the Packwood-Moynihan plan, and the duty to leave the private alone is suddenly inverted to the duty to provide for them.

And provide it would! Today the average federal subsidy to the individual public school pupil is $128. The private school student is helped too, through federal assistance in providing instructional materials, library resources, guidance and testing programs, and so on, at an average per-pupil expenditure of $40. It should be noted that increases are contained in the Elementary and Secondary Education Act Amendments passed in 1978 for both public and private schools, and improvements in "by-pass" mechanisms will further assure that privates will receive their fair share of federal aid. The original Packwood-Moynihan proposal would have completely upended these proportions by providing up to $500 for the pri-

---

*©1978, by Ernest F. Hollings. This article originally appeared in the December, 1978 issue of Phi Delta Kappan and is reprinted here by permission of the author.

vate school student--over four times what is given for the public school child. When the Senate considered it, the proposal was pared to $250. Can it really be in the public interest to provide quadruple, or in the final instance double, the aid to those attending private schools?

Not only is the amount of aid proposed disproportionate, but the kind of aid is radically different. Federal assistance consists primarily of special education programs for individual students--compensatory education, help for the handicapped, the language-deficient, and the poor. The federal government provides a floor upon which the state and local governments build. This is targeted, special-purpose aid that goes to the needy in both the public and private schools. But the tax credit for private education translates into general assistance--a windfall for an institution rather than a helping hand for a deserving child.

Public school assistance programs follow from the mandate of Congress for equal educational opportunity in the public schools. This is not required of the private schools. These latter are selective and generally choose the brightest, those without discipline problems or language problems, those from the higher income brackets, and those fleeing from the inner-city, integrated school. The public school, in contrast, must take all comers--regardless of background, regardless of special problems. Additionally, the public institution must abide by congressional laws and court decisions that the private school can ignore. Those who argue that public and private schools are directly competitive and that pupil performances can be directly compared ignore this basic difference. The public school is bound by both law and conscience to reach out to every child as a matter of his or her birthright. This is what public education is all about.

What is impressive is the record compiled by our public schools as they educate 90 percent of our youngsters, expand equal opportunity, and provide every American child the chance for a better future. The public schools have led the way.

In contrast, many private schools have been built for the specific purpose of closing the doors of economic and social opportunity. Some people call them "protest schools"; others call them segregation academies. They dot the landscape of my own back yard, and their purpose is clear to everyone. Sad to report, the best estimate is that nearly one of every five private schools is a protest school.

Packwood-Moynihan confers its benefits on 4.5 million private school students at the expense of 44.5 million public school children. Most of our private school student population is middle or upper class. In 1975 just 4 percent of all children from families with incomes of less than $5,000 were enrolled in private schools; 17 percent of all children from families with incomes of about $25,000 were in private schools; and 25 percent of those from families with incomes above $50,000. Clearly, those with the greatest ability to pay would reap the benefits. The proverbial millionaire who pays no taxes would receive a $500 (or $250) check from Washington for sending his boy to Exeter, while the 89 percent of families whose incomes are below $15,000 in the state of South Carolina would receive only 17 percent of the benefit to be paid out. That's unconscionable.

Exeter, meanwhile, boasts an endowment of $60 million; Phillips-Andover has $57 million; St. Paul's, $45 million. The endowments, holdings, and properties of many of our private schools are very great, and increasing public awareness of the extent of some of these holdings is one reason for the lack of public support for the tuition tax credit proposals.

We hear a lot of talk nowadays about cost containment and budget cutting. Clearly Senators Packwood and Moynihan are worried about neither. Theirs is a cost explosion—yet another in the long line of budget-busters. The Congressional Budget Office estimates that, should this plan take effect, within just three years the elementary and secondary tuition tax credit would cost $1.797 billion. This figure is, if anything, conservative. If tuitions are raised, or if more children attend private schools, the amount will go higher.

Certainly there is every incentive for the private schools to raise tuitions once this measure is implemented. Parents of children in private schools will have their expectations of a tax break raised high only to find themselves the conduits between the federal treasury and the private school. Common sense tells us that the private schools will raise tuitions to capture as much of this new money as they can. We need not blame them for trying. But should we provide the opportunity and open the treasury gates? And no one should be surprised if, farther down the road, politicians on the state level discover an opportunity for some federal money, too. I have served in state government. I know how easy it is to get around obstacles and amend state constitutions, and when dollars are at stake the action usually comes sooner rather than later. With over 90 percent of our children in public schools, the cost of a public school tuition tax credit would be astronomical.

Packwood-Moynihan means money and bureaucracy. Claiming a tax credit means authenticating the tax return; authenticating the return means commandeering the records of both the citizen and the school; commandeering records means another new bureaucracy; and bureaucracy means intrusion and soaring expenditure. We have been down that road so many times before that the scenery ought to look familiar. At least we ought to recognize the road signs. But somehow politicians never learn. The people, however, are onto the facts. In a nationwide Roper survey released in August of 1978, 64 percent of the American people opposed the tuition tax credit for private and parochial elementary and secondary education. And, interestingly, only 43 percent of the Catholics surveyed favored it, while 48 percent of them voiced their opposition.

Our education system cannot afford the kind of infighting that the tuition tax credit would inevitably bring between the supporters of our public and private schools. Each year at appropriations time they will square off in competition for the limited federal funds available. Once the tuition tax credit has its foot in the door, education civil war will be an annual affair. And because so many of the private schools are religious, the debates will devolve into religious wars as well.

I believe that Packwood-Moynihan should be defeated on policy grounds. It is an outlandish proposal that could only wreak havoc on our education system. The proponents know this. But, rather than address the questions of education policy or sound fiscal policy head-on, they hide behind the rhetoric of "anti-Catholic bigotry" as the reason this proposal failed to pass the Senate. That in fact is shameless pandering for purposes unrelated to the merit of this issue. They attempt to clothe opponents of their proposal as "anti-Catholic bigots." This is simply unfounded. Consider the list of organizations that opposed Packwood-Moynihan. Are they religious bigots?

The list includes the American Civil Liberties Union; American Association of Colleges for Teacher Education; American Federation of Teachers, AFL-CIO; American Association for Health, Physical Education, and Recreation; American Association of School Administrators; American Ethical Union; American Federation of State, County, and Municipal Employees; American Humanist Association; American Jewish Congress; Americans for Democratic Action; A. Philip Randolph Institute; Association for Childhood Education International; Baptist Joint Committee on Public Affairs; Coalition of Labor Union Women; Council for Educational Development and Research; Council for Exceptional Children; Council of Chief State School Officers; Council of Great City Schools; Division of Homeland Ministries, Christian Church (Disciples of Christ); Federal Education Project of the Lawyers Committee on Civil Rights Under Law; Horace Mann League; Labor Council for Latin American Advancement; League of Women Voters; National Association for the Advancement of Colored People; National Association of Elementary School Principals; National Association for Hearing and Speech Action; National Association of Secondary School Principals; National Association of State Boards of Education; National Coalition for Public Education and Religious Liberty; National Committee for Citizens in Education; National Congress of Parents and Teachers; National Council of Churches; National Council of Jewish Women; National Council of Senior Citizens; National Education Association; National School Boards Association; National Student Association; National Student Lobby; National Urban Coalition; National Urban League; Student National Education Association; Union of American Hebrew Congregations; Unitarian Universalist Association; United Auto Workers; United Methodist Church.

Just citing the list shows how ridiculous the religious bigotry charge is.

But let's review the legal precedents. The tuition tax credit is not only bad policy; it is patently unconstitutional, flying in the face of the establishment clause of the First Amendment and therefore violative of the Fourteenth Amendment also. The U.S. attorney general has written a formal opinion concluding that a tuition tax credit for families with children in private elementary and secondary schools is unconstitutional. That position is supported by most constitutional scholars, for the tuition tax credit proposed in this legislation is practically indistinguishable from the tax relief program that New York State enacted and which, in 1973, the Supreme Court held to be unconstitutional in Committee for Public Education v. Nyquist. And in 1977 the Supreme Court, in its decision in Wolman v. Walter, reaffirmed its earlier position. Although some scholars and some politicians may wish that those cases had been decided differently, most of them agree that, under those decisions, a tuition tax credit for elementary and secondary students is unconstitutional.

Senator Moynihan does not really dispute this conclusion. In January of 1978 he said, "Now I would say to you that this bill is constitutional, by which I do not mean that I predict the Court tomorrow would hold it so. I mean instead that a fair reading of our nation's history demonstrates that the First Amendment was never meant--until recently, never understood--to bar the sort of aid we propose."

This is an interesting viewpoint. It has much to commend it. For it gives each of us the freedom to make up our own minds about what the Constitution says. If we don't happen to like what the Supreme Court has ruled, we are free to ignore it--relying instead upon what we happen to deem to be a "fair reading of our nation's history." A school board might decide that a fair reading of this nation's history permits it to operate a dual school system--even though there once was a decision called Brown v. Board of Education.

I am as great a believer in liberty as Senator Moynihan. But Article III of the Constitution says that "The judicial power of the United States shall be vested in one Supreme Court," and the "the judicial power shall extend to all cases . . . arising under the Constitution." Much as I would like to be free to declare my allegiance to Ernest F. Hollings's fair reading of our nation's history, I believe that Article III provides otherwise--and makes the Supreme Court the final arbiter of the Constitution.

Finally, I should note that in an article he wrote in the spring of 1978 for Harper's, Senator Moynihan relied for support in his interpretation of the First Amendment on that eminent constitutional scholar, Ulysses S. Grant, and that renowned source of constitutional guidance, the 1876 Republican platform. I had never before realized that, in the address by Grant to which Senator Moynihan refers us--remarks before the Army of Tennessee in Des

Moines--the nation was receiving a legal disquisition of great authority. Nor had I realized that the politicians who drafted the election platform for the Republican Party in 1876 viewed themselves as resolving serious questions of constitutional law that might arise a century later.

One might think that, in determining what the First Amendment prohibits, a good starting place is recent Supreme Court decisions. Yet in his extended discussion of constitutional law in Harper's Senator Moynihan makes only the most fleeting reference to the two controlling Supreme Court decisions in this area. But in considering whether tuition tax credit legislation is constitutional, I look not to Ulysses Grant but to the Supreme Court. And I conclude--as has the attorney general--that this legislation clearly violates those decisions.

As a parent, a citizen, and an office-holder, I have always believed that public education is the best investment a nation can make. It develops a diversity, a competitiveness, a competence that is nowhere else available. Our public schools are run by over 16,000 local school boards, and theirs has always been the fundamental role. Those who pose the straw man of a public education monopoly have not traveled this land and breathed the diversity and the vitality of 107,272 public schools. No private school can boast this kind of diversity. The public school teaches the American Way as no other school can teach it. There is no substitute. Our public schools are and must remain the cornerstone of America's education system. This is not to deny or deprive private education, which can and should remain a vital part of our nation's education. But we are being asked now to discriminate in favor of the private, and what is left alone and unfunded is public education. All this to be performed by the public Congress! To borrow from Senator Moynihan's colorful rhetoric, this is horrendous, outrageous, and we shouldn't let them "get away with it."

9. Making Schools Public

John E. Coons

I would like to share a recent discovery of mine. Why I did not perceive it sooner astounds me. It couldn't be plainer, if it were my own ear, except that, like my ear, I was not able to observe it directly. My head kept getting in the way. That same dense object has blocked my perception of a basic truth about the schools called "public."

An old story may illuminate my point. Patrick and Mary O'Toole had been long and happily married. They had four strapping sons who all went to Notre Dame and became All-Americans, living out Patrick's dream. Regrettably a fifth son turned out badly. He was weak of sight and of limb and inordinately fond of books. He went to Harvard and took honors in poetry. Patrick was long suspicious about the boy, and when at last poor Mary was on her death bed he urged confession. "Mary," he said, "you're going to meet your Maker. Now is that boy an O'Toole or is he not?" He got his response: "Faith, Patrick, that boy is an O'Toole; but the other four are Finnegans."

This chestnut illustrates the eternal verity that labels do count and (with apologies to Juliet) that, an onion called a rose can be admired for its aroma. So has it been with me and "public" schools.

When the tax-supported schools were born more than a century ago they were, of course, christened. I am now convinced that they were wrongly christened. I don't argue that they should have been called Finnegan, nor should we indulge the temptation to call them illegitimate. But this much seems sufficiently clear: Whatever we call our tax-supported schools, we cannot fairly call them "public."

What is it to be public except to be accessible to all regardless of wealth or place of residence? Access: That at least for me is an essential test of a public institution. Who is eligible? May any child hope to enter this school or only a privileged few? Perhaps I am quaint in my sense of what it means to be public, but I take some consolation in Webster to whom I invite your attention at your leisure.

Now, if access be a necessary criterion, how public are our tax-supported schools? We in California have arranged ourselves in 1,041 school districts with maybe ten times that number of attendance areas. Some of the districts are famous: Beverly Hills, Palo Alto, Huntington Beach, San Clemente, Sausalito. How does one get to choose a school in such a place? By purchasing a home there. Perhaps one in ten California families can afford to live where they please. They have the power to cluster their children in isolated tax-supported schools called "public." And when they have paid their school property taxes, they can deduct them on their federal return.

Some well-to-do families don't worry about which school district to live in. They cluster their children in schools called "private" and pay the tuition. What they share with the burghers of Beverly Hills is the ability to choose. They cherish it, and they exercise it--and who can blame them?

I do not wish to suggest that all the well-to-do families of California arrange to share one another's company to the exclusion of others. Many exercise their option so as to give their children contact with children of all kinds. Thus, some choose to locate in residential areas that include various income classes and races, and they use the local tax-supported school. Others use parochial schools that enroll a higher percentage of minority children statewide (44 percent) than do the tax-supported schools (41 percent). But whatever these families do, they do by choice. And they alone do so by choice.

Those who lack the means (or the church subsidy) must go to the government schools in neighborhoods where they can afford to live. For these children the connection with the school and teacher is made not by adults who know them--nor for that matter, by any human at all. It is determined by the fact of their residence. The decision is unsullied by human intervention and is best handled by computer.

What California has managed to create is a system designed to serve the private preference of relatively few. These have choice; the rest have their marching orders. This system of tax-supported schools is "public" only in the vapid sense that it is a creature of the law. Viewed in terms of its structure and functions, it is simply a monopoly reigning over the education of the non-rich; and it is a unique monopoly making an offer the ordinary family can't refuse.

Monopoly over the common family was justified by its nineteenth century designers on two premises. One was that education would, like physics, become a science; many thought us to be on the threshold of decisive interventions that would end illiteracy and ignorance. The other premise was that Americans agreed on the good life; we had a value consensus, and it would hold and increase. Thus there was little embarrassment that the system was grossly illiberal and undemocratic; we were merely imposing with scientific efficiency what everyone wanted done anyway. It was, as David Tyack has described it, "The One Best System."

Neither premise remains today. Instead of one best system, twenty-five compete for teaching the three R's. In place of one work ethic we have a dozen ethics, only some of which value work for its own sake. Of course we agree that we should pursue the best interest of the child and foster learning, tolerance, consensus and racial integration, but there is little agreement as to what these ideals mean or how to achieve them. Education is indeterminate in its means and pluralistic in its ends. Nevertheless, we plunge on.

Those who can afford to do so choose the means and the ends for themselves; the rest choose neither and in all things await the pleasure of the educartel. More and more clearly we see that the system is animated by a third premise: Only those who can afford choice can be trusted with it. It is the creeping recognition of this systemic bias against the common man that is the bitterest pill for the managers of the system. After the rivers of democratic mythology that have baptized government schools, it is asking a great deal of the schoolmaster to accept with good humor being perceived as a despot.

What emerges from this analysis is not a simple answer to the educational problem but a clearer question. Insofar as the purposes and means of education remain conflicting and obscure, the policy question is not "What is best?". Rather, it is "How do we allocate authority to decide for the individual child?". Beyond that vague minimum about which society does agree, who should decide what and where the child shall learn? There are two candidates for this authority, the educational managers and the family. Are there reasons to prefer one to the other, or some combination of the two?

The answer could be sought on the high plain of political theory. Here everything depends on the assumptions with which one begins. Starting from an aristocratic preference one would favor decision by the few for the many. Of course, to the extent that the educational aristocracy are themselves in deep conflict, such a paternalistic decision model would seem a bit arbitrary; it means handing children over to schools merely because their managers have acquired certain credentials and not because they are the guardians of any particular ideal or because they claim any particular skill.

Every teacher in every school today <u>does,</u> of course, hold some specific ideals of his own and <u>does</u> claim some specific skills, but the child does not come to that teacher's classroom for either of those reasons. The child comes simply because he lives on 34th Street, and is told to come. And whether he gets a touchy-feely school or back-to-basics is the luck of the draw. Our present system thus fails the historic definition of aristocracy, for it lacks a common commitment among those in authority. I have on occasion called the educational order elitist. I apologize. It is, instead, Hobbes' jungle of petty tyrannies imposing private judgments. It is for the ordinary family an experience of chaos and coercion.

The alternative to Hobbes is basically Jeffersonian and democratic. Jefferson thought in terms of sturdy individual farmers. We must translate this eighteenth century image into one of individual families, few of them close to the soil and not all of them sturdy. But like it or not, family choice is the only democratic model available to an educational world so divided. If there were consensus upon specific learning goals and the tools to reach them, we could imagine an educational system that could be called democratic in the sense of majority rule. For better or worse--and I think better -- America in 1981 cannot assemble a consensus for any but the very broadest set of educational objectives and no consensus whatsoever regarding means. The only sense, then, in which democracy is possible is that of the individual choice of free and equal citizens.

Descending from political theory, it may be possible to say something more practical about the proper allocation of power over children for the pursuit of such broad majoritarian aims as can be identified. I will try. What I say will not rise to the level of theory; nonetheless, I say it because it has helped me to think about the issue, and it might help others who are similarly puzzled.

Here are my candidates for these dimly perceived social objectives: Education should promote the best interest of the child, quality in learning, liberty and responsibility for the parent, social consensus, racial integration and the good of the teaching profession. I commence with by far the most important--the child's own interest. It is the necessary (and perhaps sufficient) justification of any educational system. But, except for mastery of the three R's and some sense of our political institutions, what can the "child's interest" mean? In the absence of any social definition of a good education, it means whatever the adult with power to choose for him whould have it mean. And we are back in the circle again.

But not quite. I think it is possible in a rough way to evaluate decision-making about the child's interest simply by observing and comparing the way decisions are reached by professional systems on the one hand and parents on the other. At least one primitive principle for the allocation of power emerges from that experience: By and large individual assignments made by an adult familiar with the child are superior to assignments determined by the impersonal fact of residence. Human judgment may be fallible, but it improves upon random selection. I suppose it is too clear for argument that it is the parent who is in the better position to make a personal judgment about this child. Bureaucratic systems can provide individualization for only a very small portion of cases--and then only at great cost. If personalistic judgment is important, the parent has a great advantage.

Further, human judgment about children tends to be improved by three rather specific qualities that occur in different degrees among adult deciders. The first is the decider's capacity to hear the child's own opinion; Sugarman and I call this voice. The second is the degree to which such a decider is likely to act with altruism; we call this caring. The third is the degree to which the outcome of the decision is mutually baneful or beneficial for child and adult; we call this responsibility. I won't restate all the arguments one can make for the family in terms of voice, caring and responsibility. They are mostly obvious. It is the parent who in most cases hears the child's own opinion; it is the parent who cares the most; and it is the parent who suffers with the child when the decision is bad. It is also the parent who is most likely to take the initiative to get the child out of a bad situation; it is seldom in the interest of the managers of the school system to see students disappear from the average daily attendance count.

These arguments are not anti-professional. They merely recognize that professionalism only becomes possible when the client is free to sever the relation. Family choice, indeed, is the only way to introduce professionalism into government schools. Nor would I argue that parents do not need professional counseling in making decisions. That is precisely what they do need; what they don't need is subordination and domination by bureaucrats who have them as a captive audience. Under such conditions the interest of the child tends to become secondary to the interest of the system.

My conclusion so far is that the empowering of parents would not only make it possible at last to create a public system of education but would seem quite consistent with the best interest of the individual child. Before going on to ask whether family choice is consistent with consensus, integration and other broad social values, let us pause to ask what a system based upon family choice might look like. There is no need to describe every possible model (though I would exclude some, such as tax credits which are useful principally to wealthier families). What I will describe is the plan for my own state that many of think technically feasible and politically attractive. For convenience I will call it the California Plan.*

The structure of this plan is, first of all, conservative in this sense of that word: Unlike other reform plans, it destroys no institutions and it favors the existing government schools. These would justly be labelled "public," for no child would now be subject to an assignment forced upon him by his family's circumstance. Those who wished not to attend public schools could attend any of three other types of schools. They could, as today, opt for the traditional private school financed by tuition. In addition, however, they could now choose either the private or public form of what we call the "New Schools," both of which would be financed by state scholarships provided to families.

The important institutional innovation here is the New <u>Public</u> School which is a novel legal creature; each such school would take the form of a separate public corporation organized and designed by a local school board (or public university) and financed by the scholarships of its patrons. Its counterpart in the private sector would be the New Private School operating according to the same rules except for its entitlement to teach religion.

The public school--that is, the present model of state owned

---

*Editor's Note: The April 1981 version of the Initiative for Education by Choice proposed by Professors Coons and Sugarman is included at the end of this essay as an Appendix.

school--would be relatively favored over the New Schools, first, with more money. Scholarships for the New Schools would be worth 90 percent of what would be spent statewide in the public schools for children of similar age, grade and circumstance. Public schools could also, as today, prefer children who live in an attendance area chosen by the school board. Likewise, physically disabled children could be redirected to schools convenient to the system. New Schools by contrast would be open to all children, regardless of residence and physical handicap.

Unlike the public schools, the New Schools would also be required to set aside at least twenty-five percent of their spaces; for these spaces priority would be given to the applications of children from low income families defined as the bottom twenty-five percent on the income scale. (These children would also be entitled to reasonable cost of transport.) The rest of the spaces in a New School would be filled by application of criteria valid for public schools under the federal constitution other than residence and physical handicap.

The California Plan is, then, a way for families to choose freely among existing and new institutions. If change occurs in enrollment patterns, it will be because consumers did not like the services offered in a particular school. At last there would be a way for public institutions that have suffered brain death to expire peacefully like private schools, instead of having life sustained by artificial means including a captive clientele. Conversely there would be all the rewards of popularity for schools people like. This phenomenon is called competition, and I believe that in our society it is regarded as normal and healthy.

Another special and important feature of the New Public School is that it is permitted to operate as much like a private school as its founding school district desires. Its articles of incorporation can bind it to the parent district very closely or very remotely; thus its management could be lodged in the parents and children or, conversely, left in the hands of district administrators. Many models of governance could flourish including management by the teaching staff. If permitted by its charter, each school could hire whom it chose and deal with employees solely by contract instead of by statute and regulation. It could set its curriculum emphasizing different specialities; and it could set a code of discipline and enforce it.

California law has burdened its private schools very lightly. A fear of some opponents of educational subsidies to families has been that private schools would run too great a risk of heavy state regulation. With this fear in mind, we have inserted the following language into the initiative:

New schools shall be eligible to redeem state scholarships upon filing a statement indicating satisfaction of those requirements for hiring and employment, for curriculum and for facilities which applied to private schools on July 1, 1979; the Legislature may not augment such requirements.

This language, which would become part of the California constitution, not only would prevent such an outcome, but for the first time would offer private schools complete protection against legislative control of hiring, curriculum and facilities. The more important effect of this provision, however, is to open the possibility of deregulating some portion of the public sector; just how large a portion would depend upon the preferences of consumers. Some families will want public schools that continue to be heavily regulated; they believe such regulation contributes to child protection. Some by contrast will want New Public Schools that are deregulated to permit variation and flexibility. Consumers could have their individual ways without leaving the public sector.

Other than the admission rules the only significant regulation of the New Schools--public and private--would come in the form of information requirements and limits upon the ways in which tuition can be added on top of the scholarship. The information demands are of course crucial if the market is to be self-regulating. Consumers must have adequate knowledge to make choices, and they must be able to punish the school that deliberately misinforms them. The California plan would permit parents to levy that punishment by transferring the prorated portion of their voucher at any time to another school; it would permit the state to punish by terminating the school's eligibility to redeem vouchers upon proof of deliberate fraud.

The California plan also requires an agency independent of any school to dispense information; and it guarantees an additional subsidy to families with "special information needs"--an information voucher--to purchase counseling services in the market. The initiative is based upon respect for the judgment of all parents, but it recognizes that some families will need to overcome barriers to full participation. Many will not speak or read English well. Some will be quite unsophisticated about education, since strangers have always decided for them. Personal counseling will be the most effective means for such families to raise their level of knowledge about schools, and the counselor should be of the parent's own choosing. It is expected that a new profession of educational advisers would arise; unlike the old counseling system it would answer to the family instead of to the school. It is also predictable that volunteer organizations ranging from the YMCA to the League of Women Voters would find counseling of non-literate and immigrant parents a rewarding activity. And private accreditation groups would make it their business to rate schools upon criteria to which different parents will give varying weight.

The New Schools would be limited in another way. They could not charge extra tuition to low-income families, and the other families could be charged only according to their ability to pay. Unlimited freedom to charge add-on tuition would frustrate access by the ordinary and low-income faimly; it would recreate the present system in a new form.

The scholarships would, today, average about $2300 (though they would vary among children according to legislative judgment of need and other considerations). It is likely that some schools will be able to find families that are content to pay an extra thousand or two; though their payment would in part be a subsidy for others in the school, they would be paying far less than what it costs them today for private schools that spend at an equivalent level. The sole disincentive, if any, for such families would be the presence in the New Schools of children from all classes and races; we hope that for most families this social mix will be viewed as an opportunity for their child. For unregenerate snobs there would still be the option to stay in the old private school and pay for it.

The New Schools would be subject to one more limitation. They could not dismiss a child for academic reasons unless he or she were acquiring no substantial benefit; the school, however, could itself regulate the process of dismissal so long as its procedures were fair. Most schools would very likely establish an arbitration system for serious disputes. The school could also--with notice and fair procedure--set a code of conduct and enforce it.

For the child dismissed for academic or behavioral reasons, the California plan represents new hope. Hitherto he or she has relegated to "opportunity" schools or "continuation centers"--some good, some not so good, but in any case with few options. There would now be a strong incentive for public and private providers to organize to serve such children in new and creative ways. We should remember the historic parallel of children with learning disabilities; until the recent interventions by the judiciary and Congress, the hope, if any, for such children lay largely in the private sector. For any child who is "special" in the many senses of that euphemism, the best system is the one which can adapt and reorganize flexibly whether the providers be public, private or both.

Let me sum up what I have said about the California plan. It delivers as much power to the consumer as our ingenuity could devise. And for the producer it guarantees as much liberty as is consistent with the primary right of the family. Such a system should truly put the family in the saddle. It will be public in the fullest sense and will serve the best interest of the child.

But will it serve the other broad goals of the social order? Let me add a word as to each, beginning with the need for consensus and tolerance. Some claim that giving ordinary families the choice that the wealthy now employ would divide us as a people. The assumptions underlying this assertion are that we are presently unified and tolerant and that ordinary people tend to be bigots. There is no evidence supporting either assumption, nor is there any reason to believe that government schools are fostering consensus.

My own belief is that government that despises the values of
ordinary people and wishes to erase them by compulsion is likely to
generate more conflict than it cures; conversely a government that
plainly respects the cherished differences among people is not
necessarily divisive. Indeed, the manifestation of trust by
government will beget trust in return from families. To know that
the society supports the transmission of one's special values is to
have a reason to support the social order, not to upset it. E pluribus
unum is not a statement of satisfaction that we have abolished all
differences; it is a recognition that in human society--as in the
biological order--variety is not weakness but strength.

As for racial integration, the question can be plainly put. When
we are through doing whatever it is we will do through the courts,
should we deny opportunities for integration for those who will seek
them beyond the judicial reach? Consider the District of Columbia.
Would we have more or less integration if the children of the
District were entitled to scholarships and a bus ride to the private
school or public school of their choice -- either in or out of the
District? In many parts of California and elsewhere there are
spaces in private or public schools within reasonable distance of
children whose presence would be an integrating presence. I should
add that the most stable integration our society has experienced is
voluntary integration; and there is more of it today than is
acknowledged by those committed to busing orders as the principal,
or, worse yet, the only idea in our legal quiver.

What would family choice do for teachers? I have already said
it could make public school teaching a true profession. Let me add
that it could make it a prosperous profession. At least it would do
so in California where the cost per classroom is now approximately
$85,000 and the teacher is paid less than $25,000. In a world of free
consumer choice, state systems characterized by an enormous
commitment to administrative and para-professional personnel who
operate very large schools would begin to get competition. Families
prefer smaller schools; given free choice they would get them. Such
schools would be characterized by a heavier proportional investment
in teachers as is characteristic of private schools today. Imagine a
school of ten teachers serving two hundred children who bring, on
the average, a $2300 scholarship; it doesn't take a computer to
perceive that teacher salaries could rise. To the objection that
somebody else would then lose, I respond that the consumer is the
best one to decide which laborer is worthier of his hire.

Teachers, by the way, could be expected to form many New
Schools acting either on their own or through their unions. In the
present order teachers are not often entrepreneurs; some observers
think they lack the temperament. I think they lack the capital.
Who in his right mind would offer risk capital to finance a school
today? But given a system of scholarships there would be every
reason for private (and public) sources of capital to invest in good
teaching. This would be assisted by a special provision in the

California plan making unused space in public schools available for rent at cost to the New Schools. In an era of surplus capacity this is another important incentive. Finally, it is inevitable that the formation of New Schools will be advanced by the expertise of unions and of management consultants who will offer entreprenurial services to teachers and to the families who wish to obtain their services in various kinds of schools.

It is crucial that this society do something for the teaching profession, which is in serious intellectual decline. Since we lost the indentured service of many of our brightest women through the women's movement, and since the baby bust wrecked the teacher market, few but the dimmest of our young intellects are pursuing the path to the teaching degree and certification. Unless we change the system, within ten years it will be entirely in the hands of well-meaning mediocrities. The frightening details of this problem may be read in the recent work of Professor Timothy Weaver of Boston University.* The remedy may be read in the California plan which abolishes credentialing and tenure as requirements of law and which gives to teachers both the dignity of a free relation to a non-captive client and the opportunity for economic gain.

I will shortly describe how the plan is a blessing to taxpayers; let me now point out that the present scheme of things unnaturally depresses the level of national commitment to education. So long as the public and private sectors are arrayed in mutual economic hostility, education will be shortchanged. It has become dangerously fashionable to view education essentially as a zero sum game. According to this view, every dollar now spent for private schools diminishes the political and economic support for spending in the public sector--and vice versa. I would like to suggest, however, that a system in which the choices of families in both sectors are funded by the legislature would assemble the largest possible constituency for education. Unless change itself--any change--is perceived by the managers of the current monopolistic system as intimidating, one would have thought that they too would grasp this fundamental lesson in economics. For the initiative is in the best interests not only of the children they serve, but also of teachers and administrators in public and nonpublic schools alike.

As for impact on the institution of the family, consider first the effect of the present system on the parent of ordinary means. Until age five the child experiences that parent as authoritative and pro-

---

*Editor's Note: See Timothy Weaver, "In Search of Quality: The Need for Talent in Teaching," Phi Delta Kappan (Sept. 1979) pp. 29-32, 46. Professor Weaver also addressed this theme in his keynote address, "The Tragedy of the Commons: The Effect of Supply and Demand on the Education Talent Pool," before the February, 1981 meeting of the American Association of Colleges of Teacher Education in Detroit, Michigan.

tective. At that vulnerable age in the child's life the parent is suddenly stripped of all power, and the child is directed by strangers to report to strangers who will teach him what the strangers think best for him. Should we be surprised if he loses his healthy faith in the only people who have been his primary advocates? Can we blame children for viewing their parents as impotent, when parents can do nothing to affect the basic character of the institution which claims the prime hours of their day? There could be no more efficient device for discrediting the family in the eyes of its own members than the present regime in education.

By contrast, the family which maintains control of education has a better chance of remaining effective in all of its functions. In such a family the opinions of both child and parent can count for something; they thus become worth discussing. The family can function as the political incubator in which important questions are aired and shared. This society could do nothing better for the battered and beleaguered American family than to give it the capacity to decide for its own children. Give it counseling; give it information; give it limits; but give it power and responsibility.

Therein lies sanity and stabler social order. Don't tell us that many poor families are apathetic, stupid and delinquent. Of course they are. Don't warn that they will make mistakes. Of course they will; the rest of us do, with embarrassing regularity. Perhaps the difference between us and the poor is that we are permitted to make our own mistakes -- and learn from them. The poor are permitted no mistakes and thus have nothing to learn; their apathy and hostility is a perfectly rational response, just as the failure, violence, truancy and apathy of their children in school are responses to the indignity and foolishness of compulsory and often arbitrary assignments. If you want parents who try, and if you want children who try to learn, the surest medicine is to link them to their teachers by family choice.

I would be remiss if I said nothing about the economic cost of a system of family choice -- the California plan in particular. Let me say first that I am more interested in efficiency than cost. Let me also restate my belief that society ultimately will support education more generously if the private and public sectors can be brought more into economic harmony. But then let me stress that any plan can be designed to limit cost through a variety of devices. One is a simple ceiling on public expenditure; the California plan, for example, would impose a six year freeze on additional spending except for inflationary adjustments. Eligibility for scholarships would be phased in over that period, and the introduction of an additional percent or two of children drawn from the private sector each of those years would have minimal impact on average spending per pupil. Information and transportation would cost something, but their contribution to choice would be well worth the costs. These costs would, in any case, be minor. Even the enemies of choice have estimated the maximum added cost at less than 4 percent of the total public cost of education; and these critics have never begun to consider the savings.

These savings are potentially massive. There would be two important sources of efficiency: the size of the scholarship and the effects of deregulation. Since the scholarship is set at 90 percent of the cost in the traditional public school, student transfers from public schools to a New Public or New Private school would offset some or all costs of private school entrants. More important, the elimination of heavy statutory controls over curriculum, credentialing, tenure and facilities would permit New Schools to operate with the efficiency characteristic of private schools. Today spending per pupil in private schools is less than half that of their public counterparts; yet these low budget schools achieve what James Coleman and Andrew Greeley tell us are consistently superior results in learning.* While the costs of such schools will (and should) rise as they enter the system, competition will assure that their efficiency will be maintained with consequent benefits to their pupils and the society. Thus, a legislature that wished to maintain educational output at today's level could reduce spending; one that wished to increase output could expect to do so without changing the present public investment. In spite of deregulation there will be interesting and important decisions left for lawmakers.

If public education has had a checkered past in this country, it certainly has a future. America desperately needs public education, and I am convinced that it is politically possible to achieve it. The principal barrier is the "public" halo with which the monopoly has crowned itself. The lawmaker and the executive are in an effective position to expose this mislabeling, but they obviously run risks in doing so. It will be interesting to observe their contributions to the formation of public awareness and public opinion in the decade before us.

---

*Editor's Note: Chapter one in this volume provides a summary by Fr. Greeley of the findings of the High School and Beyond project, conducted by the National Opinion Research Center.

APPENDIX

AN INITIATIVE FOR EDUCATION BY CHOICE

The following section shall be added to Article IX of the California Constitution:

Section 17. The people of California have adopted this section to improve the quality and efficiency of schools, to maximize the educational opportunities of all children, and to increase the authority of parents and teachers.

(1) New Schools

(a) In addition to the public schools and private schools presently recognized by law, there shall be two classes of schools together known as New Schools.

(b) New Private Schools are private schools eligible to redeem state scholarships.

(c) New Public Schools are schools organized as public corporations eligible to redeem state scholarships.

School districts, community colleges and public universities may establish New Public Schools. Each shall be a public non-profit corporation governed by rules fixed by the organizing authority at the time of incorporation. Such schools are free common schools under section 5 of this article; section 6 of this article shall not limit their formation. Except as stated in this section, New Public Schools shall operate according to the laws affecting New Private Schools.

(d) New Schools shall be eligible to redeem state scholarships upon filing a statement indicating satisfaction of those requirements for hiring and employment, for curriculum and for facilities which applied to private schools on July 1, 1979; the Legislature may not augment such requirements. No school shall lose eligibility to redeem state scholarships except upon proof of substantial violation of this section after notice and opportunity to defend.

No New School may advocate unlawful behavior or expound the inferiority of either sex or of any race nor deliberately provide false or misleading information respecting the school. Each shall be subject to reasonable requirements of disclosure. The Legislature may set reasonable standards of competence for diplomas.

No school shall be ineligible to redeem state scholarships because it teaches moral or social values, philosophy, or religion, but religion may not be taught in public schools or New Public Schools; a curriculum may be required, but no pupil shall be compelled to profess ideological belief or actively to participate in ceremony symbolic of belief.

(2) Admission to New Schools

(a) A New School may set enrollment and select students by criteria valid for public schools under the federal constitution other than physical handicap, national origin, and place of residence within the state.

(b) Each New School shall reserve at least twenty-five percent of each year's new admissions for timely applications from families with income lower than seventy-five percent of California families. If such applications are fewer than the places reserved, all shall be admitted and the balance of reserved places selected as in paragraph (a) of this subsection; if such applications exceed the reserved places the school may select therefrom the reserved number.

(3) Finance

(a) Every child of school age is entitled without charge to a state scholarship redeemable by New Schools and adequate for a thorough education as defined by law. Scholarships shall be equal for every child of similar circumstance differing only by factors deemed appropriate by the Legislature; they shall reflect the educational cost attributable to physical handicap and learning disability, and, for children of low income families, the cost of reasonable transportation. Except for children enrolled in schools in which parents or other relatives have primary responsibility for instruction of their own children no scholarship shall be less than eighty percent of the average scholarship for children of similar grade level. A nonprofit New Private School shall use scholarship income solely for the education of its students. The Legislature shall provide for an appropriate division of the scholarship in the case of transfers. Nothing required or permitted by this section shall be deemed to repeal or conflict with section 8 of this article or section 5 of Article XVI.

(b) New Schools shall accept scholarships from low income families as full payment for educational or related services. Charges to others shall be consistent with the family's ability to pay.

(c) The average public cost per pupil enrolled in New Schools
shall approximate ninety percent of that cost in public schools.
Public cost here and in subsection (3)(d) shall mean every cost
to state and local government of maintaining elementary and
secondary education in the relevant year as determined by the
Department of Finance according to law; it shall not include the
costs of funding employee retirement benefits which are
unfunded on June 3, 1982.

(d) For school years 1982-83 through 1987-88 the total public
cost of elementary and secondary education shall not exceed
that of 1981-82 adjusted for changes in average personal
income and total school age population. The Controller shall
authorize no payment in violation of this sub-section.

(e) Excess space in public schools shall be available to New
Schools for rental at actual cost.

(4) Rights

(a) A pupil subject to compulsory education who attends a New
School may continue therein unless she or he is deriving no
substantial academic benefit or is responsible for serious or
habitual misconduct related to school. With fair notice and
procedures each school may set and enforce a code of conduct
and discipline and regulate its academic dismissals. No pupil
enrolled in any such school shall suffer discrimination on the
basis of race, religion, gender, or national origin.

(b) The Legislature shall assure provision of adequate
information about New Schools through sources independent of
any school or school authority. Non-literate parents and others
with special information needs shall receive a grant redeemable
for the services of independent education counsellors.

(5) Transitional Provision

The Legislature shall promptly implement this section, ensuring
full eligibility for scholarships of at least one-fourth of all
pupils in school year 1984-85 and a similar additional number
yearly thereafter.

10. Credits v. Subsidies: Comment on the California Tuition Tax Credit Proposal

John E. Coons and Stephen D. Sugarman

The National Taxpayers Union has recently sponsored an unusual educational tax limitation scheme. The proposal was circulated unsuccessfully for signatures in the form of a constitutional initiative. The California state income tax was its principal target. The proposed reform would have reduced the tax liability of corporations and individuals by awarding a tax credit for specified expenditures for elementary, secondary and higher education. Under the NTU proposal the taxpayer would qualify for the proposed credit by paying the tuition and/or "incidental expenses" of a person attending a private school or the "incidental expenses" of a person attending a public school. The individual or corporation could claim tax credit for as many--and whichever--students he or it chose. The total credit gained by all contributing taxpayers for any one pupil could not exceed $1200. Corporations could use the credit to eliminate up to half of their income tax liability to the state. Individuals could use the credit to eliminate their entire income tax liability to the state.

The Taxpayers' device has a number of unique features which are interesting for their own sake. Moreover, it provides a useful window on the relative advantages of tuition tax credits and direct educational subsidies to families, sometimes called vouchers or scholarships. Plans of the latter sort would provide families not liking their assigned public school a voucher or scholarship to be used to pay for educational costs at qualifying elementary or secondary schools of their choice both public and private. Both voucher and tax credit advocates have captured public attention of late with their talk about choice and competition. But as we will see, the intended beneficiaries of the plans differ significantly. We are unenthusiastic about the educational tax credit plans we have seen proposed--and we are especially cool to the NTU scheme. In this essay we explain why.

TAX CREDITS PROVIDE SMALLER BENEFITS TO FAMILIES THAN DO VOUCHERS.

Consider first a voucher plan that would make available to par-

*This essay appears in Family Choice in Schooling: Issues and Dilemmas, edited by Michael E. Manley-Casimir (Lexington, Mass.: Lexington Books, 1981) and is published here by permission of the authors, the editor and the publisher. © 1981 Lexington Books.

ticipating families a scholarship worth, on average, about 90 percent of what is spent on children in public schools. Such a plan has been proposed for California. In California in 1980 the average scholarship would be worth more than $2000. Now compare tax credits. In practice, such proposals presuppose far lower benefits. Recent federal proposals by Senators Moynihan and Packwood envisioned tax credits worth less than $500 per child. Plans enacted in a few states and struck down by the courts (a matter to which we will return) have provided benefits of under $200 per child. Even the NTU proposal under consideration here, while seeming to call for a substantially larger benefit--superficially, up to $1200 per child--is on its face, considerably less valuable to families than the proposed scholarship would be.

Moreover, a state income tax credit plan such as the NTU's inevitably will provide less adequate funding for schools of choice than will the California scholarship. If for no other reason, the entire pool of state personal and corporate income tax is far smaller than the total now spent on public schools; this total is potentially available for scholarship plans, if all families participate and are given scholarships worth something near to current public spending levels.

In addition, even for the rich, the $1200 figure is misleadingly high. Those whose state income taxes are lowered by a credit will have less to deduct for federal income tax purposes. Thus, for those who itemize federal tax deductions, part of the benefit from the state credit must be sent to the federal treasury. Ironically, the tax cutters' proposal becomes a form of inverse revenue sharing helping out Uncle Sam.

Consider, for example, a California family with $40,000 of yearly income and two school-age children. Today this fairly well-to-do family pays a maximum state income tax of about $2400; it will probably pay considerably less because of itemized deductions for mortgage interest, property taxes and the like. The NTU initiative would permit such a family, by spending $1200 or more on the education of each child, to wipe out all its state taxes.

However, because of the interrelation of state and federal tax laws noted above, the net cash benefit to the family would not be $2400. The family in our example will probably be in the 35 to 40 percent marginal tax rate bracket for federal tax purposes. On the normal assumption that it itemizes deductions for federal purposes, its real benefit from the NTU plan would be only about $1500, not $2400. The difference, $900, would be redirected from California to the federal Treasury.

A scholarship, by contrast, is worth its full face value to both family and school. Thus, credits generally would have to be larger than subsidies in order to deliver the same dollar benefit. Given the current level and structure of state income tax plans, however, this cannot happen. In short, people pay too little state income tax to produce this effect. This brings us to the next general point.

WHILE SCHOLARSHIPS PROVIDE EQUAL BENEFITS TO ALL, TAX CREDITS ARE HIGHLY REGRESSIVE.

We have shown above that the hypothetical well-to-do California family may benefit as much as $1500 from the NTU tax credit initiative. Now consider the outcome of the credit for other families. One with $20,000 of income in 1980 will owe roughly $440 in state income taxes (and often less if it is a homeowner family which itemizes deductions). This sum minus any increase in federal income taxes caused by the state credit—perhaps $90—represents its maximum savings under the initiative. The effect is that the state would pay only $350 to $440 toward the education of the children in the $20,000 family as compared to $1500 toward the education of the children of the $40,000 family. This is plainly regressive.

The point becomes more vivid as we move down the income scale. Families with income of $10,000 and under would receive virtually no benefit from the NTU initiative. Hence, when others exercise their choice to attend private schools with the financial support of the state, these families will not have that option. Put simply, tax credits provide no increase of choice to any family that pays no state taxes. The only way for credits to begin to be equivalent to vouchers is to make them "refundable"—that is, to subsidize families whose tax liability is too low to need the credit. Politically, this is unlikely. Tax credit plans tend to be promoted by groups whose purpose is to let taxpayers control the use of their own taxes and not to redirect those dollars to empower lower income families. Moreover, even tax credit advocates would agree that making the credit refundable would transmute their idea into a kind of complex voucher plan. In sum, since tax credits principally benefit high income families and very low income families not at all, if the objective is educational opportunity for children and autonomy for families, tax credits are a poor second choice.

THE EXTENSION OF THE TAX CREDIT TO INCLUDE EDUCATIONAL EXPENDITURES MADE BY TAXPAYERS WITHOUT CHILDREN LACKS A RATIONALE AND WILL HAVE NEGATIVE CONSEQUENCES.

Unlike typical tax credit plans, the NTU scheme does not restrict the credit to those spending on their own children. We find this puzzling. What is the point of helping corporations and nonparents avoid state income taxes by spending on the children of strangers? Why is the corporation or individual given power to decide which child and which school is worthy? Do higher income persons and corporate boards of directors have the best judgment about where the children of blue collar workers should study? No one so argues.

If the point of the initiative were to shift authority for assignment away from the public school bureaucracy, that power surely should be given to the family, as it is in any voucher plan. It should not be bestowed upon some person or corporation with little or no relationship to the child. But this is precisely what the tax credit initiative does. One is tempted to infer that the proposal is designed merely to cripple the state income tax, and that schools are incidental to its purpose.

In any event, the children who would actually benefit from stranger-choices would in many cases be children of middle and upper-middle income families. Where these have more than one child and have exhausted their own tax liability, they nevertheless could benefit from someone else's tax credit. It would be quite natural for friends to assist one another; and friends will generally be of the same social class. Corporations will institutionalize this practice by setting up special tuition fringe benefit programs for their executives.

The "stranger" tax credit provision creates yet another perverse incentive, for the opportunity for private bargaining would not be neglected. Jones pays Smith $600 in exchange for Smith's paying $1200 in tuition for Jones' son. Everyone is ahead except the state treasury and public morality. Such fraud could not be policed.

If the argument for giving tax credits to corporations and nonparents is that this would stimulate private donations to educational institutions, it must be remembered that this incentive currently exists in both the state and federal tax codes for those wanting to make an unrestricted gift to a tax exempt school. Thus, today, government already "pays" for half or more of any charitable gift made to a school by most corporations and well-to-do individuals. To be sure, this incentive might be enhanced—indeed made nearly irresistible—by converting today's charitable tax deductions into tax credits. However, we think the tradition of having government reimburse part, but not all, of one's educational gift is a wise one to preserve. Painless charity is meaningless. Moreover, if government attaches extra tax benefits to gifts for education, this will surely divert gifts away from churches, hospitals and other charities. That seems highly undesirable.

Conversely, it is not clear that the tax credit initiative will actually stimulate greater educational giving. This is because, in order to obtain the tax credit, a donor's funds have to be identified with an individual child. This earmarking, while insuring that the proposed credit is obtained, will probably destroy the charitable tax deductibility of the payment. If so, the tax advantage of the credit is eroded. Table 1 sets out the financial implications of the case of X, an individual or corporation, whose income today is $50,000 and who, we will assume, is in the 50 percent federal tax bracket and the 10 percent state tax bracket (which is roughly the case, if he is a California resident).

TABLE 1

Tax Changes:	Consequences of Unrestricted $1000 Charitable Gift		Consequences of Earmarked $1000 Gift Under NTU Initiative	
State Taxable Income	-1000		No Change	
State Tax Change		- 100		-1000
Federal Taxable Income (Assuming Itemizing)				
From Charitable Gifts	-1000		No Change	
From Lower State Taxes	+ 100		+1000	
Net Fed. Taxable Income	- 900		+1000	
Federal Tax Change		- 450		+ 500
Net Tax Change (State and Fed.)		- 550		- 500
Revenue Flows:				
To School	+1000		+1000	
From/To Federal Govt.	- 450		+ 500	
From State Govt.	- 100		-1000	
From Individual	- 450		- 500	

In sum, if the choice comes down to making an unrestricted gift and getting the charitabale deduction or making a restricted gift and getting the credit, for our hypothetical taxpayer the following points can be made: (1) In neither case is the gift free to the individual; it will cost about the same--one half--in each case. Thus, there is no increased stimulus to give; (2) The consequences to the school are relatively worse if the donor takes the credit, for the gift is restricted and not unrestricted; (3) Of course, some will prefer, at the same cost to them, to be able to earmark the gift for a particular child. As a result the social consequences are very likely to be worse. Tax-exempt schools can usually be counted on to use their donations for scholarships for the needy or for all pupils; restricted gifts will more often go to children of the middle class. Moreover, under the NTU initiative, funds will flow to schools that are not tax-exempt, and this may well be a social loss; (4) The intergovernmental impact of the tax credit route is far worse. Instead of the federal government losing $450 and the state $100, as happens with the charitable gift, the restricted gift costs the state $1000 and brings in a $500 windfall to the federal treasury. This is hardly a contribution to "local control."

Now it is true that the picture changes somewhat as we focus on less wealthy donors and small businesses. But again, if one's idea is to let individuals give to charity some of what they now pay into the state treasury, the NTU device is hardly the ideal. Instead let us have an initiative that does just that. Imagine, for example, a measure that allowed persons to direct 50 percent of their state income taxes (up to $500) to tax-exempt charities of their choice. As noted above, we would prefer a provision that also required taxpayers to contribute something out of their own pockets and not just out of their taxes; but we would surely prefer this hypothetical proposal to the NTU initiative. And, of course, we would prefer a family educational subsidy to any of these tax schemes. Scholarship or voucher plans, by empowering families, avoid all these pitfalls, while leaving in place the general tax incentive to private charitable giving.

THE EXTENSION OF THE TAX CREDIT TO COVER "INCIDENTAL" EXPENSES OF PUBLIC EDUCATION IS ILL-CONCEIVED AND LEGALLY RISKY.

What are the "incidental expenses" for which the credit may be taken under the NTU initiative? Would they include the cost of transportation, the cost of lodging if the child lives at a boarding school, the cost of lunch for school children generally, the cost of after-school tutors? None of this is made clear by the initiative, and this lack of clarity is crucial. If "incidental expenses" includes the provision of a car to a Beverly Hills sophomore, one can see how useful it will be to some income groups. Let us suppose, however, that the term is limited to such things as school supplies, musical instruments, fees for field trips and other similar school activities. Even so, the result is highly unfortunate. Rich families will get these things free by way of the credit, while welfare families will pay cash. The poor will not only pay more; they alone will pay anything.

This bizarre provision, of course, was not designed for that purpose. Its intent was to give the appearance that public school users are included in the system. It was thought that this might bring the initiative within the possible exception to the Establishment Clause barrier suggested by Justices Powell and Burger in the 1973 "aid to parochial school" cases. The Justices reserved judgment about "general" systems—i.e., those designed to help families using all kinds of schools, public as well as private. However, the "incidental expense" provision is such a transparent device it is likely to have the opposite of its intended effect. It gives the entire enterprise an aroma of deceit—worse, of amateur deceit. Presently we will speak further of the federal Constitution.

THE EXTENSION OF THE TAX CREDIT INITIATIVE TO HIGHER EDUCATION IS UNWISE AND INEFFECTUAL.

There is, of course, much to be said for the reform of educational finance at the postsecondary level. Presently, however, it is far fairer and more rational than the financing of schools. California higher education has a mature and balanced system of financing which can adapt to different tuition levels for the different kinds of state higher education systems; it thus provides reasonably tailored subsidies for the varying needs of student. There also exists an elaborate system of federal loans and scholarships (through the Basic Educational Opportunity Grant program) as well as some state scholarships for private education.

The tax credit proposed would cause serious dislocations of this system. If the payoff were sufficient, perhaps these dislocations would be justified. It appears, however, that very little, if any, thought was given to the effects upon higher education in the drafting of the NTU initiative. That was not the real interest of the sponsors. Again, it is merely a device to avoid the Supreme Court's interpretations of the Establishment Clause. In our judgment the effort is vain. It will be a very simple matter for the Justices to sever their treatment of higher education from the rest of the proposal.

TAX CREDITS AND VOUCHERS ARE NOT DISTINGUISHABLE IN THE DEGREE OF STATE REGULATION INVOLVED.

Tax credits often are advertised as simpler to administer and less of an encroachment on the freedom of private schools. It is said the in the case of tax credits, only the taxpayer has to deal with the government; the school gets its money without bureaucratic hassle. Vouchers by contrast are said to draw the school inevitably into the government net.

This is a simple misunderstanding. Tax credits can be less intrusive than subsidies to families; or they can be more intrusive. It all depends upon the conditions attached to the claiming of the credit by the taxpayer and how these conditions compare to those which limit redemption of the voucher by the school. Imagine, for example, a tax credit available only for those whose children are enrolled in racially integrated, secular, private schools that do not charge over $2000 and which must be approved by the state superintendent of public instruction. This plan plainly would involve the bureaucracy with participating schools and would force some schools to alter their basic structure in order to participate. By contrast a particular voucher scheme might involve no regulation of schools at all—direct or indirect. Schools could cash the vouchers as simply, or even more simply, than supermarkets redeem food stamps. The supposed abstract advantage of either credits or vouchers in this respect is imaginary.

In practice one must evaluate the specific regulations required by the particular proposal. Both our proposal and the NTU initiative would protect participating private schools from further regulation in the areas of curriculum, hiring and facilities. Ours would, however, impose three important additional controls on schools. They could not charge tuition in excess of the voucher amount; they would have to take all applicants--with excess demand resolved by lot; and they would have to provide public information about themselves. Not all voucher proposals contain all these rules, or any of them. We prefer them because they give the consumer control over the entry process. This furthers the objective of providing poor families, uninformed families and families with unpopular children the same opportunity as others. The school market would become truly open to all. A 1981 version of our proposal takes a somewhat different approach to the "equal access" issue. It requires voucher schools to set aside 25 percent of their places for children of low-income families and to charge those families no more than the voucher amount. The California tax credit proposal, by contrast, would encourage the rich, the talented, and other elites to use exclusive schools to buy isolation from others for their children. Which set of values you have is a personal matter, but the issues are too important to resolve solely on whether more or less regulation is required. We too have a strong bias against regulation--except where it is necessary to maintain the very freedom of the family's choice.

There is, by the way, a good reason for the anti-bureaucratic policy maker to prefer a voucher system to a tax credit. The voucher device opens a vast opportunity for deregulation of the public sector. Credits, by themselves, do not. Public voucher schools that would operate in the same deregulated fashion as their private competitors are readily imaginable. We have made just such a proposal.* For credits to achieve the same result, the idea of tuition in American public schools would have to be accepted. That is not readily imaginable, nor is it currently permissible under many state contitutions.

THE TAX CREDIT INITIATIVE IS PROBABLY NOT CONSTITUTIONAL TO THE EXTENT THAT IT ALLOWS CREDITS FOR EDUCATIONAL EXPENSES AT RELIGIOUS SCHOOLS.

Inasmuch as the U.S. Supreme Court has already held one private school tax credit plan unconstitutional (in the Nyquist case), to escape the same result new proposals must be different in ways that will matter to the Court. The strategy of the drafters of the NTU initiative is to expand the class of beneficiaries by extending the benefits of the plan to non-parents and to users of both higher

---

*Editor's Note: See Appendix to chapter nine above.

education and the public schools. We believe that this technique would fail to sanitize the proposal. As we have said, the extension to higher education can easily be severed. As for elementary and secondary schools the Court will see, just as in Nyquist, that the initiative promises no change in California's existing dual educational structure—public schools on the one hand and private, mostly religious schools, on the other. Therefore, the "primary effect," as in Nyquist, will be seen to be the aiding of religious schools and their users. The side effect of benefitting non-poor public school families and some non-parents will be just that—a side effect.

Perhaps the Court could be talked into severing religious school users from the NTU plan. The result of that, however, is a benefit limited to secular private schools, causing many religious schools to perish from the new competition. By contrast many constitutional scholars predict that a properly drawn voucher system will survive scrutiny with religious schools included. While people may differ on the desirability of these outcomes, they are plainly different in important respects.

The necessary and sufficient conditions of including religious schools lie in the extension of real choice to all elementary and secondary school families. This requires that a plan promise the creation of large numbers of new private non-religious schools and/or new public schools of choice. And it requires that working class and poor families be given the leverage, through choice, to make their existing public schools more responsive to their wishes. Only then is any benefit to religious schools and their users likely to be seen as an incidental, rather than the primary effect. While none of the tax credit initiatives have promised any of these changes, properly designed scholarship systems which aid all schools and children promise all of them; and that is why the constitutional outlook for the two is very different.

The differing constitutional prospects, in the end, reflect the differing educational aims of the plans. Tax credits really aspire to provide tax relief to current private school users. Vouchers aim to extend choice to all.

CONCLUSION

The artificiality of schemes like the credit proposal discussed here should now be transparent. As relief for the taxpayer it is weak tea. As aid to education it would be effective on behalf of the few percent of children enrolled in secular private schools. Its structure betrays its genesis. It was developed as a political device to exploit both dissatisfaction with public education and the taxpayers' revolt. In the end, it is to be recommended only to those who seek to sidetrack efforts at basic reform of our educational system and its financing.

11. Federal Scholarships for Private Elementary and Secondary Education

Stephen D. Sugarman and John E. Coons

INTRODUCTION

Through the Basic Educational Opportunity Grant Program (BEOG) the federal government provides means-tested grants that help students pay for the costs of higher education.[1] At present the grants vary in amount from $200 to $1800 per year depending upon the student's need as defined in the statute. New York Senator Daniel Patrick Moynihan has proposed that the benefits of the BEOG plan be extended to elementary and secondary education.[2]

Although Moynihan has for some time advocated that government provide financial support to users of private elementary and secondary schools, previously his efforts have focused on an income tax credit plan.[3] Despite widespread support, the education tax credit idea has so far been unable to win congressional approval. Apart from general objections to providing federal aid to private school users, critics of the tax credit plan have opposed it on distributional equity grounds, claiming that its benefits will go mainly to non-poor families. They have also argued that its application to users of religious schools would be an unconstitutional violation of the First Amendment's Establishment Clause. Further, some have objected to having the Internal Revenue Service administer what in effect could become a very large aid to education program.

Whatever the merits of these three criticisms, Moynihan's new proposal--quickly dubbed "baby-BEOG"--can be seen as a response to all of them. The grant program would be run by the Department of Education. The fact that it would be combined with aid to higher education is thought by some to aid its constitutionality. Most important, it is aimed at the working class and the poor.

We will not consider here the agency competence (or rivalry) issue. There may be good practical or political reasons to prefer one department over the other, but we leave that debate to others.

Our discussion of the effect of including college students is postponed to the end. Stated succinctly, our position is that we do not think that combining federal aid to users of higher and lower education in one program is either helpful to or necessary to the constitutionality of support to families choosing religious primary and secondary schools.

For us the most exciting aspect of the baby-BEOG scheme is its targeting of aid on the non-rich. We too have opposed Moynihan's tax credit plan, as well as Milton Friedman's voucher scheme[4], on the ground that they don't do enough for those who most need new options in education—lower income families and the very poor. What is so stimulating about the new Moynihan initiative is its responsiveness to the educational aspirations of those typically worst served by today's public schools. By focusing financial assistance on low income families, the baby-BEOG proposal forcefully counters critics of tax credits and some voucher plans who see government aid to private school users as stimulating increased economic class separation in education. Moreover, as only non-rich families would be assisted by baby BEOG, there would be less reason to insist (as we have in the case of voucher or tax credit schemes) that tuition limits and enrollment controls be included to assure the poor equal access rights.[5] At the same time the baby-BEOG idea has the political attraction of not returning tax dollars to reasonably well off and wealthy families already paying for private education.

Although its initial congressional reception was cool,[6] the baby-BEOG plan is by no means a dead letter. Indeed, as conservatives renew their push for tax credits, liberals who have opposed all proposals to aid private school users may turn to the baby-BEOG as a compromise and, indeed, as a substantial boon to their primary constituents. In short, future debate about aid to users of private elementary and secondary education could well center on federal scholarships for private elementary and secondary education.

We will not here dwell on the basic arguments for financially aiding families who enroll their children in private schools. Elsewhere we have argued at length about the merits of increasing family choice in education.[7] We do wish to emphasize that our main concern has been and continues to be the child now badly served by the public schools. We want that child's family to have the financial backing to make a credible threat to those schools: do better by our child or we will take our business elsewhere. Working class and poor families by and large cannot make such demands today; but with the right baby-BEOG plan, they could. Most importantly, giving these families economic power promises to provide the competition that can revitalize public education. Most families, we assume, will remain in public schools—but now as consumers by choice. At the same time non-rich families who prefer private education will be able to make that choice for their children. Reducing the economic burden now shouldered by low income families already enrolled in private schools, although a desirable side effect, is not the fundamental objective.[8]

This essay, in any event, has narrower concerns. Although Senator Moynihan's overall concept is excellent, the implementing features proposed so far are a bit simplistic. The details of the college BEOG plan do not fit well the needs of lower education—whatever their merit in higher education. Our central purpose here is to propose and defend somewhat different parameters for the baby-BEOG scheme.

DETERMINING NEED

The core idea of baby-BEOG is to provide need-based scholarships to children attending private elementary and secondary schools. Assume that this has been decided in principle. Who, then, should get the scholarships, and for how many dollars? One start on the problem might be to decide which children are poor--perhaps all those living at or below the official poverty level--and then simply offer to pay the full costs of their private schooling. There would be a number of serious problems with such a tactic.

First, need for assistance with school costs is neither restricted to children living in poverty, nor does need sharply cut off at any specific income level. Thus to have an all or nothing rule for benefits creates both substantial injustice and work disincentives. In short, for a worker to earn $100 more than the poverty level and as a result have his child lose a scholarship worth far more than that is bad policy. The scholarship amount, like food stamps, should phase out as family income increases. The present college BEOG program adopts this approach; its phase-out rate may not be appropriate for elementary and secondary education, however, as we will see.

Second, a scholarship award for the full cost of schooling gives the eligible family a powerful reason to select the most expensive school. Putting a ceiling on the amount of the scholarship is one possible response to this pressure. But if the limit isn't generous, many desired schools will be out of the reach of the poorest families, thus defeating a central purpose of the plan. Further, a limit simply encourages the family to select a school at that limit rather than to "shop for price." A full scholarship scheme also runs the risk of having the family feel that it has less invested in the choice it has made for its child than it might feel if at least some of its own cash is on the line. The folk wisdom that things that are free aren't worth so much to you, and that you're more likely to demand good performance from something that you've put your money into, has a ring of truth to it. Together this second set of concerns argues for a matching plan that combines a family contribution with the scholarship to pay for the cost of the school. BEOG's matching arrangements, we will argue, are inappropriate for baby-BEOG.

The analysis thus far gives us two general principles to be used in awarding scholarships: (1) Even the poorest family should make some (even token) financial contribution toward even the lowest cost school. (2) As either family income or school cost increases, so should the family's contribution.

Third, suppose now that family has more than one child in private school? How should that affect its total contribution? At least three alternatives are worth considering. (a) A single contribution on behalf of the first child could suffice for the rest, or (b) each additional child in private school could impose on the family an obligation equal to that expected for the first child, or (c) a reduced contribution could be required for additional children. This is a difficult issue. On the one hand it can be argued that, in a needs-based program, once we have asked the family to contribute all it fairly ought to pay toward the education of its first child in private school, there will be no more money left that we can fairly ask to be contributed toward the education of the others. On the other it may be argued that it is only fair for a family to dip further into its funds (thus lowering its living standard) in order to send additional children to private schools; the additional government aid should be conditioned on additional family contributions. We lean toward the rule that one family payment serves for all its children. However, the BEOG program for higher education has adopted a compromise position calling for extra but reduced contributions for each additional child; to simplify discussion we will here accept that position for baby-BEOG.

Having described the principles, we must turn to the crucial details. At just what rate should the family's contribution increase as its income increases? At just what rate should the family contribution increase as its chosen school's costs increase? Just how much extra should a family contribute if it has more than one child in private school? What counts as income for these purposes? And how should accumulated family assets (wealth) be counted, if at all? We will address these issues from three perspectives: How has BEOG resolved them? In what respects are these solutions inappropriate for elementary and secondary schools? What parameters for baby-BEOG would be desirable?

HOW THE HIGHER EDUCATION BEOG WORKS TODAY

One child in college

Suppose a couple has one child and the child is about to attend college. Suppose further that the family has less than $25,000 in assets and that the child's annual college expenses will exceed $3600, two factors the importance of which will be explained in due course. Simplifying slightly, if the family's annual income, as defined in the statute, is in the range of 0 to $5400, the child will be eligible for the maximum $1800 grant.[9] As the family's income increases, the amount of the grant slowly declines until it reaches the minimum award level of $200. The rate at which the student's grant declines is 10.5 cents for every extra dollar the family has in income above $5400. For our hypothetical family the minimum grant level occurs once its income reaches about $20,000. If family income is greater, the child is ineligible.[10]

The basic theory behind this grant formula is of course simple: the poorer the family, the higher the grant should be--because the family is less able itself to pay for the child's education. But the details require separate explanations.

First, why is the initial $5400 in family income disregarded? BEOG adopts the idea that the amount the family ought to be able to contribute to its child's education depends on its <u>discretionary</u> income--its total income less an amount needed for the essential living expenses of the family members. In other words, until it meets its basic living expenses a family cannot contribute to college costs at all; and $5400 is a subsistence amount assumed by the law to be reasonable for a family of three. Consistently, when there are additional children in the household, the $5400 figure increases under the statute. Table 1 sets out the amounts for families with up to five children.

TABLE 1

BEOG

DISREGARDED INCOME FOR BASIC LIVING EXPENSES

Number of Children (in Two-Parent Family)	Disregarded Income Amounts
1	$ 5,400
2	$ 6,850
3	$ 8,050
4	$ 9,150
5	$10,100

For 1979-80. These numbers are adjusted over time. They are based on national low income family definitions which are somewhat greater than the official government poverty level. The disregarded income amounts are increased as the CPI increases.

Second, why does the student's grant phase out at the rate of 10.5 cents for each dollar of family income above the statutory disregard? This rate is the vector of a variety of competing considerations. Some would ask the family to put <u>all</u> of its income above the subsistence level towards its child's college education. This would call for a far more rapid grant phase-out rate--$1 for each $1 of income above subsistence. Others disagree and think it fair for low income families to have somewhat better net standards of living as their income rises. They would not ask families to contribute all of their discretionary income toward college costs.

In addition to fairness considerations, there are incentive concerns. If the family had to put all its discretionary income toward college costs in order for the child to have a chance to afford to attend, the family might refuse and the child would not attend (or the child might feel too guilty to ask that much from his parents). But the congressional purpose behind BEOG is to stimulate children of low income families to pursue further schooling by reducing the financial barrier they might otherwise face. There are also the usual work disincentive concerns, suggested earlier, that arise with programs having rapid benefit phase-out rates--also called "high implicit tax rates." Put simply, what is the point of the parent earning a dollar more if it reduces the grant by an offsetting amount? Moreover, it must be remembered that BEOG is laid on top of other means-tested plans for which many BEOG families are eligible, thereby creating the risk of implicit marginal tax rates in excess of 100 percent.

A further consideration in deciding the grant phase-out rate is the distance up the income scale it is thought appropriate to provide financial assistance for school costs. If, for example, Congress decides that families with $18,000 of income ought to get some help, then assuming an income disregard of only a subsistence amount, this necessarily implies a grant phase-out rate of very much less than 100 percent. In fact, the practical reason that the BEOG phase-out rate today is 10.5 percent instead of 20 to 30 percent, as it was originally set, is that Congress in 1978 decided to extend some benefits of the plan to so-called middle income families; and to do so it simply reduced the implicit tax rate.[11] This simultaneously, of course, improved the benefits provided to students in somewhat poorer families. As those who study means-tested programs know, the maximum grant amount, the phase-out rate, the amount of the income disregard and the "break even" level (the income level where benefits cease) are all interrelated so that any three of these parameters pretty much determine the fourth.

A final consideration relevant to setting the BEOG phase-out rate is one's view of the family's proper contribution when more than one of its children is in college. Plainly, if for the first child a 100 percent phase-out rate is applied, this leaves no room to imply a greater family contribution for additional children. By contrast, a modest phase-out rate such as BEOG employs makes it feasible to ask more from the family when an additional child attends college.

Third, why does BEOG provide a maximum grant of no more than $1800? The short answer, of course, is that this limits federal cost. But, as we have seen, an alternate approach to cost reduction is to increase the grant phase-out rate. The $1800 maximum, therefore, can be seen as representing a choice; for the same federal costs Congress provides at least some funds for middle income students rather than providing larger grants to poorer students.

In any event, since the fair family contribution plus the grant cannot under the statute exceed $1800, the rest of the student's costs must be raised elsewhere. If the program intended the family to pay for these extra costs, this could alter dramatically our previous evaluation of BEOG's fair family contribution feature.

However, Congress did not contemplate that the parents would pay the excess; rather it assumed that the money would come from any of a variety of other sources. These include the student's own work, perhaps through the federally subsidized work-study program; student borrowing, perhaps through the federal student loan programs; and scholarships and/or loans from the student's own chosen college. These are traditional and widely available sources of college student income that BEOG drafters presumably did not want to displace. Put differently, it was thought fair for poorer college students to have to win school scholarships, take out loans and/or work in order to complete the payment for higher education. BEOG implies a fair student contribution as well as a fair family contribution. Note also, unless a poor student receives an additional scholarship, the $1800 limit plainly gives that student an incentive to attend an inexpensive college.

Fourth, a student's grant is limited not merely by the difference between the family's fair contribution and $1800; in addition, the grant may be no greater than 50 percent of the student's educational costs. What is the purpose of this limit? Once more, limiting federal costs is not the only objective; rather, the half-cost rule symbolizes a federal role of junior partner with other sources. In practice, it serves primarily to cut the grants of the poorer students attending lower cost schools; this is because of the way the $1800 maximum and the half-cost features (and a third limit) are linked.

Specifically, the BEOG grant is equal to the least amount among these three: (a) $1800 minus the family's fair contribution, or (b) one half of the student's educational costs, or (c) the difference between school costs and the family's fair contribution. As a result, whenever costs exceed $3600 all students must be impacted by the $1800 limit before they run into the one half of educational costs limit. Similarly, the third limit does not operate when costs exceed $3600. Since "costs" for BEOG purposes include both tuition, books and living expenses, it is thus obvious to anyone who has paid any attention to the cost of going to college that only the $1800 maximum will be relevant in most cases; after all, in elite private schools tuition alone exceeds $3600.

Nonetheless in some cases, when students attend public colleges with low or no tuition, they will feel the bite of the other limits. Notice, now, how the crunch is almost entirely reserved for the child from the very low income family. A student otherwise eligible for a $1200 grant is impacted by the half cost rule only by attending a school costing $2400 or less; a student otherwise eligible for a $600 grant is impacted by the third limit only by attending a school costing $1800 or less (the half-cost rule would only apply when costs were $1200 or less and hence is inapplicable). Yet the bite of the half-cost rule applies to a student otherwise eligible for the maximum $1800 grant as soon as his costs fall below $3600.[12]

Putting aside now any objections to the specific BEOG limits, it should be clear that the limits together create the need for what we have called the student's fair contribution--and do so in a way that causes the student to have a financial interest in the cost of the school attended. To sum up, Table 2 illustrates BEOG's operation for a variety of families with one child who is in college.

TABLE 2

PAYING FOR COLLEGE COSTS IN FAMILIES WITH ONE CHILD

FAMILY INCOME		School Costs				
		$1200	$1800	$2400	$3600	$4800
$ 5,400	BEOG	600	900	1200	1800	1800
	Family Contribution	0	0	0	0	0
	Student Contribution	600	900	1200	1800	3000
$10,000	BEOG	600	900	1200	1300	1300
	Family Contribution	500	500	500	500	500
	Student Contribution	100	400	700	1800	3000
$15,000	BEOG	200	800	800	800	800
	Family Contribution	1000	1000	1000	1000	1000
	Student Contribution	0	0	600	1800	3000
$20,000	BEOG	0	300	300	300	300
	Family Contribution	1200	1500	1500	1500	1500
	Student Contribution	0	0	600	1800	3000

More Than One Child in College

Now suppose the family has two students in college. The BEOG drafters concluded that the fair family contribution is to be increased by 40 percent and that half of the total should be allocated to each of the children. In other words, instead of 10.5 percent, the family is now expected to contribute 14.7 percent of discretionary income, or 7.35 percent per child. Put more precisely, the grant for each is $1800 less 7.35 percent of the family's discretionary income (subject to the two other limits already discussed). As suggested earlier, the idea is that while it is fair to ask the family to contribute something towards the second child's college costs, that contribution should be less than for the first child. This principle is carried out for additional children in college. Table 3 illustrates this feature.

TABLE 3

BEOG FAIR FAMILY CONTRIBUTIONS

# of Children in College	Fair Family Contribution/Child (% of discretionary income)	Total Fair Family Contribution (% of discretionary income)
1	10.5	10.5
2	7.35	14.7
3	5.25	15.75
4 (or more)	4.2	16.8

Some Additional Details

A few final BEOG features need to be explained.

(i) If the family has more than $25,000 in qualifying assets, 5 percent of that extra is counted as available for contribution to the child's education. The student's grant thus is reduced by 5 percent of qualifying family assets over $25,000. This is defended in part on the ground that all the income the family could earn from these assets though a simple savings account ought to be put toward college costs. House equity also counts for BEOG purposes. This may, in economic argot, represent the imputed rental value of home ownership; or maybe, more prosaically, it is assumed that housing costs for homeowners are less. In any event, in inflationary times the rule is important: a family with house equity of $61,000 is disqualified from BEOG on that basis alone—even if its discretionary income is 0 and it has no other assets. Of course, not too long ago anyone with over $60,000 in house equity was probably quite well-to-do. But in many parts of the country houses that were bought for $10,000 now cost $80,000—yet their occupants are far from rich.

(ii) Because of presumed work expenses, the amount that the family can subtract for basic living expenses is greater if both parents work.[13]

(iii) A smaller sum for basic living expenses is allowed when there is one instead of two parents in the household.[14]

(iv) Income for BEOG purposes is determined as follows. Take the family's (last year's) adjusted gross income for federal income tax purposes, and subtract its federal income taxes; then add certain non-taxed items such as social security and public assistance payments and subtract certain allowable "unusual" expenses, if any, that the family had.[15]

(v) Although the BEOG formula rests on the idea of a fair family contribution, in fact this family contribution need not actually be made. Congress did not want to bar a student from the program if his parents did not in fact provide their fair share; the result in such cases, of course, is that the student must himself raise the parental portion. Likewise, if the hypothetical family contribution is low in terms of what most parents actually pay, then students generally will have to raise less than expected. In the end, for college students, tinkering with the fair parental contribution may not matter much since the student can generally sacrifice to close the gap. But at the elementary and secondary schools things would be quite different.

BABY-BEOG: HOW IT SHOULD WORK

We have described the BEOG rules at length because appreciation of their details suggests how these rules ought to be altered if the basic BEOG idea is to be applied to lower education.

At the elementary and secondary level it would be incongruous for the grant formula to be structured so that there is a gap between the fair parental contribution and total school costs. Non-parental sources available to college students are typically unavailable to younger pupils; the concept of a "fair student contribution" would make little sense even in high school. Likewise substantial family borrowing to finance primary or secondary students is hard to imagine. It is simply not a part of our culture; ask any bank. And private schools simply cannot provide scholarships to all who would need financial assistance. In our view, they should not even be asked to shoulder this burden; the private school scholarship generally comes indirectly from other families in the school community, while the point of a government scholarship plan at the primary and secondary school level should be fully to distribute the cost of empowering the needy family. Unlike BEOG grants, baby-BEOG should largely supplant existing private school scholarship sources.

If the BEOG formula were simply carried over to elementary and secondary schools, parents would be expected to make both the family and student contributions, and the poorest families would have to contribute a grossly disproportionate share of their income towards the cost of schooling. This not only offends our sense of equity but would assure that the neediest children either would be concentrated in the lowest cost schools or, far more likely, would not even consider leaving or threatening to leave public school. Our policy objectives for baby-BEOG, therefore, would be frustrated.

Our objection to the implied demand for further parental contributions could be met if the basic BEOG restrictions--the $1800 maximum and the 50 percent of costs rule--were simply eliminated. But this solution runs into a different and important objection raised at the outset. As we said earlier, the family should have an incentive to shop for price; and limits like the 50 percent rule and the $1800 ceiling do remove the incentive to spend indefinitely. Yet, for lower education there is a better way to assure that the fair family contribution plus the BEOG equal full school costs while at the same time insuring that the family contribution fairly increases as both income and school costs go up.[16]

To explain how this better formula would work, let us identify first a "standard" (or average) cost school; say it costs $1800 to attend. A family with one child who sends the child to such a school would be required to make an "appropriate" contribution and the grant would be 100 percent of the difference. At this point let us assume that the contribution would be set at the 10.5 percent rate that the BEOG formula now contemplates as the family's fair contribution out of discretionary income.

Suppose now the family chooses a school costing more or less than $1800. In that case an index number would be applied to its appropriate contribution to the standard cost school in order to determine the family's contribution to the school with different costs. This index number would be the ratio of the chosen school's cost to the cost of a standard school; for a school costing half the $1800 standard the index number would be 1/2. Hence, if family A's contribution, given its need, would be $400 in a standard cost school, it would become $200 in a $900 school; ($900/$1800=1/2 and 1/2 of $400=200). On the other hand, if it selected a $2700 school, its contribution would be $600; ($2700/$1800=3/2 and 3/2 of $400=$600). For family A the grant program would match every $2 of family contribution with $7 worth of scholarship.

Suppose a wealthier family B's appropriate contribution to a standard cost school to be $800; it would have to contribute $400 in a $900 school and $1200 in a $2700 school. For this less needy family the program would match every $2 of the family's contribution with a $2.50 scholarship. Stated differently, for every $9 of extra school spending, family A pays $2 and family B pays $4--the program makes up the difference. This means, for example, that to shift its child from a $1200 school to an $2100 school would cost family A $200 more and family B $400 more.

If the family had more than one child in school, then let us assume that its contribution for each additional child would be the same proportionate increase now provided for in the BEOG formula. Table 4 illustrates this hypothetical proposal for three school cost levels, for two-parent families with 1 and 2 children (both in school) and with varying incomes. For simplicity, however, we have used 10 percent rather that 10.5 percent as the contribution rate, and we have used $5000 and $7000 as the family size related income disregards instead of the BEOG figures in Table 1.

TABLE 4

HYPOTHETICAL BABY-BEOG INDEXED PLAN
FOR 3 TUITION LEVELS

		1 Child School Costs			2 Children School Costs Per Child		
Family Income		$900	1800	2700	900	1800	2700
$ 7,000	Family Contri- bution per child	100	200	300	0	0	0
	Grant per child	800	1600	2400	900	1800	2700
$10,000	Family Contri- bution per child	250	500	750	105	210	310
	Grant per child	650	1300	1950	795	1590	2380
$15,000	Family Contri- bution per child	500	1000	1500	280	560	840
	Grant per child	400	800	1200	620	1240	1860
$20,000	Family Contri- bution per child	750	1500	2250	455	910	1365
	Grant per child	150	300	450	445	890	1335
$30,000	Family Contri- bution per child	900	1800	2700	805	1610	2415
	Grant per child	0	0	0	95	190	285

A glance at Table 4 illustrates how the proposal serves the various principles we have advocated for a scholarship plan. First, the family contribution increases as its income goes up. Second, the family contribution increases as school costs go up. Third, the family contribution plus the grant equal total school costs. And fourth, as the number of its children in school increases, the family's contribution per child declines.

This hypothetical indexed plan, however, might be thought to be too expensive to the government. It may also be thought to require too little from families in certain cases, regardless of the availability of federal funds. Let us consider then a variety of possible adjustments in its parameters.

At least six types of alterations can be made to the hypothetical indexed grant plan that would shift costs more toward the family and away from government. First, the fair family contribution could be set as a greater proportion of discretionary income. Rather than 10 percent for the standard cost school, the rate could be higher. Put differently, the 10 percent rate could be established for a school costing less than $1800 (our hypothetical plan imposes only a 5 percent contribution rate for a $900 school). We explained earlier that the phase-out rate selected is ultimately an arbitrary compromise of a variety of values. In that vein we will propose for purposes of serious legislative discussion a fair family contribution rate of 12 percent for a $1000 school. On the proportionality principle explained earlier, this implies a 24 percent rate for a $2000 school and so on.

Second, the fair family contribution could be escalated at more than a proportional rate as school costs increase. In other words, the government matching rate could decline as the family spends more. For example, if the contribution rate is 12 percent for a $1000 school, it could be made more than 24 percent as proposed above for a $2000 school—say, 30 percent. Adjustments of this sort involve changing the amount of the price subsidy. Not only do they save public funds for a given cost school, but also they reduce the family's incentive to select a costlier school. Yet we see no particularly good reason to prefer such a decline in the matching rate, for our legislative proposal will continue to apply the proportionality principle.

Third, the amount of income disregarded can be reduced. That could be justified on the ground that the BEOG disregard is too generous a definition of discretionary income, being set above the poverty level. This is a difficult judgment to make. We like instead the idea that by lowering the disregard we can assure that virtually all families contribute some modest sum toward the cost of private education they use. The income offsets we propose for families of various sizes are set out in Table 5. (Compare Table 1).

TABLE 5

FEDERAL SCHOLARSHIP (BABY-BEOG) PLAN

PROPOSED INCOME DISREGARDS

Number of Children (In two-parent family)	Disregard
1	$4000
2	6000
3	7000
4	8000
5	9000

In addition to imposing some contribution on lower income families, this adjustment has the effect of (a) increasing the amount of the family contribution for all participating families and (b) lowering the family income maximum for participation in the plan. All these effects reduce costs.

Fourth, the extra family contribution for additional children attending private schools can be increased. For reasons described earlier, however, we prefer to stay with the BEOG rates.

Fifth, the definition of school costs can be tightened. We agree that ordinary living expenses (e.g., room and board) that sensibly count as costs for higher education, should not be subsidized by federal elementary and secondary scholarships. In short, boarding school opportunities should not be the object of this program. On the other hand, restricting the program to tuition alone seems too narrow. We would prefer to include as well school books, other school fees, reasonable transportation costs and essential school supplies.

Sixth, a ceiling could be placed on the amount of school costs toward which the government would contribute. If such a ceiling is established, it should take into account both the present cost of public schooling and the cost to start a new private school. Suppose we set the ceiling at $1000. This is more than the tuition cost of many private—especially religious—schools today. This observation, however, neglects the fact that without endowment sources, it is very difficult to start a new school from scratch with tuition levels of $1000. Especially since a central purpose of the plan is to empower poor and working class families credibly to threaten departure from public schools, a $1000 ceiling would be too low. Given typical public school costs across the nation today, we think it should be appropriate at the outset for our indexed plan to have a cost matching ceiling of $2000. We recognize that low income students wanting to attend more costly schools would have to receive additional scholarships from those schools or find the money elsewhere. We have some confidence, however, that the costlier schools would in most cases provide some supplemental financial assistance.

We have not considered here cost-reducing strategies that would involve changing the BEOG definition of income, the BEOG treatment of work expenses and so on, because they are largely satisfactory to us for these purposes. We do, however, favor a change in the assets contribution rule -- which, it will be noticed, we have ignored so far for baby-BEOG purposes. Specifically, we think the home equity rule is wrong. Either home equity should be ignored, as it is in many needs-based programs; or else a separate additional home equity exemption (say, $50,000) should be allowed. One thing to remember here is that while BEOG assumes that parents with home equity might borrow against it, this seems far more likely for college than for lower education, if for no other reason than the significant difference in the number of years of education involved.

Putting together the various provisions just discussed, we can now set out in tabular form how a federal scholarship plan to our liking would work for private elementary and secondary school. Table 6 assumes in each case that all the family's children are in private school.

TABLE 6
PROPOSED FEDERAL SCHOLARSHIP (BABY-BEOG) PLAN

Family Income		1 Child (School Costs)				2 Children (School Costs per child)				3 Children (School Costs per child)			
		500	1000	2000	2500	500	1000	2000	2500	500	1000	2000	2500
$ 5,000	Family Contribution Per Child	60	120	240	740	0	0	0	500	0	0	0	500
	Grant Contribution Per Child	440	880	1760	1760	500	1000	2000	2000	500	1000	2000	2000
7,500	Family Contribution Per Child	210	420	840	1340	63	126	252	752	15	30	60	560
	Grant Contribution Per Child	290	580	1160	1160	437	874	1748	1748	485	970	1840	1840
10,000	Family Contribution Per Child	360	720	1440	1940	168	336	672	1172	90	180	360	860
	Grant Contribution Per Child	140	280	560	560	332	664	1328	1328	410	820	1640	1640
15,000	Family Contribution Per Child	500	1000	2000	2500	378	756	1512	2012	240	480	960	1460
	Grant Contribution Per Child	0	0	0	0	122	244	488	488	260	520	1040	1040
20,000	Family Contribution Per Child	500	1000	2000	2500	500	1000	2000	2500	390	780	1560	2060
	Grant Contribution Per Child	0	0	0	0	0	0	0	0	110	220	440	440

CONSTITUTIONALITY OF OUR BABY-BEOG PROPOSAL

Our proposal ought to pass First Amendment scrutiny by the Supreme Court in spite of the inclusion of religious schools. It is safer by far than the typical educational tax credit proposal for four reasons. First, its purpose is plainly nonreligious; it is based on a simple traditional philosophy favoring family choice of schools, whether public or private. Second, unlike tax credits, which benefit private schools only, our version of baby-BEOG is designed to improve public education. The greater opportunity for lower families to "exit" would stimulate public schools to stop taking them for granted and to improve the quality of service. Third, while the other schemes favor existing schools (mostly religious) by forgiving tuition already paid, our baby-BEOG proposal would put the subsidy directly in the hands of the consumer. Fourth, the scholarship will be big enough to stimulate the growth of new schools--including many nonreligious schools. These factors together demonstrate that aid to religion will only be a side effect. This will be reassuring to a Court which in the past has been presented with schemes that have had as their primary purpose and intended effect the bailing out of existing religious schools.

TRANSITION: A MORE MODEST PROPOSAL

In 1980, Senator Moynihan's baby-BEOG plan failed to win Senate approval. With Ronald Reagan as the new President and a shift in Senate personnel, congressional friends of private education will surely try once more to adopt some plan that will help families who opt out of the public schools. We fear that a modest non-refundable tax credit plan will be adopted. Apart from being poor public policy, this scheme is likely to be held unconstitutional by the U.S. Supreme Court. Congress can do better. Our version of baby-BEOG might become a compromise vehicle drawing together conservatives and liberals. For the short run, however, there is yet another simpler and more modest proposal which could appeal to both groups and which would represent a significant first step toward empowering ordinary families.

As a transitional measure, we propose that Title I of the Elementary and Secondary Education Act be converted to a "voucher" system. Now costing more than $3 billion annually, Title I has succeeded reasonably well as a non-stigmatizing public employment scheme. As a compensatory education device, however, it has little to show for itself. More promising is an arrangement whereby individual needy families control their child's share of the federal budget in the form of a mini-voucher. This could be easily managed.[17]

Turning Title I funds into mini-vouchers would help poor, low achieving children in private schools finally get their fair share of the pie. Indeed, for many poor families the voucher would be enough to pay for all or most of their basic private school tuition—something which should be permitted under the program. Other poor families will be able to switch from public to private schools of choice by having a Title I voucher. Finally, the bulk of poor families, whose children would remain in public schools, would gain a measure of influence over their children's education. They could, of course, tender their voucher to the local public school for the enrichment program the school offers. Alternatively, however, they could choose from an array of part time, after school, weekend or summer programs that will become available and are specially designed for low achieving students.

Title I vouchers and our baby-BEOG plan share common themes—focusing on lower income families in a way that permits them either to choose private schools for their children or to put pressure on public schools to reform. Seen in this light, a revamped Title I can be an important first step toward our proposal for federal scholarships for private elementary and secondary school users.

NOTES

1. 20 U.S.C. Sec. 1070a (1976), as amended by 20 U.S.C. Sec. 1070(a) (Supp. II 1978).

2. Moynihan's proposal was first contained in S. 1101, 96th Cong., 1st Sess. (May 9, 1979). Moynihan then testified on behalf of the proposal on October 23, 1979 before the Subcommittee on Education, Arts, and Humanities of the Senate Committee on Labor and Human Resources.

3. Although many proposals to provide a federal income tax credit for certain educational expenses have been introduced, the leading contender of late has been styled the Packwood-Moynihan bill (after its sponsors). In the summer of 1978 it failed in the Senate by eight votes. Senators Moynihan and Packwood reintroduced this legislation in the 97th Congress as S. 500.

4. See Milton Friedman, Capitalism and Freedom (Chicago: University of Chicago Press, 1962), ch. 6, p. 85. We do favor other voucher plans, however. See generally, John E. Coons and Stephen D. Sugarman, Education by Choice: The Case for Family Control (Berkeley: University of California Press, 1978).

5. We have proposed voucher plans in California that either (1) prohibit schools from charging more than the voucher and generally require schools to serve all applicants with excess demand resolved by lot or (2) guarantee low income children 25 percent of the spaces in voucher schools and require excess tuition charges to be assessed on the basis of ability to pay.

6. On June 23, 1980, Moynihan brought his proposal to the floor of the Senate by way of an amendment to the Higher Education Act that then was before the body. Moynihan engaged in a lengthy debate with Senator Hollings, and on June 24, 1980 the amendment

was defeated 71-24. Senator Metzenbaum, a supporter of the Moynihan proposal, had earlier tried unsuccessfully to add it by amendment in committee.

7. See generally, Coons and Sugarman, Education by Choice (1978).

8. By contrast, Senator Moynihan, in the floor debate on his proposal, emphasized the desirability of helping out low income families currently using private schools. See 126 Congressional Record S7838-55 and 7964-74, (daily ed., June 23-24, 1980).

9. These numbers are taken from the 1979-80 grant period. See generally, BEOG Program Determination of Eligibility Index 1979-1980 (HEW Office of Education, Bureau of Student Financial Assistnace). For 1980-81, because Congress did not fully fund the program, grants did not exceed $1750. For 1981-82 the grant maximum is scheduled to go to $1900, subject to full Congressional appropriation. Further increases in subsequent years, up to $2600 in academic year 1985-86, are also now in the law. Sec. 402(b) (1) of the Education Amendments of 1980, Pub.L. 96-374, 94 Stat. 1402.

10. In certain circumstances, college students can show themselves financially independent from their parents so as to qualify for "independent student" status and thereby have their grant determined apart from parental income and assets. We will ignore this provision since it is irrelevant for lower education purposes.

11. See the discussion of the Middle Income Student Assistance Act at 1978 U.S. Cong. and Ad. News 5314 (House Rep. 95-951).

12. Objections to this impact caused Congress in 1980 to adjust the half-cost limit starting in 1982-83. The limit is scheduled to be 60 percent of costs then and to rise to 70 percent of costs by 1985-86. Sec. 402 (c)(1) of the Education Amendments of 1980, note 9 supra.

13. Fifty percent of the earnings of the parent with the least earnings up to a maximum of $1500.

14. A single parent with two children is treated like a two parent family with one child and so on.

15. Unusual expenses include some catastrophic losses and extra large medical expenses as well as unreimbursed elementary and secondary school costs.

16. Our proposal here is based upon the "family power equilizing" idea we first introduced more than a decade ago. See generally, John E. Coons, William Clune III, and Stephen D. Sugarman, Private Wealth and Public Education (Cambridge, Mass: Harvard University Press, 1970), pp. 256-268. For a more detailed discussion see Coons and Sugarman, "Family Choice in Education: A Model State System for Vouchers," 59 Calif. L. Rev. 321 (1971).

17. See Stephen D. Sugarman, "Education Reform at the Margin: Two Ideas," Phi Delta Kappan (Nov. 1977) at p. 154.

12. Information Inequities:
A Fatal Flaw in Parochiaid Plans

Michael A. Olivas

"In a system with no options, ignorance
might be bliss. In a system based on
choice, ignorance is ruin."
Education by Choice
J. Coons and S. Sugarman, 1978

Although educational vouchers and other American governmental means of financing private elementary and secondary schools
can trace their intellectual roots to Adam Smith and Tom Paine,[1]
actual voucher experiments and serious legislative proposals have a
more recent history. In 1972, a modified voucher plan was
implemented in San Jose, California, but was limited to the public
elementary schools in the Alum Rock Union Elementary School
District.[2] Postsecondary vouchers have existed since the GI Bill,
and federal legislation establishing Basic Educational Opportunity
Grants (BEOG's) in 1972 created a massive entitlement program that
has incorporated many features common to voucher plans.[3]

In the late 1970's however, two legislative plans proposed
quantum leaps in governmental assistance to the private elementary
and secondary education sector: a state voucher plan in California
and federal legislation to extend the BEOG program to parents
whose children attended private elementary and secondary schools.
Although neither plan was enacted into law, and although the
constitutionality of the plans is untested, it is clear that political
agendas will include increasing attention to these parochiaid plans,
at all levels and in many administrative guises. This essay explores
these two strands--federal and state--of parochiaid plans, and
evaluates the fundamental premise upon which all "free market"
proposals are based, namely, that adequate information systems can
generate true choice to allow poor and rich, majority and minority,
and educated and uneducated parents to make informed, reasoned
judgments on the quality of schools to which they would send their
children. A convincing web of evidence shows this premise to be
flawed. Recent litigation on public aid to private schools suggests

---

*The research for this essay was supported in part by the Fund
for the Improvement of Post-Secondary Education (FIPSE) and by
the Tinker Foundation. The views expressed are those of the author
and not necessarily those of FIPSE or the Tinker Foundation.

that little judicial attention has been paid to information provisions; instead, courts have concentrated upon measuring plans against constitutional standards. Analyzing the allowance and disallowance patterns of courts enhances an understanding of the administrative complexity of parochiaid plans and points to the need for comprehensive public information programs, whatever the administrative configuration.

JUDICIAL VIEWS: PAROCHIAID AS A CONSTITUTIONAL END RUN

Depending upon one's view, legal commentators characterize the Supreme Court's record in parachiaid cases as a "drunkard's reel"[4] or as "a landmark in the history of religious liberty and church-state separation in our country."[5] The truth, whatever it may be, is probably between these two poles. Indeed, the Court has zigzagged and developed new tests over time, but Court composition, societal change, intractability of evolving positions, and increasing sophistication of legislators and litigants have undoubtedly contributed to confusion among court watchers and practitioners in a number of educational legal areas.

That the Court has shifted course in other areas does not, of course, serve as solace to those who seek guidance in fashioning legislation or in proposing information systems to support parochiaid plans. Since Everson v. Board of Education,[6] a 1947 decision upholding a New Jersey transportation plan, state legislators have become more adept at the cat and mouse game: drafting legislation increasing aid to private schools, appropriating funds until litigation is initiated, arguing the case all the way to the Supreme Court, and beginning the process over.[7] For example, Ohio's tuition grant program was held unconstitutional in Essex v. Wolman;[8] its revised tax law for parochial school credits was invalidated under Grit v. Wolman the same year;[9] the state's plan to supply standardized tests and scoring services was upheld in Wolman v. Walter.[10]

In the record of the Ohio legislation, as in other states, information inequities were not considered, for the usual mode of assistance proposed has been categorical program aid or aid directly to schools. Therefore, whether the Court allowed a textbook law (Board of Education v. Allen)[11] or disallowed a textbook law (Marburger v. Public Funds[12], Meek v. Pittenger[13]), disallowed salary payments to teachers (Lemon v. Kurtzman, Sanders v. Johnson),[14] or disallowed a facilities maintenance program (PEARL v. Nyquist),[15] these programs were for specific services or supplies. Information inequities are less likely to exist in categorical programs enacted by legislatures, for benefits accrue either to the students in the form of services and supplies or to the professional personnel who administer tests. Few delivery problems, discretionary allocations, or queuing difficulties occur when all the children are tested, all receive books, or all attend schools kept in better repair.

Although the instances in which tuition assistance, tax benefits, and voucher plans were scrutinized have been virtually uniformly declared invalid, the issue of inherent inequity in the administration of the programs has not been examined by the courts. Thus, in a tuition law (Essex v. Wolman),[16] tax credit program (Grit v. Wolman),[17] indirect grant program (PEARL v. Nyquist, Sloan v. Lemon),[18] or tax exemption program (Beggans v. Public Funds),[19] the issue at stake has been whether the schemes violated the Establishment Clause.[20] The test, enunciated most recently in PEARL v. Regan, is:

> Under the precedents of this Court a legislative enactment does not contravene the Establishment Clause if it has a secular legislative purpose, [if] its principal or primary effect neither advances nor inhibits religion, and if it does not foster an excessive entanglement with religion.[21]

This test, ostensibly simple, is less so in practice, as the permutations of the legislative proposals indicate. While a detailed analysis of these cases is unnecessary here, it is important to note that the California Voucher Initiative and the BEOG proposals have a scope far surpassing the incremental programs or tax plans previously allowed or disallowed by the Supreme Court.[22] The increased scope of both plans has implications for information inequity, previously unconsidered by courts.

In sum, although the legislative and litigative history of parachiaid plans constitutes an imperfect source for predicting the constitutionality of radical proposals such as the California Voucher Initiative or BEOG bill,[23] courts have had occasion to scrutinize information plans in non-categorical programs, but have not done so. Yet this unexamined component of parochiaid plans may be the most crucial equity element in the radical new proposals. The following sections develop the view that the two parochiaid plans, though quite different in their scope and focus, have an important premise in common: that information systems are adequate to ensure equitable free choice in the parochiaid programs. Precedents in a previous voucher plan, existing BEOG trends, and social service delivery literature suggest strongly that the premise upon which the plans are based is fatally flawed.

MAJOR PROVISIONS OF PAROCHIAID LEGISLATIVE PROPOSALS

This portion of the essay summarizes the major components of the educational voucher proposals of Professors Coons and Sugarman and of the BEOG proposal of Senator Patrick Moynihan.

The California Initiative

The 1980 attempt to place a voucher initiative upon the California ballot has several important contexts, including national and state factors. In many states, spending and tax limitations measures have become commonplace. In 1978, twelve of the sixteen states that held elections to consider eighteen such measures passed laws, amended state constitutions, or enacted other means to limit public spending or to alter school finance.[24] This nationwide phenomenon had a federal counterpart in the tax limitation measure proposed in the U.S. Congress, the "Kemp-Roth" bill, although this proposal has not yet been enacted into law.[25]

California's situation is important for understanding parachiaid proposals. In this state, voters may circulate petitions to amend the state constitution, and this popular referendum procedure has become the vehicle for radical tax and educational finance reform.[26] This method of cutting tax liabilities has obvious applicability for school finance reform, particularly in the state where major school finance litigation had forced educators and legislators to confront inter-district inequities in their method of paying for public elementary and secondary education.[27] In addition, a limited voucher program has been in operation in a California school district since 1972,[28] so the voters had a categorical precedent upon which to base their approval or disapproval.[29] Although Coons and Sugarman failed to gather sufficient signatures to place their "Initiative for Family Choice in Education" on the California ballot, they and others in other states are continuing their efforts at state and school finance reform through voucher proposals.

Although the proposals differ in their details and approach,[30] the important elements of the California Initiative include: (1) modifying the California Constitution to eliminate property taxes as the major vehicle for funding elementary and secondary education, (2) placing expenditure ceilings upon state educational expenditures, including administration of the Department of Education, (3) establishing three classes of schools (public, independent, family choice) and certificates redeemable at independent or family choice schools, and (4) requiring information services (independent of school systems) for parents. In sum, the proposal would create a hybrid "independent" school category, and allow parents a certain sum of money to enable their children to attend this incorporated, public, non-profit school or a private school, incorporated as a public benefit or mutual benefit corporation. Children who did not enroll in these two categories of schools would enroll in the public school sector, approximating the present public school system. This plan would almost certainly introduce a dynamism into the system, and would probably increase options for parents, to the extent that public funds would be available to spend upon more goods in the marketplace. In this regard, the proposal shares a major purpose with the BEOG proposal--the deliberate stimulation of competition between public and private schools through public entitlements that can be redeemed in private schools.

The BEOG Proposal

Senator Moynihan's proposal sought this end through a different means, an amendment to the Higher Education Act of 1972, which was reauthorized in the 96th Congress for five years.[31] Moynihan's proposal, though broader in scope than the California Initiative, is deceptively simple. His program would extend the BEOG eligibility to parents with children in a private elementary and secondary school, provided the school is incorporated as an IRS 501(c)(3) non-profit organization. The plan, then, simply extends BEOG benefits to a larger pool of users, whose incomes would be analyzed for the family's ability to contribute. This "needs analysis" would then be computed by formulas to match the cost of attendance with the grant allowance. In this fashion, eligible parents would receive non-reimbursable grants to enable their children to attend private elementary and secondary schools. Each child would be eligible for twelve academic years worth of BEOG eligibility; the existing BEOG program allows college students four academic years (five in special circumstances).[32]

The legislative simplicity of the BEOG proposal belies the complexity of the eligibility and application process.[33] Parents whose children are enrolled in eligible private schools would complete a standard financial aid form, itemizing expenditures, deductions, and a host of financial data. This form would be sent to central form processing facilities, which would compute the eligibility index and forward the report to the schools, whose financial aid offices would calculate the amount of the grant and assemble a "financial aid package," which would include institutional resources, scholarship awards, and other financial assistance. Extensive programs exist to distribute applications, process the forms, and calculate eligibility for parents of postsecondary students (or for students who are eligible and declare themselves "independent" of their parents). The negotiation of these systems has particular relevance in judging the merits of extending the BEOG program to elementary and secondary students, for the major appeal of the plan is its proposed linkage to already existing administrative mechanisms.

Therein lies a major rub, for there is available an increasing body of literature that suggests that information systems are inadequate to administer either an expanded BEOG program or the California voucher plan. The evidence suggests that either plan would severely stratify existing systems by primarily assisting those with enhanced access to information, technical assistance, and professional influence. The information-rich would inevitably and disproportionately include the wealthy, nonminority people, and highly educated parents. In order to examine these information inequities in "free market" systems, four measures of information systems are available: 1) inequities in access to information, 2) inequities in the nature of descriptors, 3) problems of other "free market" information models, and 4) potential conflict considerations.

INFORMATION INEQUITIES AND MARKETPLACE CONSIDERATIONS

Before examining the four indices by which information systems can be measured, it is useful to consider briefly the reasons why information is such a crucial issue in parochiaid proposals. Henry Levin, a proponent of postsecondary vouchers, has proposed three major dimensions for assessing such plans: finance, regulation, and information.[34] Of the information dimension in voucher systems, Levin has noted, "In order for such a system to work effectively, there must exist useful and accessible information on these choices for both the individual participants and for the institutions and enterprises that wish to offer postsecondary education and training programs."[35] Stephen Klees has noted that information systems play a significant role in voucher plans: "Imperfect information in a market system may cause serious inefficiencies and inequities. These problems will be of greater-than-normal concern in a market system for educational services."[36] Gary Bridge has characterized information imperfections as the "Achilles' Heel of Entitlement Plans." Although his focus is upon postsecondary plans, his concern would be heightened by K-12 entitlement programs: "Information imperfections are a problem which will not be solved easily, and they may prove the fatal weakness of theoretically sound proposals to increase free market competition in education in order to achieve greater economic efficiency and social equity."[37] The essential role of information in parochiaid plans is also acknowledged by voucher proponents. Coons and Sugarman, whose views on this dimension of vouchers form the epigraph of this article, have noted, "unless artfully designed, information systems can themselves vitiate the variety that choice is intended to promote."[38]

Even without reference to considerations of equity, economics literature has measured duplication, inefficiency, and waste due to imperfect information and inability of marketplaces to correct these imperfections.[39] While time and increased information can improve choice in a free market, in a system deliberately designed to stimulate dynamism and to increase users, consumers have a greater, not lesser, chance of receiving incorrect information.[40] In a social system as important and complex as schools, the margin for error is very small and unlikely to correct itself in a dynamic marketplace. As an equity concern, therefore, the method of dissemination is a crucial consideration, for unless all groups have equal access to information, including ability to decipher the data, there is no real choice operating in the marketplace. This is especially problematic when the choice involves schools, in which, unlike grocery stores, products cannot be easily compared and chosen.

Research evidence in several social service programs gives an insight into the inadequacies of information systems for the poor and disadvantaged. When these findings are combined with data on the condition of education for minorities and disadvantaged populations, it is clear that educational information inadequacies will disproportionately affect those already undereducated.[41] Further, there is no reason to believe that dynamism introduced deliberately into the school system for all parents would generate a more equitable information distribution than would programs administered specially for disadvantaged populations.

Inequitable Access to Information

It is axiomatic that wealthy persons have more resources to purchase information and hence, more access to additional resources than do poor persons. It has also long been acknowledged that minority populations, particularly bilingual populations, utilize different sources of information than do majority populations.[42] Therefore, information systems in voucher plans that do not incorporate equitable and comprehensive dissemination programs will be unequal in their effect. Information systems, even those that have outreach and advertising components, may miss the mark. This has been the case in food stamp programs, with simple eligibility criteria requiring no choice among services on the part of clients. Studies of underparticipation by extremely poor families in these programs have attributed the low rates to poorly designed information dissemination.[43] Similar findings have been reported for social service entitlement programs, suggesting the poorest potential clients have little access to basic information concerning their eligibility for programs, to assistance in securing application forms, or in documenting their financial need. These programs have included welfare, housing subsidies, elderly benefits, and a wide range of social services that are legislatively designed for poor populations but administratively implemented so that extremely impoverished clients are never made aware of their entitlements.[44] Yet the poor do develop sources of information, particularly in minority communities, where the ethnic press, bilingual advertising, minority radio programming, church-related channels, and folk-grapevines are employed to disseminate information.[45] The highly oral (and frequently bilingual) nature of these networks provides clues as to how difficult, if not impossible, it will be for voucher plans or BEOG proposals to incorporate comprehensive information dissemination into their complex programs. One study of a low income program for nursing mothers discovered that 95 percent of the women had heard of the program by word of mouth, although an extensive print media campaign had been undertaken.[46] A study of food stamp recipients found that the most frequent source of program information was not formal, institutional dissemination, but informal, oral communication with friends and relatives.[47] A survey of low income participants in social service programs revealed that persons employed in private households had a higher awareness of such programs than did other employed individuals, suggesting that frequent contact with more "information-rich" employers increased general awareness of the employees' eligibility for entitlements.[48] The recurrent theme throughout this literature is that the dissemination of program information to disadvantaged populations is a crucial component for delivering service to these populations. A corollary theme is that poor persons use informal, oral, familial networks and are less likely to have access to information resources than are more advantaged populations.

That this would be true for relatively simple entitlement programs widely known for their subsistence benefits does not bode well for complex educational vouchers or BEOG plans. While social service programs tend to stabilize their procedures and improve their information services over time,[49] as the target populations spread the word among themselves, voucher plans deliberately create a dynamic mix of choices so that parents may have the widest range possible from which to choose. Therefore, instead of increasing the efficiency of low income participation in the program, a complex voucher system would more likely decrease the participation by low income families, as oral information and informal networks would be inadequate to convey complicated data on school characteristics or parental prerogatives to organize and establish new schools.

Formal systems of communication would likely exacerbate the already existing information gap. Robert Yin, in a study of information delivery systems in education, concluded: "The equality of access, however, generally benefits information-rich (or advantaged) populations to a greater degree than information-poor (or disadvantaged) populations; although both populations will gain in absolute terms, there is a differential gain that appears to increase the inequity between these populations."[50] If this gap is inevitable, or if it cannot be effectively lessened by formal communications provisions, then serious consideration must be given to supporting informal networks. If such formal support is impossible to administer, then complex voucher or other parochiaid plans will be inequitable in design and in effect.

Inequitable Nature of Education Descriptors

The very nature of the information needs and available networks for disseminating information requires an extraordinarily efficient and effective message be communicated to parents. Theoretically, widespread dissemination programs could be designed and undertaken with special attention to information needs of minority and disadvantaged communities, although evidence strongly suggests this task is too difficult and expensive to succeed. However, an even more serious problem may be the message to be communicated. What information is needed? The voucher proposal would require, at minimum, information on costs (over and above the voucher amount), transportation, racial composition, teacher quality, curriculum, school history (e.g., college-bound graduate rates), entrance requirements, adequacy of facilities, location, school environment (e.g., open classrooms or traditional arrangements), and many more qualitative and quantitative criteria. Of course, these judgements are currently made by parents who enroll their children in private schools or, where there is flexibility, in one of several public schools. Indeed, one of the major appeals by parochiaid proponents is that this kind of shopping is currently necessary, and that not enough parents have enough "choice" in the school selection.

However, the elements of "choice," the information required to create true choices, and the means to disseminate these bits of information cannot be and are unlikely to be met by existing technology and information systems, and cannot be dismissed as a minor consideration. When one examines the complexity of parochiaid plans and their information requirements, the focus must be upon reaching the disadvantaged populations with information that is rich enough to enable them to make informed choices. This focus requires an analysis of the descriptors necessary for making choices, and an understanding of the evaluation skills of disadvantaged populations.

Negotiating complex forms (required by BEOG plans) and organizing or choosing a school require high levels of reading, mathematical, and evaluation skills. Anyone who has completed an income tax return realizes the degree of reading and mathematical skills necessary for completing the forms, even if a standard deduction is used. Completing the necessary financial aid forms is even more complicated than completing tax forms, and requires more calculations, including complex data requirements that compute the expected parental contribution. Further, there are multiple forms for financial aid for federal, state, local, and institutional aid, and the federal form is actually one of three possible forms: the Financial Aid Form (FAF) of the College Scholarship Service, the Family Financial Statement (FFS) of the American College Testing Program, or the federal BEOG form.[51]

Not only is descriptor information by its nature difficult for anyone to evaluate, but disadvantaged populations would be required to make qualitative and quantitative judgments on a range of established and recently-started schools (in a voucher system) or to participate in a complex program calibrated upon expected family contributions (in a BEOG plan). In neither case would the likely outcome be true choice for most poor families, for obvious socio-economic reasons. Marc Bendick and Mario Cantu, for instance, have conservatively estimated that over 75 percent of the U.S. poverty population have less than eighth grade reading skills. They also analyzed application forms and program information for over eighty social welfare programs, and found that only 11 percent of these materials could be read and understood by the clients with eighth-grade reading skills.[52] If so few disadvantaged persons can read and understand materials for an entitlement program designed exclusively for poverty populations, it is highly likely that more complex forms requiring them to shop among schools and to interact with intermediaries (the agencies calculating parental "need") would prove an insurmountable administrative barrier. Moreover, unlike colleges and universities that typically provide services for students seeking financial aid, most elementary and secondary schools have not established such offices. The start up costs and inexperience in dealing with the financial aid bureaucracies would combine to make it less likely that such services would be provided to more disadvantaged populations than to those parents who have access to accounting assistance and other technical expertise. In short, the research literature, existing administrative procedures, and likelihood of the wealthy having access to information and technical assistance suggest that disadvantaged populations would be unlikely to participate fully in information systems essential for parochiaid plans.

This is not to suggest that some of the plans do not incorporate provisions for information. For example, the voucher models proposed by Christopher Jencks and James Coleman have included provisions for educational information vouchers.[53] And the Coons-Sugarman California initiative contains provisions for "Information to Parents" that must assure "adequate information through sources independent of any school or school authority." This provision is sketchy, however, and no details are available to voters to identify the "grants" redeemable for information, to outline the network of "independent" counseling, or to explain how a separate administrative structure squares with other provisions in the initiative for reducing expenditures, limiting administrative costs, and entitling new students to public funds. The BEOG proposal apparently envisions utilizing existing government and private networks for extending eligibility to the parents of elementary and secondary students.

It is important to understand how either parochiaid plan would extend information without increasing costs, because existing networks would be affected, and could conceivably collapse under a BEOG plan or have to be restructured in a dynamic voucher plan that encouraged parents to form their own schools at public expense. To examine the strain on existing systems, it is helpful to understand better the present governmental programs for higher education information services.

Problems of "Free Market" Information Models

Recognizing the need for information dissemination systems, legislators have made such provisions a part of many social service or entitlement programs. Many programs also contain "truth in advertising" provisions in recognition of the need to provide supportive services and to disseminate truthful and helpful information. For instance, the screening and selection provisions of Job Corps programs require dissemination through existing agencies and community-based organizations. And student assistance program legislation requires specific consumer items and financial aid officers "who shall be available on a full-time basis" to counsel students.[54] In addition to these provisions within legislation for social services, there are federal programs specifically intended for educational counseling and information, such as Talent Search and Educational Opportunity Centers.[55] Examining the oldest of these programs, Talent Search, in more detail will suggest the limitations inherent in information programs and inadequacies of these models for adaptation to parochiaid plans.

First funded in 1966, Talent Search is designed to seek out and "identify qualified youths of financial or cultural need" and to "publicize existing forms of student financial aid."[56] An extensive network of institutions and community-based organizations has been established, and professional counselors in Talent Search provide students and parents with technical assistance in completing complex financial aid forms and institution applications.[57] In 1978, the 131 Talent Search projects served approximately 186,000 students with a total appropriation of nearly $12.5 million. Eighty percent of the clients served in 1976 were minority, and two thirds of the clients families had annual incomes of less than $6,000.[58] The 1978 resources available per client averaged $67, giving a rough approximation of the cost of such information services.[59]

Although the per-client amounts seem high, it is estimated that less than 10 percent of the eligible population will be served by the Title IV support programs, even if additional appropriations were to be made by Congress.[60] Further, if appropriations are a quantifiable index of legislative support, then Talent Search and other educational information services enjoy little support. Talent Search appropriations were frozen at $6 million from 1973 to 1976, and at $12.5 million in 1978 and 1979.[61] These information programs, however, are intended to assist students in the awarding of over $2.5 billion dollars of need-based financial assistance. Finally, these programs are not entitlement programs, based upon relative wealth of students in a state or region, but are categorical programs for which applicants compete. The proposal process is highly competitive, and may or may not provide systematic coverage to disadvantaged populations in a geographic region or service area. In 1978, for example, 131 of 190 Talent Search proposals were funded,[62] and although program staff undoubtedly attempt to fund proposals so as to provide service on an equitable geographic basis, the staff are constrained by lack of money, reviewer recommendations, and political considerations. The major constraint to establishing a comprehensive information network may be that the funding staff can only react to proposals submitted for consideration. If an area is not served, it may be because no organization or institution initiated a proposal to serve that region. Thus, existing educational information programs have not enjoyed adequate support to meet the need of disadvantaged populations, and the categorical nature of the competitive proposal process is not likely to correct market inequities. This model would seem to paint a pessimistic picture for accommodating additional clients either for a federal BEOG program or for a state voucher plan, even one that incorporated an information voucher component.

Additional evidence of the inability of these programs to correct information inequities may be inferred from recent BEOG data that suggest a decline in low income BEOG applicants and an apparent decline in low income college enrollments.[63] Of course, it is not merely information inequities that contribute to the decline of disadvantaged students, for the problem is complex. However, the passage of the Middle Income Student Assistance Act extended the eligibility of students in federal financial assistance programs to families making $25,000 and above, threatening the resources of existing information systems and institutional financial aid offices.[64]

While evidence of federal resources is pessimistic, local efforts in a voucher system also suggest that information inequities would arise in parochiaid plans. The Alum Rock voucher program was an excellent experiment in information systems, for the San Jose community was predominantly minority and the program was limited to the public schools, a system neither as dynamic nor complex as that proposed by the Coons-Sugarman initiative. Despite extensive bilingual advertising, Mexican American families were less familiar with the program than were blacks, who in turn were less aware than were white families. As one might imagine, parents with lower levels of education were less well informed than were more highly educated participants. These disadvantages increased over the length of the program.[65] The findings from the Alum Rock experiment tend to corroborate the findings in other equity literature: "[S]ocially advantaged individuals have access to more sources of information; and as a result they end up having more information about their alternatives; and a dynamic, changing market system tends to raise the information imperfections which occur most often among socially disadvantaged groups."[66]

The research literature and administrative experiences with financial aid counseling programs and a recent controlled voucher plan should be a warning that radical shifts in the systems of public and private education cannot be accommodated by existing information networks. The present systems are underfinanced and meet only a small part of the need with present target populations. Only the voucher plan proposes an information dissemination component, yet either would strain the networks upon which they are premised. Additional compelling evidence of the inability of a dynamic "choice" system to incorporate a comprehensive information plan is the difficulty a voucher program would have in articulating with categorical programs for disadvantaged students or students with special needs. These and other conflict considerations form the final section of this essay.

Conflict Considerations

Any major change in a way of doing business is bound to disrupt any system. A large scale voucher plan or BEOG proposal, however, would deliberately introduce dynamism into the system, and would overload existing information networks. Moreover, the voucher initiative would likely disrupt many categorical programs enacted over time to target services toward disadvantaged students. A system based upon "choice" may be impossible to coordinate with one based upon established categorical need-based programs. The information requirements of these programs deserve attention, for it is not only unclear how the information needs will be met, but it is unclear how newly-established schools envisioned under the Coons-Sugarman initiative would treat their responsibilities to enroll disadvantaged students.

Although the initiative includes language concerning categorical factors, it is vague and uncertain: "The redeemable amount may also differ by such factors as grade level, curriculum, bilingualism, special needs and handicaps, variations in local cost, need to encourage racial desegregation, and any other factor deemed appropriate by the legislature so long as the right of every child to enroll in any school remains unaffected by his or her family's capacity to purchase education." In these programs, the putative "rights" of children may be denied by the administrative means available. Under the initiative, parents could choose single-race schools, for information on the racial composition would be difficult to obtain until the classes were assembled. For school systems not in compliance with court orders to desegregate, a dynamic "choice" plan would enable parents and administrators to thwart court-drafted desegregation programs. In such a situation, the chances of useful information reaching disadvantaged parents, a disproportionate number of whom would be minorities, would be very small. The same administrative problems would occur in diagnosis of language minority children for bilingual education classes, which require clusters of limited-English or non-English speaking children.[67] Another predominantly minority consideration that would be affected by information inequities would be migrant programs for children of agricultural farmworkers. This highly mobile population follows the crops, often crossing many state lines. While these children remain an extremely disadvantaged population, initiation of a computerized records system and the development of a migrant education network have begun to focus attention on the need for extraordinary administrative procedures.[68] However, the mobile characteristics of farmworker families and low educational attainment of adult migrants will effectively preclude migrant parents from receiving or evaluating information on the voucher schools. Migration and reverse migration of Puerto Ricans from the island to the 50 states would cause similar problems for an information system.[69] Another inevitable conflict consideration is the method by which private schools or the California hybrid independent schools would meet and advertise their responsibility for enrolling handicapped children.[70] The list could continue, for most programmatic and administrative activities would be affected by the parochiaid proposals, not all of which have information implications. For example, it is unclear how the lotteries and waiting lists envisioned for over-subscribed schools would operate, or how this queuing could be an efficient use of facilities. Accreditation and evaluation activities would surely lie fallow until the system became organized. Although the Moynihan proposal has a provision prohibiting national origin discrimination, it omits gender as a consideration. The California initiative includes gender, but omits national origin, a serious omission for a state with a significant Mexican American population.[71] In my judgement the voucher proposal and the Moynihan BEOG proposal would create severe disruption of categorical programs and strain informational systems that rely upon centralized administration to coordinate the activities.

CONCLUSIONS

It is evident that the California initiative and the BEOG proposal would meet at least two goals thought to be desirable by parochiaid proponents: public assistance to the private education sector, and a dynamic marketplace from which parents could choose a school to their liking. While this paper has not examined the appropriateness or constitutionality of these goals, it has examined the administrative structures and information systems these plans will require, and has found them inadequate for the increased load they would be forced to bear. The appeal of both plans is, in large part, their apparent simplicity and employment of existing resources. One need not invoke Greek mythology to imagine the consequences of simple plans gone awry, introducing dynamism into information systems that cannot handle their present load and that fail to reach the disadvantaged and information-poor.

Research evidence, however, suggests strongly that this is exactly what would happen under either parochiaid plan. Information is a crucial element for participating in the programs and for giving parents effective choice. Yet access to technical assistance and counseling for BEOG eligibility is presently available to only a few hundred thousand. Further, the existing financial aid network is only operative in the postsecondary sector. For parents to receive information in a voucher system, a new information network would have to be constructed and regulated. Under either system, those parents most likely to participate by receiving information and by possessing the skills or resources to secure skills would be advantaged parents. To suggest otherwise is to ignore the evidence and the experience of earlier voucher experiments.

Can the goals of the parochiaid proponents be met in ways less detrimental to the existing system, or less likely to have information inequities? The developing debate has not provided a clear answer. My fears notwithstanding, there is clear merit to the debate that has been triggered by parochiaid proposals. For instance, in support of several options to improve the range of choices available to parents, Henry Levin has noted, "If the voucher proposals stimulate both the development of these public choice approaches as well as the citizen awareness and political effort to implement them, the debate on vouchers will have performed an important public service."[72] As Levin suggests, public school systems can provide more options by creating more schools, mini-schools, or other curricular and programmatic options. The debate may cause more legislators to question the false economy in establishing underfunded information networks or in supporting bills that promise to cut expenditures while overloading existing delivery systems.[73] Many of the proposals that would improve choice could incorporate information systems targeted at disadvantaged populations, provided the systems were more specific and comprehensive than those presently in use. However, if Coons' and Sugarman's admonition, quoted in the epigraph, is correct--and evidence suggests it is--then many legislative proposals to direct government money to private schools will fail to achieve the very purpose they are intended to accomplish, enhancing the opportunity of quality education for all. In Coons' and Sugarman's terms, such plans would inevitably be ruinous.

NOTES

1. D. West, "Tom Paine's Voucher Scheme for Public Education," Southern Economic Journal, 33 (1967), 378-382.
2. Daniel Weiler, A Public School Voucher Demonstration: The First Year at Alum Rock (Santa Monica: Rand, 1974).
3. Scott E. Sterling, "The G.I. Bill: An Education Entitlement," in Norman D. Kurland, ed., Entitlement Studies (Washington, D.C.:

NIE, 1977), 123-144; Keith Olson, The G.I. Bill, The Veterans, and the Colleges (Lexington: University of Kentucky Press, 1974).

    4. Nathan Lewin, "Disentangling Myth from Reality," 3 J. L. and Ed. 107 (1974).

    5. Joseph B. Robinson, "Little Room Left to Maneuver," 3 J. L. and Ed. 123 (1974).

    6. 330 U.S. 1 (1947).

    7. Robinson, note 5 supra, at 123-128; Leo Pfeffer, "Aid to Parochial Schools: The Verge and Beyond," 3 J. L. and Ed. 115-121 (1974).

    8. 342 F. Supp. 399 (S.D. Ohio 1972), summarily aff'd., 409 U.S. 808 (1973).

    9. 353 F. Supp. 744 (S.D. Ohio 1972), summarily aff'd., 413 U.S. 901 (1973).

    10. Ohio Rev. Code Ann. Sec. 3317.06 (J); 433 U.S. 229 (1977).

    11. 392 U.S. 236 (1968).

    12. 358 F. Supp. 29 (D.N.J. 1973), summarily aff'd., 417 U.S. 961 (1974).

    13. 421 U.S. 349 (1975).

    14. 403 U.S. 602 (1971); 403 U.S. 955 (1971).

    15. 413 U.S. 756 (1973).

    16. Note 8 supra.

    17. Note 9 supra.

    18. Note 14 supra; 413 U.S. 825 (1973).

    19. 442 U.S. 907 (1979).

    20. "Congress shall make no law respecting the establishment of religion......." U.S. Const., Amend. I. The clause is applicable to the states through the 14th Amendment. Cantwell v. Connecticut, 310 U.S 296 (1940).

    21. 444 U.S. 646, 653 (1980).

    22. For more detailed analyses of entitlement or voucher plans, see George La Noue, ed., Education Vouchers: Concepts and Controversies (New York: Teachers College Press, 1972); John E. Coons and Stephen D. Sugarman, "Family Choice in Education: A Model State System for Vouchers," 59 Cal. L. Rev. 321 (1971); Harvard Center for the Study of Public Policy, Education Vouchers (1970) in David Kirp and Mark G. Yudof, Educational Policy and the Law (Berkeley: McCutchan, 1974) 62-68. For more detailed criticism of the California Initiative, see Henry M. Levin, Educational Vouchers and Social Policy (Stanford: Institute for Research on Educational Finance and Governance, 1979).

    23. Nevertheless, scholars have ventured opinions on how the Court would react to a voucher case. See, for example, Pfeffer, note 7 supra; Eldon Wedlock, Jr., and Dennis D. Jasper, "Parochiaid and the First Amendment: Past, Present, and Future," 2 J.L. and Ed. 377-393 (1973). See Kirp and Yudof, Educational Policy and the Law, note 22 supra, 32-84.

    24. Education Commission of the States, Legislative Review (Denver; ECS, November 1978).

25. In the 96th Congress the "Kemp-Roth" proposal was pending before the House Ways and Means Committee (H.R. 1598) and the Senate Finance Committee (S. 33). The Republican Party adopted a major plank in its 1980 platform to limit federal spending and to cut taxes. And the Reagan administration has announced its firm intention to implement this policy.

26. See James Catterall and Thomas Thresher, Proposition 13: The Campaign, The Vote, and the Immediate Aftereffects for California Schools (Stanford: Institute for Research on Educational Finance and Governance, 1979). For background on the initiative process, see Cal. Educ. Code Sec. 4000-23 (West Supp. 1975), implementing Cal. Const. Art. IV, Sec. 25; for the referendum process, see Sec. 4050-57. See generally, Craig N. Oren, "The Initiative and Referendum's Use in Zoning," 64 Cal. L. Rev. 74-107 (1976); Max Radin, "Popular Legislation in California: 1936-1946," 35 Cal. L. Rev. 171-190 (1947).

27. Serrano v. Priest, 5 Cal. 3d 584, 487 P. 2d 1241 (1971).

28. Note 2 supra.

29. Roger Cobb and Charles Elder, Participation in American Politics: The Dynamics of Agenda-Building (Baltimore: Johns Hopkins University Press, 1972) p. 122; see generally, Lewis A. Coser, Continuities in the Study of Social Conflict (New York: Free Press, 1967).

30. See, for example, the failed Missouri Constitutional Amendment Proposal H, a voucher plan for public, private, and parochial schools.

31. Education Amendments of 1980. Pub. L. 96-374, 94 Stat. 1367.

32. The Moynihan proposal is printed in 126 Cong. Rec. S 7838-39. The proposal was debated on June 23 and 24, 1980, and was defeated in the Senate by a vote of 71 to 24. See 126 Cong. Rec. S 7839-68 and S 7964-74 (daily ed. June 23 and 24, 1980).

33. For a summary of federal assistance programs, see Virginia Fadil and Julianne Thrift, Federal Student Assistance and Categorical Programs (Washington, D.C.: National Association of Independent Colleges and Universities, 1978).

34. Henry M. Levin, "Postsecondary Entitlements: An Exploration," in Kurland, ed., note 3 supra at 1-51; and Levin, Educational Vouchers and Social Policy, note 22 supra.

35. Levin, "Postsecondary Entitlements," note 34 supra, at 32.

36. Stephen Klees, The Role of Information in the Market for Education Services (Stanford: Occasional Paper in the Economics and Politics of Education, 1974), 41.

37. Gary Bridge, "Information Imperfections: The Achilles' Heel of Entitlement Plans," School Review, 86 (1978), 522.

38. John E. Coons and Stephen D. Sugarman, Education by Choice: The Case for Family Control (Berkeley: University of California Press, 1978), 148.

39. G. Stigler, "The Economics of Information," Journal of Political Economy, 69 (1961), 213-225; A. Alchian, "Information

Costs, Pricing, and Resource Unemployment," in E.S. Phelps, ed. Microeconomic Foundations of Employment and Inflation Theory (New York: Norton 1970).

40. S.A. Ozga, "Imperfect Markets Through Lack of Knowledge," Quarterly Journal of Economics, 74 (1960), 29-52.

41. Michael Olivas, The Dilemma of Access (Washington, D.C.: Howard University Press, 1979); George Brown, Susan Hill, Nan Rosen, and Michael Olivas, The Condition of Education for Hispanic Americans (Washington, D.C.: National Center for Education Statistics, 1980); Lorenzo Morris, Elusive Equality: The Status of Black Americans in Higher Education (Washington, D.C.: Howard University Press, 1979).

42. Leonard Bloomfield, Language (New York: Holt, Rinehart, and Winston, 1933); Joshua Fishman, Language Loyalty in the United States (The Hague: Mouton, 1966).

43. Harold Love, "The Reasons Participants Drop Out of the Food Stamp Program: A Case study and its Implications," American Journal of Agricultural Economics, 52 (1970), 387-394; Maurice MacDonald, Food Stamp Participation in Wisconsin (Madison: Institute for Research on Poverty, 1975).

44. Susan Welch, Michael Steinman, and John Comer, "Where have all the Clients Gone?" Public Welfare, 31 (1973), 48-54; Peter Taylor-Gooby, "Rent Benefits and Tenants' Attitudes," Journal of So/.al Policy, 5 (1976), 33-48; T.G. Staples, "Supplementary Security Income: The Aged Eligible," Social Security Bulletin, 7 (1973); Frances Piven and Richard Clowart, Regulating the Poor: The Functions of Public Welfare (New York: Random House, 1971).

45. Adalberto Aguirre, "The Sociolinguistic Situation of Bilingual Chicano Adolescents in a California Border Town," Aztlan, 10 (1975), 55-67; M. Childers and T. Post, The Information-Poor in America (Metuchen, NJ: Scarecrow Press, 1979); Evelyn Lee, "Mental Health Services for the Asian Americans: Problems and Alternatives," in Civil Rights Issues of Asian and Pacific Americans: Myths and Realities (Washington, D.C.: U.S. Commission on Civil Rights, 1979), 734-756; Joan Ablon, "Relocated American Indians in the San Francisco Bay Area: Social Interaction and Indian Identity," in Howard Bahr, Bruce Chadwick, and Robert Day, eds., Native Americans Today: Sociological Perspectives (New York: Harper and Row, 1972), 412-428.

46. Marc Bendick, Toby Campbell, Lee Bawden, and Melvin Jones, Towards Efficiency and Effectiveness in the WIC Delivery System (Washington, D.C.: Urban Institute, 1976).

47. Welch, Steinman and, Comer, note 44 supra.

48. Oliver Moles, "Predicting Use of Public Assistance: An Empirical Study," Welfare in Review, 7 (1969), 13-19. See also Nancy Mudrick, The Interaction of Public Assistance and Student Financial Aid (Washington, D.C.: College Board, 1980).

49. ABT Associates, Participation in a Direct Cash Assistance Program (Cambridge: ABT Associates, 1974); Jacqueline Anderson

and Rocco D'Amico, "Use of AFDC by Eligible Families: A Predictive Model," Welfare in Review, 7 (1969), 25-26; N. Ausmus "Occupational Information Systems and the Department of Labor", Journal of Employment Counseling, 14 (1977), 54-48.

50. Robert Yin, "The (In)equity of Information Delivery Systems in Education," paper presented at NIE Conference on Equity in Educational Information Dissemination, Washington, DC, February 23, 1979, p. 2.

51. There are also state forms that can be used for federal application, such as that of Pennsylvania Higher Education Assistance Agency. Janet Hansen, Student Aid and the Urban Poor (Washington, D.C.: College Board, 1980). For an analysis of rural disadvantage, see H. Gilingren, "Perception of Changes of Farm Emigrants Before and After Migration," Rural Sociology, 34 (1968), 223-228.

52. Marc Bendick and Mario Cantu, "The Literacy of Welfare Clients," Social Science Review, March 1978, 56-68. See also Laura K. Gordon, "Bureaucratic Competence and Success in Dealing with Public Bureaucracies," Social Problems, 23 (1975), 197-208; Nancy Mavrogenes, Earl Hanson, and Carol Winkley, "But Can the Client Understand It?" Social Work, 22 (1977), 110-112.

53. Christopher Jencks, "Educational Information: Part 22," Testimony Before the Senate Select Committee on Equal Educational Opportunity, 92d Cong. 1st Sess., (1971); James S. Coleman, "Choice in American Education," in James S. Coleman, ed., Parents, Teachers, and Children: Prospects for Choice in American Education (San Francisco: Institute for Contemporary Studies, 1977), 1-12.

54. Comprehensive Employment and Training Act of 1973, Title IV, Sec. 404 (a); Higher Education Act of 1965, Title IV, Part F, Sec. 493 A. (a) (1).

55. Paul Franklin, Beyond Student Aid (Washington, D.C.: College Board, 1980); Opportunity Programs for the Disadvantaged in Higher Education (Washington, D.C.: American Association for Higher Education, 1975); Fadil and Thrift, note 33 supra.

56. Higher Education Act of 1965, Title IV, Subpart 4, Sec. 417 B. (b) (1).

57. Descriptive Study of the Talent Search Program (Triangle Park, N.C.: Research Triangle Institute, 1975), Vol. III.

58. Factbook (Washington, D.C.: Bureau of Higher and Continuing Education, 1978), 17-22.

59. Talent Search: $12,455,000/186,266 clients = $66.87; Educational Opportunity Centers: $5,246,000/86,675 clients = $60.52. Factbook, note 58 supra, at 17-22.

60. Ibid., pp. 2-3.

61. Ibid. p. 17. See also testimony of Michael Olivas and David Lessard in Department of Labor, HEW, and Related Agencies: Appropriations for 1981, Hearings before the Subcommittee on Labor, Health, Education and Welfare, and Related Agencies of the

House Committee on Appropriations, 96th Cong., 2d Sess., (1980), vol. 12, pp. 299-300.

62. Factbook, note 58 supra, at 20.

63. Larry Gladieux and Charles Byce, "As Middle-Income Student Aid Expands, Are Low-Income Students Losing Out?" (Washington, D.C.: College Board, 1980). For evidence of the stratification of college students by income, see Michael Olivas, The Dilemma of Access, note 41 supra, at 34-38.

64. Gladieux and Byce, note 63 supra.

65. Bridge, note 37 supra.

66. Ibid., p. 517.

67. Beatriz Arias, "Issues in Tri-Ethnic Desegregation," paper presented at American Educational Research Association, Boston, April 1980; Abdin Noboa, "Hispanics and Desegregation," paper presented at the Forum for Responsible Federal Educational Policy, Washington, D.C., June 3, 1980; Joseph M. Montoya, "Bilingual-Bicultural Education: Making Educational Opportunities Available to National Origin Minority Students." 61 Geo. U.L.J. 991-994 (1973).

68. Brown, Hill, Rosen, and Olivas, note 41 supra, at 32-33; Doris Slesinger, Health Needs of Migrant Workers in Wisconsin (Madison: Wisconsin Bureau of Community Health, 1979); Glenn Hinkle, Robert Tipton, Terrence Tutchings, eds., Who Cares? Who Counts? A National Study of Migrant Students Educational Needs (Washington, D.C.: USOE Teacher Corps, 1979).

69. José Hernández, "La Migración Puertorriqueña Como Factor Demográfico: Solución y Problema," Revista Interamericana, 4 (1975), 526-534; José Hernández, "Hispanic Migration and Demographic Patterns: Implications for Educational Planning and Policy," Hispanic Migrations from the Caribbean and Latin America (New York: ERIC Clearinghouse on Urban Education, 1979), 2-6.

70. The Education for All Handicapped Children Act of 1975, 20 U.S.C. Sec. 1401 et seq. (1979). See generally, David A. Montgomery, "The Education of Parochial School Handicapped Children and the Establishment Clause, 8 J.L. and Ed. 457-494 (1979); Leroy Peterson, Richard Rossmiller, and Marlin Volz, The Law and Public School Operation (New York: Harper and Row, 1978), 328-329; Kirp and Yudof, note 22 supra, at 717-719.

71. Montoya, note 67 supra.

72. Levin, note 23 supra, at 25.

73. It may also lead legislators to question the false economy of "consolidation" legislation that collapses categorical programs into general support budgets. See S. 2270 (6 February 1980), "The Education Simplification Demonstration Act," for an example of the consolidation genre.

Discussion

PROFESSOR COONS: I'd just like to say I agree with almost everything that Dr. Olivas says except for his conclusions. Certainly you need information, as I made clear in my essay. Vouchers or any other scheme should be tested by the standard of information which is supplied. For that very reason we are opposed to legitimating a scheme in which the information is supplied by the producer of the education. We would require the information to come from an independent source, who would be responsible to the family whom he is supposed to serve. If you do that, and if you make the form of delivery personal instead of written, you have answered every one of the important problems that Dr. Olivas has raised.

ROBERT BALDWIN, EXECUTIVE DIRECTOR, CITIZENS FOR EDUCATIONAL FREEDOM: We have discussed over and over the differences between public and private education and the commitment to public education versus private education. And I believe, first of all as a parent, that the commitment of the government should be to the education of children. The primary concern should not be the institution in which that education is provided, but rather the education of those children. I am not a Catholic, I am a Baptist. And as a parent of four children, I am concerned about the education of my children. I am not willing, as a parent, to wait five years or ten years to find the solutions that public education promises. I will not jeopardize my children's education for that purpose.

As a parent, I am required by law to send my children to a school; I am required by law to contribute part of my hard-earned income to pay for education; and then I am prohibited by law from using my educational tax dollars to educate my children in the school of my choice. And I believe that our concern must be for the education of children. As Professor Coons has said, the most qualified person should be the one who decides where that child is educated. And I believe that every parent in this country ought to be able to share in the benefits that are provided, the public benefits of the tax dollars to educate his child in the school of his choice.

Tuition tax credits are one possibility. Vouchers would be another possibility. The mechanism is not nearly as important as solving the problem in education. And right now the problems in education are not being solved. We talked about minorities and the problems of minorities. Forty-seven percent of the inner-city blacks in this country graduating from high school are functionally illiterate, unable to fill out a job application or read a newspaper. Is that solving their problem? If we gave those blacks in the inner city the opportunity to freely choose to educate their children in a school like Mrs. Taylor's that is providing a quality education, I think that most of them would jump at the opportunity.

And all these arguments about separation of church and state and the arguments about segregation and the arguments about elitism are absolute hooey. I challenge Dr. Olivas to produce the statistics supporting his argument. During the recent congressional hearings on the IRS and the allegations of racial discrimination in private schools, no federal government agency could provide the Congress of the United States with any evidence of racial discrimination to any significant extent in nonpublic schools. And the evidence that was presented by Father Blum and Father Greeley suggest that the nonpublic schools in the inner cities are doing a pretty good job for minority children. The evidence is that public schools are failing to educate the children in this country. And as a parent, I believe that the parents in this country want the opportunity to educate their children in the best way they can.

JUDGE MIKVA: I happen to be supportive of public assistance for nonpublic schools. When I was in the Congress, I introduced a tax deferral scheme that I thought might help enhance freedom of educational choice. But I very much disagree with the way you premised the proposition and I want to tell you why. You kept putting in "as a parent." "As a parent" you have certain rights. You do have all kinds of rights as a parent, but the equation of public education cannot be stated as one between parents and state; it's that kind of statement of the equation that leads to Proposition 13s and other kinds of misconceptions of what public education and funding of public education is all about.

If the challenge to support education is only between parents and the state, then all those people like me who are now empty-nesters would have the right to say, "Well, then, stop taxing me. I've paid my share." And yet we know that if we are going to preserve a free society, we're going to continue to have to share the burden of public education not just between parents and the state but between everybody and the state. That's the only quarrel I have with you. I am not about to defend all aspects of public education in its current state. And I leave it to Dr. Olivas to give his statistics. But I get very edgy when somebody says, "I'm a parent and therefore I have certain rights as to how my tax money should be spent." You're a taxpayer. And that's the basis upon which we finance public education.

MR. BALDWIN: I'm not questioning that. I don't question that all taxpayers should support education. My concern is that we are mandated by law to educate our children.

JUDGE MIKVA: Well, you're mandated by law to pay the taxes to educate everybody's children.

MR. BALDWIN: That's correct. But then we are prohibited from using our tax dollars to educate our children in the school of our choice.

JUDGE MIKVA: They're not your tax dollars.

MR. BALDWIN: They are the tax dollars that I would use to educate my child if I were not taxed.

JUDGE MIKVA: They're also my tax dollars. And I've already educated my children—or, at least I have seen them through as much education as the public school system will provide. If they have been over-educated, that has escaped me. But my quarrel is not with your desire to improve public education, or even with your desire to innovate as to how we maintain and enhance our pluralism. I quarrel only with the concept that suggests that because you're a parent you have some special say as to how those tax dollars should be raised or spent. With that I disagree.

MR. BALDWIN: No, I only have a quarrel as to where my child shall be educated. And that's the point I'm trying to make.

DR. OLIVAS: In response to Mr. Baldwin's comment concerning statistics on segregation in nonpublic schools, I can only say that segregation is increasing. The data are incontestable. I have them right here for Hispanic children.* Segregation has increased significantly in all sectors of the country.

PROFESSOR COONS: If segregation is increasing, Dr. Olivas, why do you wish to preserve the system which is the segregator? I'm not quite sure I follow. Surely you don't prefer segregation. Therefore what follows from that?

DR. OLIVAS: I begin with the premise that it is wrong to segregate.

PROFESSOR COONS: But the present system is segregating.

DR. OLIVAS: Yes.

---

*Editor's Note: The data to which Dr. Olivas refers are contained in Table 2.05 of George Brown et al., The Condition of Education 1980 (Washington, D.C.: National Center for Education Statistics, 1980).

PROFESSOR COONS: Well, if the major premise in your syllogism is that segregation is wrong, and the minor is that the present system is segregating, what follows as your conclusion?

DR. OLIVAS: There are a number of alternatives which do not require scrapping the present system in order to rectify the wrong of segregation. I spoke to these in my paper.

PROFESSOR COONS: I'd love to hear some of those alternatives, because I am dubious that coercion alone will solve this problem. I happen to believe that freedom of choice will do a lot more for racial integration than some of my opponents do. But as I suggested in my paper, one is entitled to espouse a pessimistic philosophy of the human person if one wishes to.

STEVE CURTISS, AMERICAN LEGISLATIVE EXCHANGE COUNCIL: I'd like to direct my question to Professor Coons. Do you know of any state legislators that are presently thinking of introducing a voucher system into the state?

PROFESSOR COONS: No, but I know lots who have been asked. And they say, "Oh, that's a very good idea. But I'm very busy; my agenda is overwhelming. But if you get it to the floor, I'll vote for it. But don't ask me to front for it." Now why is that? Perhaps it is partly because the California Teachers Association and the AFT and the administrators' union are the largest political contributors in California.

MRS. MAE DUGAN, CITIZENS FOR EDUCATIONAL FREEDOM (ST. LOUIS, MO., CHAPTER): Judge Mikva, I would like to state for the record that the parental right of choice in education is recognized as a human right by the United Nations' Universal Declaration of Human Rights. Artical 26, Secton 3 of that document reads: "The parents should have the prior right to choose the kind of education they want for their children." Unfortunately, parents cannot exercise this right under the present system.

JUDGE MIKVA: You know, one of the nice parts about being a judge is that I don't get the mail anymore. I write my opinions and they are then cast upon the waters and only law professors read them. And I don't have to try to make myself perfectly clear. But let me try one more time. I did not say that parents don't have rights. What I said is that the social equation is not between the state and parents who pay the taxes so their children can be educated, but between the state and citizens who pay taxes so that everybody's children can be educated. That's the only point about which I was challenging Mr. Baldwin.

And it is not that parents shouldn't have rights to educate their children as they see fit. I have exercised those rights; I have used the private schools for my children, both at the secondary level and at the level of higher education. Far be it from me to say that people shouldn't have the right to choose the kind of education they want. But when we pay our taxes (and we don't have the right to choose to pay or not to pay), we pay them not because there's a contract between you and the state to educate your children. The social equation is that we are all paying for the education of everybody's children. That's why I continue to pay taxes even though I no longer have children of school age.

DR. ROY FORBES, DIRECTOR, NATIONAL ASSESSMENT OF EDUCATIONAL PROGRESS; EDUCATION COMMISSION OF THE STATES: I think some statistics that were quoted a few minutes ago by Mr. Baldwin may have come from a study we did. One of the standards that we have suggested that evaluators follow is that when we hear our statistics misused, we should try to correct it. If the figure of 48 percent illiteracy came from our data, I have to say that the National Assessment of Educational Progress assesses all 17-year-old students, including those that go to both public and private schools. So to quote this statistic as if it were a measure of public schools' accomplishment or non-accomplishment would be incorrect.

I am also with the Educational Commission of the States. And one of the projects we have deals with migrant education. It's one which I've become very close to in the last four or five months. And I think that we're beginning to make some progress in helping those particular students, who seem to be the most disadvantaged in this country right at the present time—students whose parents have chosen to be migrant workers or are locked into the migrant stream. So I would like to ask Jack Coons about the way that his voucher plan would affect the migrants.

PROFESSOR COONS: Dr. Olivas, I think, disagrees with me and I'd like to hear why, but Steve Sugarman and I believe that there would be nothing more salutary for the migrant workers and their children with respect to education than to have the opportunity to organize their own peripatetic school, that would travel with them, that would be organized around the system and culture in which they live. We think that migrant workers should be able to choose their own teachers, who would teach—in addition to English—in whichever form, bilingual or Spanish, was thought best, perhaps in different ways for families that felt differently about it. It seems to me that peripatetic education has a future. But it has a future only if education can be organized in such a flexible, non-district, non-geographically constrained way that it can respond to the needs of those particular people. I think that's one of the real possibilities that vouchers represent.

MS. ROBYN HICKEY, GRADUATE STUDENT, GEORGE WASH-INGTON UNIVERSITY: Where in the voucher system is there really a guarantee for the familiar notion of "equality of educational opportunity"? If, in fact, low income people want to be integrated, that's fine; but that's an assumption. What is to prevent those types from all going to one set of schools and possibly those who can afford to pay more from going to another?

MR. DOYLE: There is no single voucher system. There are many voucher systems. And each different voucher system reflects the policy objectives of its framers and formers. So Ms. Hickey's interest can be addressed systematically and responsibly in a voucher system. In fact, Jack Coons has made great efforts to do so in the one that he's designed.

PROFESSOR COONS: Well, I agree that there is no perfect system, and there will always be people who will make bad judgments. But what I would say is that you don't give up on humans by adopting the presumption that they belong to the class of the "stupid and uncaring" simply because their income isn't high enough to buy their way out. The 80 percent of people who are not rich enough to pay for private schools must not be treated as if they are all invincibly ignorant and uncaring. Some are, but most are sufficiently smart and they are caring, and they try. Now let us suppose that they are given a chance and they run with it, and they run away from the 25 percent of the ignorant or uncaring. Then the next question is, "Are the twenty-five percent invincibly that way, or will the example of their peers and a good information system make a difference over time?" Maybe Dr. Olivas is right that a good information system is impossible. And maybe these people will never change. But is our society to be built on the assumption that those people must forever be paternalized and decided for? Or are we going to let them make some mistakes and learn? We choose the latter course in the rest of life outside of education. We let people make their own mistakes and through their mistakes become more mature, and ultimately some of them become autonomous. That's what a really exciting life is about: to offer freedom to people who have been told all their lives what they're going to do and where their kids are going to go to school; to say to them for the first time, "You've got something to choose"; to offer to them both freedom and restraint at the same time, because they are not free any longer not to choose; paradoxically society would say, "You must be free. You must choose."

I would think that to say this would be the most healthy thing for the American family. Children have seen their parents as impotent people who are useless with respect to controlling formal education. They have grown used to thinking that their parents have nothing to say about this important experience in the child's life outside of the family. If we told these parents, "You have the power to choose, "for the first time many of their children would begin to see their parents as important and authoritative creatures, playing the role of a parent and relating to their children in the way that the family in mythology is supposed to do. I think the family can work that way. But you've got to give those people real power and real freedom. If you expect nothing from people, nothing is what you'll get.

MRS. MARILYN LUNDY, PRESIDENT, CITIZENS FOR EDU-CATIONAL FREEDOM: I would like to go back to this question of educational financing and the reason why an adult whose children have graduated from school still pays taxes. I think it really hinges on this question of parental control and the rights of the child. Contrary to the idea that we're paying for the present generation's education, actually educational financing is the reverse of Social Security. In Social Security the individual pays during his or her earning years and gains the benefit in his retirement years. Educational financing is reversed — the child gains the benefits during his learning years and pays back during his earning years or during the rest of his life. So the important thing to recognize is that the child forever after pays back for the investment made in him to make him a better citizen in a better society. But if no money is invested in that person's education, it's pretty unjust to have him or her pay back for the rest of their lives. And this correlates with the parent's right, which was established in <u>Pierce v. The Society of Sisters</u>.* I think that the parent has the right to choose where their education tax dollars should go. I think we have to understand that. My answer to the question of why we still pay taxes is that we're repaying the investment that was made in us. But if society has made no investment in the education of the millions of children who have attended nonpublic schools, then society cannot expect these people to support public education generously and gladly.

JUDGE MIKVA: This discussion has been very useful. It has shed more light than heat; and that is, indeed, very unusual for this subject matter.

---

*Editor's Note: 268 U.S. 510 (1925). See Stephen Arons, "The Separation of School and State: <u>Pierce</u> Reconsidered," <u>Harvard Ed. Rev.</u> 46 (1976) 76-104; and Donald P. Kommers and Michael J. Wahoske, Eds., <u>Freedom and Education: Pierce v. Society of Sisters Reconsidered</u> (Notre Dame, Ind.: Center for Civil Rights, 1978).

PART THREE
CONSTITUTIONAL PERSPECTIVES

Introduction

The Hon. J. Skelly Wright

This section of the volume should be of keen interest not only to judges and lawyers, but also to policy makers and to all citizens concerned with nonpublic education. The essays gathered here probe the underlying foundational, or constitutional, reasons for constraints on the government's role in nonpublic education.

In order for government action in nonpublic education to survive First Amendment scrutiny under the Establishment Clause, it must have a secular legislative purpose, it must not have a primary effect that either advances or inhibits religion, and it must not foster an excessive entanglement with religion.

This the Supreme Court taught us all almost ten years ago; and, of course, there is more or less general agreement on this basic principle. How this principle is to be applied to a particular governmental action affecting nonpublic education, especially at the elementary and secondary school level, still divides us.

No easy or false consensus emerges from a reading of the two lead essays, provided by ranking sub-cabinet officials in the Office of Legal Counsel (the federal government's constitutional law office, so to speak), during the Ford Administration (Professor Scalia) and the Carter Administration (Mr. Hammond). The confrontation between these two evenly matched advocates leads not to general confusion on constitutional principles, but to a sharp and vigorous exchange on how to apply those principles to the complexities of public policy that beset the political branches of our government as they carry out the distinct roles assigned to them by the constitution.

The three responses to the essays of Mr. Hammond and Professor Scalia likewise provide much food for reflection. Two of the most experienced and most able litigators in the church-state field, Nathan Dershowitz of the American Jewish Congress and Charles Wilson of the Washington firm of Williams and Connolly, provide a stimulating and thoughtful exchange that is enriched by their extensive experience in constitutional litigation, often on opposing sides of leading First Amendment cases. Finally, a well known constitutional historian, Professor Walter Berns, provides the view not of a litigant or a lawyer, but of a scholar concerning the purpose and meaning of the religion clauses of the First Amendment.

I have, on occasion, been called upon in my judicial capacity to decide complex cases arising under the religion clauses of the First

Amendment.* From this experience I am, of course, aware that there are often no easy or at least no simplistic answers to the difficult questions that are posed by virtue of the unresolved (and perhaps unresolvable) tension between the prohibition against a governmental establishment of religion and the constitutional guarantee that the government should not impede the free exercise of religion. The papers gathered in this volume and the open, lively discussion of the central themes exlored here from many points of view should remind all of us that reflection along the lines of this discussion, vigorous but not hostile, strongly stated but open to dialogue, will always be a desirable goal in a free and open society that strives to acknowledge religious values without allowing the government to define the content of those values or to impose those values upon anyone.

---

*Editor's Note: See, e.g., King's Garden, Inc. v. FCC, 498 F.2d 51 (D.C. Cir. 1974); Founding Church of Scientology v. United States, 409 F.2d 1146 (D.C. Cir. 1969); and Application of the President and Directors of Georgetown College, Inc., 331 F.2d 1000 (D.C. Cir. 1964).

13. The Constitutionality of Federal Aid to Sectarian Elementary and Secondary Schools: A View from the Justice Department

Larry A. Hammond

I have been asked to summarize several major questions that have been presented to the Justice Department in very recent years involving the Federal Government's authority--or lack of authority--under the Establishment Clause of the First Amendment to provide assistance to nonpublic elementary and secondary schools. The Department of Justice has been called on in a variety of contexts to address these important and difficult constitutional questions. I will focus my remarks primarily on four programs, two that have been embodied in legislative proposals that have yet to receive congressional approval (grants under the Basic Educational Opportunity Grant program and tuition tax credits), and two congressional enactments that are now the subject of litigation (Title I of the Elementary and Secondary Education Act and portions of the Department of Labor's job program under the Comprehensive Employment and Training Act). On those matters presently in litigation in which the Justice Department is representing the Government, my remarks necessarily will be limited to a review of the issues these cases present and to an explanation of the central reasons for our positions.

A general foreword here might prove useful. In most of the circumstances in which we have either offered an opinion upon legislative proposals or litigated the constitutionality of federal statutory enactments, there have been individuals who have thoughtfully studied the constitutional questions, including Senator Moynihan and Professor Scalia, and have found the guidance in the Supreme Court's recent opinions less than adequate. Not infrequently, the claim has been made that the Court has failed to articulate and to adhere consistently to any set of standards for approaching cases under the Establishment Clause. As a general proposition, this is a view of the Court's decisions with which we disagree.

Unlike Senator Moynihan and others, I do not believe that the Supreme Court's decisions in this area are, to use his flat word, "wrong." I do not believe that these decisions are unprincipled. And I do not believe that they are the product of Justices whose decisions are the product of biases, of a preference for public education over private education. Indeed, I believe that in every one of the major cases decided in the last 30 years, the Supreme Court and each of the Justices have done their level best to identify the controlling constitutional principles and apply these principles to the legislative programs they were called upon to review.

Unlike Professor Scalia and others, I do not think that the decisions of the Supreme Court are chaotic or unintelligible. I do not think that responsible lawyers cannot understand them, cannot comprehend them, and cannot apply them. In fact, I think that in most of the areas discussed in this symposium and in most of the cases that come before courts in this country, the decisions of the Supreme Court under the Establishment Clause are intelligible and that the results are predictable.

Although the Court has certainly not resolved all of the possible questions, and although the Court has emphasized that each case—each program—must be evaluated on its own facts, we have found that the decisions do provide standards that can be comprehended and applied. Because we do find guidance in the Court's opinions, we have rejected the approach suggested by some that those who occupy positions in the Legislative and Executive Branches ought to feel free to support whatever programs are deemed desirable, leaving any constitutional scrutiny to the Supreme Court. Instead, we have found reasonably applicable guidance in the Court's opinions, and both Attorneys General Bell and Civiletti have felt constrained by that guidance. With that brave preface—expressing a viewpoint I know that many do not share—I will turn to the particular programs.

BASIC EDUCATIONAL OPPORTUNITY GRANTS (BEOGs)

In an opinion sent to Secretary of Education Hufstedler in 1980, Attorney General Civiletti reconfirmed the view of the Department of Justice that legislation that has been proposed during the last two Congresses to extend Basic Educational Opportunity Grants to students enrolled in private elementary and secondary schools, in addition to those enrolled in institutions of higher education, would be unconstitutional.* This opinion reflects the judgment of the Office of Legal Counsel that we have not been able to identify any substantial arguments that would distinguish such grants from similar programs heretofore invalidated by the Supreme Court. Whatever the merit of the several persuasive arguments that have been made in favor of the desirability of such grant programs, we do not see how the Court could fail to decide that they have an impermissible "primary effect" that aids the religious mission of sectarian schools. The Supreme Court's 1973 decision in Committee for Public Education v. Nyquist,[1] and a companion case, Sloan v. Lemon,[2] remain the leading authority for the conclusion that unrestricted grants to parents of children attending sectarian ele-

---

*Editor's Note: The opinion of Attorney General Civiletti was cited by Senator Moynihan and entered into the record of the debate on the Senate floor concerning the BEOG proposal. 126 Cong. Rec. Sec. 7857-59 (daily ed. June 23, 1980).

mentary and secondary schools, given to reimburse them for tuition paid to such schools, violates the principles of the Establishment Clause.

Two suggestions have been made to distinguish the New York statute in Nyquist and the Pennsylvania statute in Lemon from the bill that was before Congress in the baby BEOG proposal, but neither suggestion is, in my judgment, persuasive. The first attempt to differentiate the BEOG proposal from the enactments invalidated in Nyquist and Lemon focus on the fact that the BEOG proposal is a federal proposal rather than a state proposal. I simply have been unable to find a reason to believe that the fact that it is a federal program rather than a state program is of any constitutional significance. There is nothing in the history of the First Amendment that would suggest that a more stringent standard should apply to a state government than would apply to the federal government in Establishment Clause cases.

The second suggestion that has been made is that the baby BEOG program might be distinguished because it was incorporated into the program of grants to allow low-income parents to send their children to public and nonpublic colleges. The argument here is that a court would fail to distinguish between colleges on the one hand and elementary and secondary schools on the other. The flaw in the argument is that the entire history of the Supreme Court's decisions over the last 30 years has been to the contrary. Whenever a case has come up that has involved colleges, the Court has looked at it differently than it has when elementary and secondary schools have been at issue. Senator Moynihan has suggested that that was because the Court had concluded that a 19-year-old is less susceptible to religious influence than is an 18-year-old. I do not believe that his statement can be found in the Supreme Court's cases. What you will find, among other things, is that the Supreme Court found that colleges and universities have historically not been as pervasively sectarian in their orientation as have been elementary and secondary schools -- a proposition that I think most people would not disagree with.

The Court's more recent pronouncements have reaffirmed our view that tuition grants--at least insofar as the largest beneficiary is the class of parents who elect to send their children to religiously-affiliated schools--cannot be sustained.

TUITION TAX CREDITS

In 1978 the Department was also asked to review a bill then known as the Packwood-Moynihan bill that would have made tax credits available to the parents of children attending nonpublic schools. For much the same reason that compelled us to question the constitutionality of grants, we concluded that such a program of tax credits would not survive scrutiny under the Establishment Clause. Again, the case most directly on point is the 1973 Nyquist decision. There the Court struck down tax benefit programs at the state level primarily on the ground that such benefits would have much the same practical effect as direct government grants, or that they would have the effect of advancing the religious mission of sectarian schools. The Court has also noted that programs of this sort create a potential for political entanglement and divisiveness along religious lines. As recently as 1979, the Supreme Court summarily affirmed Beggans v. Public Funds for Public Schools,[3] a case in which the Third Circuit relied heavily on Nyquist to strike down a New Jersey program of tax exemptions for parents of children enrolled in nonpublic elementary and secondary schools. Thus, we have no reason to expect the Supreme Court to take a new direction in this area.

Before leaving the area of recent legislative proposals, I should mention that the Department has also been called on to evaluate the constitutionality of proposed legislation providing direct grants exclusively to nonpublic schools for textbooks, standardized tests, speech and hearing diagnostic services, diagnostic psychological services and counseling, instructional materials, and transportation to and from school. In 1978, we concluded that direct grants to nonpublic schools for these purposes would be found unconstitutional, as opposed to provision to students of, for example, textbooks, as approved in Board of Education v. Allen,[4] or transportation, as upheld in Everson v. Board of Education.[5] We have not been called on to reconsider this view, and we do not expect that under recent case law our opinion would differ regarding direct grants related to the secular educational functions of a school. We recognize, however, that Committee for Public Education and Religious Liberty v. Regan,[6] upheld a New York statute directing the reimbursement of nonpublic schools for the costs incurred in administering state-mandated testing and certain other administrative activities.

COMPREHENSIVE EMPLOYMENT AND TRAINING ACT JOB PLACEMENTS IN SECTARIAN SCHOOLS

The Department is currently defending court challenges to the constitutionality of two major federal programs involving sectarian elementary and secondary schools. In Decker v. United States Department of Labor,[7] the United States District Court for the Eastern District of Wisconsin struck down all use of Title II Public Service Employment funds provided in the Comprehensive Employment and Training Act (CETA) for placement of CETA workers in sectarian elementary and secondary schools, primarily on the ground that it creates excessive government entanglement with religion. On appeal to the Seventh Circuit, the United States argued that the District Court erred insofar as CETA monies are used to fund noninstructional positions.

CETA is a general welfare program with a large class of beneficiaries only a small number of whom work in sectarian elementary or secondary schools. The CETA program pays the salaries of unemployed or underemployed individuals; the monies are not provided directly to the sectarian schools. We relied on a number of recent decisions, including Meek v. Pittenger,[8] for the proposition that where the activity in question is noninstructional and does not create an impermissible risk of fostering religious views, the government surveillance required to assure that a primary effect of the services is not to foster religion will not create excessive entanglement between church and state. We argued that there is direct Supreme Court authority for the Government's position regarding four of the categories of noninstructional positions at issue: cafeteria workers, health and safety service employees, speech and hearing diagnosticians, and clerical positions associated with the administration of state tests and federal programs. We found sufficient authority to justify the defense of two other noninstructional categories of employment: speech and hearing therapists and custodial day-care workers.

The District Court in Decker relied heavily on the potential for political entanglement in the CETA program when CETA workers are available to sectarian schools.[9] Although this is a pertinent factor, the Supreme Court in Nyquist considered political entanglement only a warning signal.[10] Thus, for those limited categories of positions described above, the Department of Justice has maintained that the program is constitutionally defensible. Arguments were heard in the summer of 1980 pursuant to an expedited reviewing schedule. Although this case is neither well known nor likely to have direct impact on important federal programs, it is nonetheless an important case, if for no other reason than that it will require the Court of Appeals—and possibly eventually the Supreme Court—to reconsider a very wide range of employment programs that may indirectly benefit nonpublic schools.*

TITLE I OF THE ELEMENTARY & SECONDARY EDUCATION ACT

As I have noted, the Government has not presented to the court in the CETA case the question of the propriety of providing teaching and related instructional services. That question, however, is very much at the heart of the case recently decided by a three-judge court in New York in the latest chapter of the PEARL litigation. The plaintiffs in that case have challenged aid to nonpublic schools provided under Title I of the Elementary and Secondary Education Act. Title I provides for instruction and counseling by public employees for low income, educationally disadvantaged children. The

---

*Editor's Note: On September 9, 1980, the Seventh Circuit affirmed the ruling of the District Court and remanded the case to that court for further proceedings.

The students are initially selected for participation and then the programs are located in schools in areas with high concentrations of eligible students. The program is predominantly located in public schools, but the Act requires provision of comparable services to children attending private schools. The program has existed since the mid-1960s and affords states and localities considerable flexibility to provide programs tailored to local needs.

Provision of these services in sectarian schools has been challenged in a number of law suits around the country, but the major focus of this litigation has been the New York case, National Coalition for Public Education and Religious Liberty (PEARL) v. Hufstedler.* The three-judge court in PEARL has now upheld the constitutionality of the Title I programs in New York City sectarian elementary and secondary schools based upon an extensive fourteen-year-record of operations.[11] The court confined its ruling to the facts presented to the court with respect to the particular attributes of New York City sectarian schools and with respect to the functioning of Title I in the City.

Among the factors relied upon by the three-judge court in its lengthy opinion were the following. In New York City, Title I services are provided on the premises of sectarian schools during regular school hours. The New York City Board of Education adopted this arrangement after attempting to provide services to these students after regular school hours on both public and private school premises and finding that they were unable to provide the statutorily mandated comparable services in such a setting for reasons such as student fatigue. The instruction was provided by peripatetic teachers and did not duplicate any of the regular classroom work. The classrooms were purged of religious symbolism and the teachers were closely supervised by the Board of Education and not by the religious school personnel. Supplies were segregated, preferably locked away, from the regular materials in the school.[12]

The court noted that the Title I program adheres strictly to what is known as the "child benefit principle," and does not provide aid directly to the sectarian schools. It also noted that during 1978, for example, only 4 percent of the national Title I expenditures were for nonpublic school students. In New York, this figure was 8 percent. Most interesting was the Court's conclusions that the New York City sectarian schools do not fit the "pervasively sectarian" profile of the Supreme Court's decisions. This conclusion alone was not sufficient to the court to ensure that the Title I program will not promote religion, but it was a factor in the court's conclusion that the restrictions imposed on the Title I program were sufficient to prevent provision of services from having a primary effect of aiding the religious mission of the schools.[13] The court concluded

---

*For a fuller description of the history of this litigation, see the note on pages 189-190.

that "the evidence establishes that the results feared in other cases has not materialized in the City's Title I program."[14]

The court's conclusion that the New York City schools are not pervasively sectarian facilitated its decision that excessive entanglement would not result from efforts to ensure that Title I funds are not diverted for religious use. The court also concluded that the program did not create a danger of excessive entanglement because funds were not dispersed to nonpublic schools or their employees, and the evidence established that Title I personnel have not fostered religious views in the past.[15] The Court concluded:

> While Title I could conceivably engender a program that did not satisfy Establishment Clause standards, this Court will not rule on the basis of abstract propositions. No constitutional infirmity has been revealed on the facts of this case. Accordingly, both the statute and the City's program survive judicial scrutiny.[16]

The plaintiffs filed a jurisdictional statement with the Supreme Court, but not in timely fashion. Apparently for this reason the Court dismissed the appeal on October 6, 1980,[17] and it denied rehearing on December 1.[18] Because the Supreme Court has decided not to hear the PEARL case, litigation in the many suits around the country challenging Title I, all of which had been stayed pending the outcome of the New York case, will undoubtedly be recommenced. Although the PEARL decision has precedential value only in the Southern District of New York, it is my view that the reasoning of District Judge Tenney in that case may go a long way toward providing guidance on the scope of permissible federal programs designed to aid children enrolled in nonpublic elementary and secondary schools.

NOTES

1. 413 U.S. 756 (1973).
2. 413 U.S. 825 (1973).
3. Public Funds for Public Schools of New Jersey v. Byrne, 444 Supp. 1228 (D.N.J. 1978), aff'd., 590 F.2d 514 (3d Cir.), summarily aff'd., 442 U.S. 907 (1979).
4. 392 U.S. 236 (1968).
5. 330 U.S. 1 (1947).
6. 444 U.S. 646 (1980).
7. 485 F. Supp. 837 (D.Wis. 1979).
8. 421 U.S. 349 (1975).
9. 485 F. Supp. at 841, 843.
10. 413 U.S. at 794-98.

11. National Coalition for Public Education and Religious Liberty v. Harris, 489 F. Supp. 1248 (S.D.N.Y.), appeal dismissed for want of jurisdiction, 449 U.S. __, 101 S. Ct. 55, rehearing denied, 449 U.S. __, 101 S. Ct. 601 (1980).

12. 489 F. Supp. at 1255-57.

13. Ibid. at 1258-65.

14. Ibid. at 1265.

15. Ibid. at 1265-70.

16. Ibid. at 1270.

17. 449 U.S. __, 101 S. Ct. 55 (1980).

18. 449 U.S. __, 101 S. Ct. 601 (1980).

14. On Making It Look Easy by Doing It Wrong: A Critical View of the Justice Department

Antonin Scalia

The 1978 opinion of the Justice Department's Office of Legal Counsel regarding the tuition tax credit legislation and its 1980 opinion regarding the extension of BEOGs to elementary and secondary school students (both of which were adopted by summary affirmance, so to speak, of the Attorney General) are wrong. They are wrong in the way good lawyers have been trained to be wrong, not so much in what they say as in what they leave unsaid. They make the best case against the constitutionality of the legislation but fail to give the devil, or what the Carter administration evidently regarded as the devil, his due.

It is, in fact, impossible to say with any assurance that this legislation would be struck down by the present Supreme Court. It is equally impossible to· say with any assurance it would not be struck down. The reason why this is so was expressed quite clearly by Justice White in the concluding paragraph of the most recent Supreme Court opinion dealing with the general subject:

> Establishment Clause cases are not easy, they stir deep feelings, and we are divided among ourselves, perhaps reflecting the different views on this subject of the people of this country. What is certain is that our decisions have tended to avoid categorical imperatives and absolutist approaches at either end of the range of possible outcomes. This course sacrifices clarity and predictability for flexibility, but this promises to be the case until the continuing interaction between the courts and states produces a single, more-encompassing construction of the Establishment Clause.[1]

An extraordinary admission in a majority opinion, but indeed, as one might expect, somewhat understating the case.

CHAOS AND CHANGE

The fact is that Supreme Court jurisprudence concerning the Establishment Clause in general, and the application of that clause to governmental assistance for religiously affiliated education in particular, is in a state of utter chaos and unpredictable change.

The chaos is demonstrated easily enough by a recitation of the Supreme Court's commandments to the States in the aid to education field: Thou mayest provide bus transportation to and from school for parochial school students;[2] but thou shalt not provide bus transportation to and from field trips.[3] Thou mayest furnish textbooks for use in sectarian schools;[4] but thou shalt not provide other instructional materials and equipment, such as maps.[5] (Senator Moynihan has raised the question, "What do you do with a map that's in a textbook?"; the Supreme Court has not yet addressed that fine issue.) Thou mayest exempt from real estate taxes premises devoted exclusively to worship of the Almighty;[6] but thou shalt not, in certain circumstances at least, permit parents an income tax remission for tuition payments to schools whose function consists in part of sectarian education.[7] I envision these commandments not as engraved upon tablets of stone but as scribbled on one of those funny pads that children use, with a plastic sheet on top that can be pulled up to erase everything and start anew.

The chaos is just as apparent if one wanders in the Establishment Clause field beyond the narrow area of aid to education. Thus, we are told that the so-called neutrality principle controls the government's attitude towards religion. That is to say, the government must not only abstain from favoring one sect over another, but it must also not favor religion over irreligion.[8] Yet when Wisconsin sought to compel Amish parents to send their children to school beyond the eighth grade [9] and when South Carolina sought to withhold unemployment compensation from a Seventh Day Adventist who was unemployed only because she would not accept Saturday work,[10] the First Amendment was held not merely to permit but, indeed, to require special dispensation for these religious beliefs, dispensation that would surely not be accorded to persons who abhor high school education or Saturday work for mere philosophical or temperamental reasons. And how is it, one might ask, that the term "religion," which appears only once in the relevant constitutional provision,[11] is interpreted very broadly to cover even philosophical dispositions of conscience when freedom of religion is at issue, but is interpreted very narrowly to include virtually nothing but theistic belief when establishment of religion is at issue?[12]

So much for the chaos. As for the change: Perhaps I am wrong to mention this as an element separate from the chaos, because I suspect it is ultimately the one that causes the other -- that is to say, in each successive era of change the cases from the prior era are not overruled, possibly for the very good reason that the Court realizes it is writing on a funny-pad and that the prior era may soon return. In any event, recurrent and substantial change characterizes even the most fundamental aspects of Establishment Clause jurisprudence. For example, the neutrality principle that I just described was set forth in 1947, in the Everson case, in which the Court said: "The state [must] be a neutral in its relations with groups of religious believers and non-believers....State power is no more to be used so as to handicap religions than it is to favor them."[13] Five years later the Court had changed its mind and wrote the following:

> We are a religious people whose institutions presuppose a
> Supreme Being....When the state encourages religious
> instruction or cooperates with religious authorities by
> adjusting the schedule of public events to sectarian needs,
> it follows the best of our traditions. For it then respects
> the religious nature of our people and accommodates the
> public service to their spiritual needs....The government
> must be neutral when it comes to competition between
> sects....It may not coerce anyone to attend church, to
> observe a religious holiday, or to take religious instruc-
> tion. But it can close its doors or suspend its operations
> as to those who want to repair to their religious sanctuary
> for worship or instruction.[14]

By 1963, the neutrality principle was back in favor again, at least
verbally, in the Schempp case, though it is difficult (no, let us be
frank, impossible) to reconcile Schempp with cases such as the
Amish and Seventh Day Adventist decisions that I referred to above.

An even more pronounced condition of constant change is
apparent in the aid to education cases in particular. The 1978
opinion of the Office of Legal Counsel concerning tuition tax credits
attempts to give the appearance of pyramid-like antiquity and
solidity to the current law by observing that the three-part test of
Lemon v. Kurtzman[15] "has been repeated in every significant
Supreme Court decision in this area during the last decade." (It was
actually only seven years at that time, but let that go; even a full
decade is breathlessly short enough, considering the major issue of
social policy involved.) But in fact the three-part test has not been
consistently followed since 1971, or at least not in the fashion in
which it was written. As originally expressed, the test was as
follows:

> First, a statute must have a secular legislative purpose;
> second, its principal or primary effect must be one that
> neither advances nor inhibits religion....; finally, the
> statute must not foster "an excessive government entan-
> glement with religion."[16]

Note that the second test refers to "its principal or primary effect,"
connoting a single, main effect. This meaning is reaffirmed later in
the opinion, when the Court refers to "the principal or primary
effect of the programs."[17] The Court gave the test the same
meaning in another opinion issued on the same day when it upheld
(except in one limited respect) the federal Higher Education Facilities Act: "[W]e consider four questions:...Second, is the primary
effect of the Act to advance or inhibit religion?"[18]

But look what happens to the test within two years: It is used in 1971 to validate a federal program. In 1973, when it is used to invalidate state aid to education legislation, it is expressed quite differently:

> [T]he propriety of a legislature's purposes may not immunize from further scrutiny a law which has a primary effect that advances religion....[I]t simply cannot be denied that this section has a primary effect that advances religion in that it subsidizes directly the religious activities of sectarian elementary and secondary schools....[Earlier] cases simply recognized that sectarian schools perform secular, educational functions as well as religious functions, and that some forms of aid may be channeled to the secular without providing direct aid to the sectarian....Of course, it is true in each case that the provision of such netural, nonideological aid, assisting only the secular functions of sectarian schools, served indirectly and incidentally to promote the religious function....But an indirect and incidental effect beneficial to religious institutions has never been thought a sufficient defect to warrant the invalidation of a state law.[19]

Note how nicely the test of "the principal or primary effect," meaning, quite obviously, the main effect, has been transmogrified into a test of "a primary effect," in the sense of a direct or immediate rather than an indirect or secondary effect. The two "tests" are, of course, quite different. On the other hand, the Court's latest decision on the point may have gone back to the original test, since it repeats the original formulation that a statute is valid "if its principal or primary effect neither advances nor inhibits religion." Several times the opinion of the Court refers to "the primary effect."[20] So even the decade-old Gibraltar of doctrine to which the Justice Department's opinion refers, turns out to be only seven years old, or less than a year old in its latest reincarnation, and surely more like a chameleon than a rock.

But the major omission in the Justice Department's appeal to the firm and unshakable principle of the three-part test is its failure to note that the test (except, perhaps, the first part of it) really doesn't say very much. What is "excessive entanglement"? And what is "the principal or primary effect" of legislation? Or, depending on which precedents the Court cares to follow, what is "a primary or a direct effect" of legislation? (A good proportion of all tort litigation is attributable to the utter indeterminateness of such a cause-effect standard.) The Supreme Court itself, with characteristic understatement, acknowledged in Tilton the limited utility of its "test":

There are always risks in treating criteria discussed by

the Court from time to time as "tests" in any limiting sense of that term. Constitutional adjudication does not lend itself to the absolutes of the physical sciences or mathematics. The standards should, rather, be viewed as guidelines with which to identify instances in which the objectives of the Religion Clauses have been impaired. And, as we have noted..., candor compels the acknowledgment that we can only dimly perceive the boundaries of permissible government activity in this sensitive area of constitutional adjudication.[21]

DISTINGUISHING FEATURES OF BEOG

How, then, is one confidently to predict the outcome of the next Supreme Court opinion in an area so characterized by chaos even as to the most fundamental principles and by constant and multi-directional change? The answer, I suggest, is that one quite obviously cannot confidently predict it, even when the facts of the case are foursquare with those of earlier decisions; and much less so when, as in the present case, there are significant differences of the sort that can be expected to alter the Justices' "feel" for the matter. Yet despite the fact that the Supreme Court has not invalidated federal legislation such as the BEOG legislation or the tuition tax credit proposal, the Justice Department opinions of 1978 and 1980, without even an expression of uncertainty, categorically assert the unconstitutionality of federal legislation then being considered by the Congress. Such a cavalier prediction of what the Court would do is simply too much to be believed. The significant factors I refer to that distinguish the BEOG proposal from any other aid to education program declared unconstitutional by the Court are twofold, and in combination they render the prediction of unconstitutionality a very risky bet.

Broadness of Coverage

The first significant difference between the BEOG proposal and statutes such as the one invalidated in Nyquist is that the former has a broad base. It does not benefit exclusively, or even primarily, students who attend church-related schools, much less the schools of a single denomination. More than 95 percent of all the BEOG funds, it is estimated, would be distributed to students attending colleges and universities, where church-related schools are a small minority--if, indeed, for constitutional purposes sectarian schools at the post secondary level need even be distinguished from public or private nonsectarian schools. I do not have precise figures regarding the number of church-school students versus the number of non-church-school students who would be benefited under BEOG, but it is clear that the latter will vastly predominate. By contrast, the situation noted by the Court in Lemon v. Kurtzman, was that 95 percent of the students benefited by the Rhode Island statute were in Catholic schools.[22]   In Nyquist, 85 percent of the schools attended by the students receiving tuition grants and tax benefits under the New York law were church-related, and "all or practically all" of the schools entitled to direct maintenance and repair grants were Catholic.[23]   In Sloan v. Lemon, at least 90 percent, and perhaps as many as 96 percent, of the students qualifying for the Pennsylvania "parent reimbursement" payments attended church-related schools, "most of these...affiliated with the Roman Catholic Church."[24]

It was not inadvertence or verbosity that prompted the Court to recite these statistics in those opinions. One of the bases the Court has used for distinguishing state laws granting tax exemption to church property, which are constitutional under the Walz case, from those state aid to education programs that it has declared invalid is the fact that the former are not restricted to a class composed exclusively or even predominantly of religious institutions but apply to all property devoted to religious, education, or charitable purposes.[25]   In Nyquist, by contrast, the Court said that the benefits "flow primarily to the parents of children attending sectarian non-public schools." The Court continued:

> Without intimating whether this factor alone might have
> controlling significance in another context in some future
> case, it should be apparent that in terms of the potential
> divisiveness of any legislative measure the narrowness of
> the benefited class would be an important factor.[26]

And the Court has used this same factor of broadness of benefited class to distinguish the invalidated programs from the state school busing and textbook loan programs that have been upheld. As Justice Powell wrote in Sloan:

> Our decision...is not dependent upon...speculation. Instead
> we look to the substance of the program, and no matter
> how it is characterized its effect remains the same. The
> State has singled out a class of its citizens for a special
> economic benefit....[A]t bottom its intended consequence
> is to preserve and support religion-oriented institutions.
> We think it plain that this is quite unlike the sort of
> "indirect" and "incidental" benefits that flowed to
> sectarian schools from programs aiding all parents by
> supplying bus transportation and secular textbooks for
> their children. Such benefits...provided no special aid for
> those who had chosen to support religious schools.[27]

This distinguishing factor of the broadness of the group benefited may be somewhat stronger with respect to the tuition tax credit legislation than it is with respect to the BEOG proposal, for in the former case the entire program of tuition tax credits for elementary and secondary school students as well as for college students would have been created by the same enactment, whereas the BEOG proposal would add elementary and secondary students (mostly in church-related schools) to an existing program currently limited to higher education. But it seems to me this should make no difference. The "broadness" or "narrowness" of benefit coverage for purposes of the Court's distinction should be determined by the total scope of a logically and conceptually unitary program, and not by the scope of one or another individual amendment to it. For the "broadness" or "narrowness" factor speaks to the presence or absence of preferential purpose and effect, and it can hardly be called preferential to add to an existing program a group that could logically have been included there in the first place. That is to say, far from being "preferential" to a class that is heavily weighted toward church-related schools, the BEOG proposal would merely eliminate a pre-existing discrimination against that class.

If I were to indulge the assumption, for purposes of this discussion, that the Court's opinions display some pattern of reason and consistency, then I would note that the foregoing analysis of the "broadness" and "narrowness" issue is endorsed by the Supreme Court. For example, the New York statute authorizing the loan of secular textbooks to children attending church-related schools was upheld in the Allen case because it was a broad-based statute that extended to private school students a program already available for public school students.[28] Similarly, the Pennsylvania textbook loan program upheld in Meek v. Pittenger did nothing but "extend to all schoolchildren the benefit of Pennsylvania's well established policy of lending textbooks free of charge to elementary and secondary school students."[29] Although it does not appear in the Everson opinion, the New Jersey school-busing program approved in that case likewise seems to have consisted of an extension to private-school students of a benefit that already existed for public-school students. That is certainly the case with respect to state school-busing measures enacted since Everson.

The attempt of the Justice Department's 1978 opinion to explain away this clearly distinguishing feature, explicitly enunciated in Supreme Court decisions, is unconvincing. Indeed, this piece of lawyer-like advocacy is so feeble as to prove nothing but the tendentiousness of the opinion itself. The Department's first argument is as follows: "The Supreme Court has repeatedly drawn a distinction between grants to sectarian colleges and universities and similar grants at the pre-college level." But of what possible relevance is that? Even disregarding the fact that the textbook and busing cases referred to above involved only pre-college students, the Department's argument makes no sense at the level of theory alone. If we did not know we were dealing with a "suspect class," so to speak, there would be no need to demonstrate that that class was sufficiently diluted in a broader group to begin with! That is to say, the "broadness of benefit" distinction enunciated by the Court assumes, and is surely not refuted by, the constitutionally more questionable status of the narrow group alone.

The Justice Department's opinion argues further that the effects of the proposed legislation will be different at the elementary/secondary and college levels, and that the legislators know that the two areas are different. I take it to be the point of these statements that the program in question does not qualify for the "broadness of benefited class" validation because it does not meet the requirement I suggested earlier, of being "logically or conceptually unitary." If that were clearly true, it would support the Department's out-of-hand dismissal of the "broadness of benefit" distinction. Undoubtedly, one could not invoke the distinction in support of a measure that adds parochial school aid (of a sort that public schools do not enjoy) to a broad-based highway funding program. But is the difference between aiding college tuition payments and aiding elementary and secondary school tuition payments really of that magnitude? Surely many federal regulatory requirements, and many federal assistance programs, apply to schools at all levels, and are not thought to be contrived by virtue of such coverage. The GI Bill, it may be noted, has long paid for both high school and college education. And the difference between colleges and elementary/secondary schools is certainly less than the difference between churches, on the one hand, and hospitals, museums and opera houses on the other; but in Walz the latter aggregation was held sufficient to support church tax exemptions on "broadness of benefit" grounds.

The Department of Justice opinion concludes triumphantly that "the court has stated clearly that to [display an unconstitutional] 'primary effect' a law need not result exclusively or even predominantly in religious benefits. Rather, a primary effect can exist even where there are any number of other appropriate and praiseworthy consequences of the legislation." That is an accurate quotation, but it is wrenched out of context. It pertains not to the inclusion in the legislation of secular beneficiaries who far outnumber the religious, but rather to "other effects" achieved through benefiting the narrow religious class. For example, secular educational effects might be achieved by direct grants limited to Catholic schools, but such a program by virtue of its discriminatory limitation would be invalid. In any case, the point here is not that broadness of coverage always assures constitutionality, but that it often may. It is therefore impossible to assert that prior Supreme Court decisions cover the tuition tax credit proposal or the BEOG proposal.

Federal Action

The second reason why this legislation presents a distinctive case is even more persuasive. No Supreme Court opinion disallowing a program of tuition assistance has involved a <u>federal</u> statute. In fact, only one minor feature of any federal aid to education program has ever been invalidated on Establishment Clause grounds, that being a feature under which the federal government would have paid for the construction of buildings that could ultimately be used for outright worship purposes.[30] For some reason that escapes me, the federal government's Department of Justice doesn't seem to appreciate the state-federal distinction. So a word or two is in order about "The Importance of Being Federal."

Realistically, the Court is much less inclined to slap Congress on the wrist than a state legislature. In the entire history of the Republic only about one hundred federal laws have been declared unconstitutional. There are reasons for this other than the mere self-protective instinct of the federal courts. As Justice Holmes put it many years ago:

> I do not think the United States would come to an end if we lost our power to declare an Act of Congress void. I do think the Union would be imperiled if we could not make that declaration as to the laws of the several States.[31]

In the area of the Establishment Clause in particular, a stricter vigilance over the states makes special sense. At that level of government, the mere fact that a single religious sect is often a majority or a substantial plurality of the population, may present a real danger that legislation will aid a particular religion under the guise of pursuing secular, or at least nondenominational, goals. It is no accident that the Supreme Court decisions striking down state tuition plans in states with large Catholic populations repeatedly make a special point of the high proportion of the benefited students who attend Catholic schools. But in the national legislature, by contrast, no single sect predominates, and the Court can more readily allow educational or freedom-of-choice considerations to be expressed in tuition grant legislation, without fearing that these policy choices are really subterfuges for an imposition by a particular sect upon their fellow citizens.

It is not unheard-of that a constitutional provision should have stricter application to the states than to the federal government. That is the case, for example, with the Equal Protection Clause, as it applies to disabilities imposed by government upon aliens. The federal government can impose such disabilities much more freely than the states, since it is more generally justified (by reason of its exclusive power over foreign affairs, immigration and naturalization) in taking the characteristic of alienage into account.[32]

A similar theoretical basis supports greater freedom for Congress than for the states in the area of educational policy. One of the justifications—perhaps the most important justification—behind legislation extending federal educational subsidies to children in private schools is the assertion that without some such subsidy, state support of exclusively public schools has the effect of impairing the freedom of religion of those who wish to attend, or wish their children to attend, different schools. The argument is that it wrongfully constrains freedom of religion to condition such a choice upon the relinquishment of a significant educational subsidy to which these people would otherwise be entitled—just as in the Sherbert case the Court ruled that the State of South Carolina had wrongfully constrained the Seventh Day Adventist's selection of Saturday as the day of rest by withholding unemployment compensation.

One may agree with this justification or disagree with it, but it unquestionably underlies much of the support for private school subsidies. And the point is that the Constitution gives Congress, not the states, special authority to pass legislation designed to remedy state-created impairment of freedom of religion. The Supreme Court has so held even where such impairment does not rise to the level of unconstitutionality. For the Fourteenth Amendment, which is the source of the application of the freedom of religion clauses to the states, provides that "The Congress shall have power to enforce, by appropriate legislation, the provisions of this article."[33] This power has been held to permit Congress to alter (within certain limits) the judicially defined line between the requirements of the equal protection clause on the one hand and the constitutional power of the states to fix voting qualifications on the other.[34] One may argue that this power should equally permit Congress to alter (within certain limits) the judicially defined balance between the competing values of nonestablishment and freedom of religion. Thus, as in the alienage cases, congressional action might go beyond what the state legislatures could do.

I do not necessarily endorse this last theory—mostly because I do not endorse the notion of a legislatively expandable Fourteenth Amendment that the Katzenbach and Mitchell cases establish. I would prefer to ground the preferential treatment of federal statutes in the educational policy field upon the deference generally to be accorded constitutional determinations of the national Congress—determinations, incidentally that need not be deemed to approve equivalent action by the states, unless the Congress explicitly says so.

CONGRESS'S ROLE IN CONSTITUTIONAL INTERPRETATION

Thus, two alternative theories exist, with solid foundation in the case law, for distinguishing the proposed federal tuition tax credit and the BEOG proposal from state programs previously held invalid. Even if, as we have assumed up to now, the only significant constitutional question were "Given its past holdings and dicta, would the present Supreme court declare these proposals to violate the First Amendment?," the answer would have to be: "Not necessarily." But in fact, that is not the right question at all. The parsing of cases and the nit-picking of aberrant dicta in each opinion that flows from the pen of the Court is all good clean fun, a profitable living for some of us, and a respectable enterprise for lawyers representing or advising parties. But the issue here is not whether some private individual may or may not take a particular action with impunity. It is whether Congress may and should pass a particular law. And Congress has its own responsibility of constitutional interpretation, quite independent from that of the Court, and flowing from the same high source, namely, its members' oath of office to support and defend the Constitution.

For the purpose of determining whether Congress should pass a law, it is not appropriate to hang upon every word that drops from the latest, shifting majority of Justices in a deeply divided Court unable to frame any consistent, principled basis of decision. Indeed, for Congress to perform its solemn constitutional obligation by running back and forth to the beat of that syncopated drum would be positively grotesque. This is not to say that in the performance of its independent responsibility to interpret the Constitution, Congress should ignore the Court. Of course, a long, principled line of consistent decisions has great weight, and should inform the judgment of the legislative branch. Even an eccentric, unprincipled five-to-four decision that is directly on point might be permitted to guide that judgment, if all of the five are still alive. But neither of those conditions exists here. Congress is not faced with a judicial precedent directly at odds with the BEOG proposal or the tuition tax credit proposal. And it most assuredly is not confronted with a long, principled line of consistent decisions on the subject.

The major role of Congress in interpreting the Constitution is not, I think, widely enough acknowledged. Even members of Congress themselves underestimate it. Their role is enormously important, more important ultimately than the role of the Court. The fact is that no theory of constitutional interpretation consistently pursued by Congress has ultimately failed, even when it has initially flown in the face of a coherent body of Supreme Court jurisprudence. Examples of this truth include the expansion of the commerce power, the effective disappearance of the doctrine of unlawful delegation of legislative authority, and, most recently, the death of the doctrine that laws must be "color-blind." Even greater should be the power and the responsibility of Congress when it is dealing with an area in which the Court itself has come as close as decorum will permit to acknowledging that it doesn't have the foggiest idea what it is doing and requires solid guidance.

The real constitutional question, then, is not whether one can predict that a particular bill will manage to attract a majority on the current Court, but rather, whether a legislative proposal accords with the constitutional traditions and beliefs of our people. Only when the false question of predicting the behavior of an erratic court in an unsettled area has been eliminated can the congressional

responsibility for constitutional interpretation be faithfully ful-
filled. My view of what that responsibility requires in the present
case can be stated in the form of a brief inquiry. What would be the
constitutional status of BEOG legislation that provided tuition
assistance only for students in non-religious elementary and secondary private schools? It would unquestionably be constitutional,
would it not? In order to oppose the Moynihan BEOG proposal on
constitutional grounds, then, one must believe that the First
Amendment, which was adopted out of a special solicitude for
religion, has the effect of not merely permitting but requiring a
special discrimination against religion. Only students who wish to
attend religious schools not only may but absolutely must be
excluded from a subsidy available to all others. That bizarre,
antireligious result is simply too much to derive, it seems to me,
from the mere prohibiton of an establishment.

Legislators who do not agree with that and want to be fair in
this matter must explain, I think, why federal tax exemptions
generally applicable to other charitable institutions must not be
withheld from places of worship. In truth, the present case is no
different. But at least these issues should be discussed in Congress
at a principled level. They should not be foreclosed by lawyerly
hair-splitting of selected hairs and brash judicial entrail-reading of
the sort represented by the Justice Department opinions.

NOTES

1. Committee for Public Education and Religious Liberty v.
Regan, 444 U.S. 646, 662 (1980).
2. Everson v. Board of Education, 330 U.S. 1 (1947).
3. Wolman v. Walter, 433 U.S. 229 (1977).
4. Board of Education v. Allen, 392 U.S. 236 (1968), and Meek
v. Pittenger, 421 U.S. 349 (1975).
5. Wolman, note 3 supra.
6. Walz v. Tax Commission, 397 U.S. 664 (1970).
7. Committee for Public Education and Religious Liberty v.
Nyquist, 413 U.S. 756 (1973).
8. Everson, note 2 supra, and Abington School District v.
Schempp, 374 U.S. 203 (1963).
9. Wisconsin v. Yoder, 406 U.S. 205 (1972).
10. Sherbert v. Verner, 374 U.S. 398 (1963).
11. "Congress shall make no law respecting an establishment of
religion, or restricting the free exercise thereof." U.S. Const.,
Amendment I.
12. See generally Richard E. Morgan, "The Establishment Clause
and Sectarian Schools: A Final Installment?" 1973 Supreme Ct.
Rev. 57, and Paul James Toscano, "A Dubious Neutrality: The
Establishment of Secularism in the Public Schools," 1979 Brigham
Young L. Rev. 177.

13. Everson, note 2 supra, 330 U.S. at 14-15.

14. Zorach v. Clauson, 343 U.S. 306, 313-14 (1952).

15. 403 U.S. 602, 612 (1971).

16. Ibid. at 612-613.

17. Ibid. at 613 (emphasis added).

18. Tilton v. Richardson, 403 U.S. 672, 679 (1971).

19. Nyquist, note 7 supra, 413 U.S. at 774-75 (emphasis added).

20. Regan, note 1 supra, 444 U.S. at 653, 658.

21. Tilton, note 18 supra, 403 U.S. at 678.

22. Lemon v. Kurtzman, 403 U.S. 602, 609 (1971).

23. Nyquist, note 7 supra, 413 U.S. at 768.

24. Sloan v. Lemon, 413 U.S. 825, 830 (1973).

25. Walz, note 6 supra, 397 U.S. at 673.

26. Nyquist, note 7 supra, 413 U.S. at 794.

27. Sloan, note 24 supra, 413 U.S. at 832 (emphasis in original).

28. Allen, note 4 supra, 392 U.S. at 243.

29. Meek, note 4 supra, 403 U.S. at 682-84.

30. Tilton, note 18 supra, 403 U.S. at 682-84.

31. Oliver Wendell Holmes, Jr., Collected Legal Papers 295 (1920).

32. Compare Mathews v. Diaz, 426 U.S. 67 (1976) with Nyquist v. Mauclet, 432 U.S. 1 (1977).

33. U.S. Const., Amendment XIV, Sec. 5.

34. See Katzenbach v. Morgan, 384 U.S. 641 (1966), and Oregon v. Mitchell, 400 U.S. 112 (1970).

15. The Case for the Consistency of the Court and the Inconsistency of the Justice Department

Nathan Z. Dershowitz

There is obviously a basic conflict between the positions that have been asserted by the Office of Legal Counsel of the Department of Justice during the Carter administration and the positions asserted by someone who formerly served as Assistant Attorney General for the Office of Legal Counsel in the Ford administration. I find myself in disagreement with at least half of what Mr. Hammond has said, and I think in total disagreement with what Mr. Scalia has said. I find it a little bit difficult to respond to everything that has been said in the brief space of this comment, but I would like to highlight three points.

My first point relates to the tension in the Justice Department's positions concerning pending legislation and current litigation. I think that the essay of Mr. Hammond makes clear that when the Justice Department comments on pending bills, it makes a relatively accurate assessment of constitutional requirements. When it finds a case directly on point and it cannot draw any logical distinction between that case and the proposed legislation, it offers the advice that the bill would be found unconstitutional. For example, if it finds Nyquist directly on point, it will recommend (or at least conclude) that tuition tax credit bills are unconstitutional because of a dispositive Supreme Court decision. It also did that with respect to the so-called "baby BEOG" proposal. But when the Justice Department is called upon to defend in court legislation that has been enacted, for example, Title I of the 1965 Elementary and Secondary Education Act, it suddenly takes less principled positions.

For example, in discussing the distinctions to be made with respect to tax credits, Mr. Hammond stated that he really saw no distinction between the constitutional argument applicable to state legislation and the one applicable to federal legislation. Since the Justice Department has apparently reached the conclusion that the constitutional restraints on both federal and state provisions are the same, I wish the Department would apply it to the Title I cases, such as PEARL v. Hufstedler. Since the Supreme Court has held state statutes modeled on Title I to be unconstitutional, it is difficult to see why the federal provision should not also be unconstitutional. But, apparently, the Justice Department sees some distinction between state and federal when it comes to Title I, but not when it comes to tax credits.

The same thing happens to be true, I think, if one looks at the CETA legislation and the Decker case. I think that if the Justice

Department had done an evaluation of CETA as a bill, as opposed to being called upon to justify the statute in the <u>Decker</u> case, it would have reached a different conclusion. So there is a tension in the Justice Department's positions that requires some sort of an explanation.

My second point is a comment on the whole concept of the inconsistency of the Supreme Court that has been presented by Mr. Scalia. I think he is being extremely unfair to the United States Supreme Court. If one reviewed that Court's determinations over the last ten years in virtually any area other than the religion clauses of the First Amendment and tried to find a consistent pattern, I think one would be shocked as to the number of cases where decisions by the present Court are fundamentally inconsistent with what one thought was the law only a few years ago. One example of this phenomenon would be the libel area. There have been flip-flops on the prevailing view as to the appropriateness of summary judgment, and flip-flops in the substantive law of libel and privacy. And the same phenomenon occurs in other areas of the law as well. For example, who could have predicted the result in the Supreme Court's ruling in the <u>Prune Yard Shopping Center</u> case by examining the history of the prior shopping center cases?

By comparison with these areas in which the Court has run a zig-zag pattern, I think that objective and fair commentators would find a great deal more consistency in the Church-State cases than Mr. Scalia is prepared to acknowledge. In fact, I think there is a prevailing pattern in this area of the Court's determinations.

There is another point that needs to be made in this area. Every time the Supreme Court came down with a determination that a statute or program was unconstitutional, the state legislatures went back over the Supreme Court's decision with a fine tooth comb and sought to find a loophole, a method of getting around it. So it is inevitable that, in an area fraught with delicate questions requiring the balancing of competing values, it will be very difficult for the Court to be fundamentally consistent, especially when state legislatures are continually trying to get around the Court's decisions.

If one steps back and looks at the broader picture of the work of the Supreme Court as a whole, one will conclude that, in general, it is relatively easy, compared to other areas, to predict which way the Supreme Court is going to go on church-state cases. Of course, there will be tough questions, some very carefully drawn distinctions, and some problem areas. But I think that it is really unfair to sit and to pick at every single word within those decisions in order to demonstrate inconsistencies, without recognizing a greater inconsistency in other areas of the Court's work.

My third point concerns the regulatory burden that typically accompanies federal financial assistance. To a very large extent, most of the presentations in this volume are directed at the problem of how to get federal money to nonpublic schools. There is hardly any mention as to what would happen to the independence of the nonpublic schools if they were to receive federal funds.

What I'm talking about is this: when the federal government dispenses funds in any form, it does not grant total freedom to the receiving institutions to use the funds as it sees fit. There are responsibilities and restrictions on how one uses that money. There are limitations on what kind of judgments an institution can make when it receives funds. I am referring specifically to issues such as whether an institution can discriminate on the basis of race or religion, and whether it has responsibilities under the National Labor Relations Act and other labor legislation and a whole range of other federal regulatory activities.

No serious discussion of the question of federal aid for nonpublic schools would be complete without paying attention to what would happen if federal monies were made available to church-related schools. What would happen to the composition and character of nonpublic schools when the federal government, by necessity, starts creating and enforcing rules and regulations which today apply only to the public schools? Will nonpublic schools retain the basic composition that they now have? Will their quality remain the same? Will their independence remain the same? Or are we engaged in a desperate search for dollars which would ultimately lead to the destruction of these important institutions?

I personally do not believe that receipt of federal money will be the panacea that some supporters of such aid for church schools think it will be. There is a lot of money that is presently available for the public schools, and the public schools are having serious problems with respect to some of the federal regulations that come with the federal aid. To take some of those problems and add them to the burdens of the private schools would create fundamental problems, not just for the administrators of these schools, but for the very nature of private education in this country.

16. The Facts Matter: The Case for Accurate Records in Constitutional Adjudication

Charles H. Wilson

I am afraid I find myself in the uncomfortable position of agreeing somewhat with Mr. Dershowitz despite the fact that we are on opposite sides of the Title I litigation. I must say that I too agree with some of the things that come out of the Office of Legal Counsel and disagree with other positions that Office takes. In fairness to Mr. Hammond and his Office, however, I should add that the suggestion made by Mr. Dershowitz that his Office has acted inconsistently with regard to tax credits, on the one hand, and Title I, on the other hand, is not well taken. I think Mr. Dershowitz's complaint concerned the position that the Justice Department took when the PEARL litigation was filed back in 1976, a year after Meek v. Pittenger was decided. The position of Mr. Dershowitz's organization was that Meek necessarily established a per se rule invalidating Title I. The Justice Department did not accept that view and proceeded to defend the constitutional challenge to Title I brought by Mr. Dershowitz's organization. We now have a unanimous decision of a three-judge court agreeing with the position taken by the Department of Justice. According to the District Court in PEARL v. Harris, Meek did not establish a per se rule invalidating Title I, and the programs funded under Title I, at least as implemented in New York City, have been found constitutional.*

---

*Editor's Note: This Title I action was commenced in 1966, a year-and-a-half after Congress enacted the ESEA. The District Court dismissed the action for lack of standing by the taxpayer plaintiffs. Flast v. Gardner, 271 F. Supp. 1 (S.D.N.Y. 1967). The Supreme Court reversed this judgment in Flast v. Cohen, 392 U.S. 83 (1968). The case was remanded to the District Court, but the matter was not pursued any further by the plaintiffs until February of 1976, when they recommenced litigation in the wake of Meek v. Pittinger, 421 U.S. 349 (1975). The plaintiffs then moved for a preliminary injunction to terminate provision of Title I funds to localities to finance educational services in religious schools during school hours. On March 3, 1978, the District Court denied this motion because a preliminary injunction would work an unwarranted hardship on the defendants and would harm the public interest in the continuity of educational programs, and because the long interval between the initial filing of the complaint in 1966 and the renewal of litigation in 1976 suggested to the court that the plaintiffs had not

I disagree, however, with Mr. Hammond's statement that the decisions of the Supreme Court are not chaotic or confusing. They are confusing. "Chaotic" may be too strong a term, but they are confusing. And when I use the word "confusing," I use it not in the sense that a lawyer cannot understand what the Court is trying to say, but confusing because the Court seems to be addressing in its decisions concerns that are not really part of the world that we are concerned with. When I use the word "we," I am talking about myself as an attorney and others who have been litigating these issues for many years.

If, however, the Court seems not to be dealing with the real concerns of this issue of aid for parochial schools, or nonpublic schools, I think it is largely the fault of the lawyers who are responsible for the litigation. Many of us think it is unfortunate that the Supreme Court has such a strong and powerful voice on this issue. After all, the major concern of this symposium is with policy questions, not legal questions. Unfortunately, the Supreme Court has the final word on these issues because it is the final arbiter of the constitutionality of legislation. It gets that final word by the very process of litigation. And I feel that the reason why the Court's decisions are confusing and inconsistent, and give little guidance, and have the lack of predictability that Justice White referred to in the PEARL v. Regan decision,* is that the lawyers who litigate the cases really are not meeting their obligations. They are not meeting their obligations because they do not present the Court, the final arbiter of this issue, with an adequate factual record

---

made a clear showing of the threat of "irreparable harm" fundamental to the granting of a preliminary injunction. National Coalition for Public Education and Religious Liberty v. Califano, 446 F. Supp. 193, 195 (S.D.N.Y. 1978). The plaintiffs also moved for summary judgment, but the court denied this motion on the ground that there were significant factual disputes between the parties concerning the use and administration of the Title I funds and concerning the details of the challenged programs. Ibid. 446 F. Supp. at 196. After a full trial on these disputed issues, the three-judge court ruled on April 19, 1980, that neither the ESEA nor the New York City program violated the Establishment Clause of the First Amendment. National Coalition for Public Education and Religious Liberty v. Harris, 489 F. Supp. 1248 (S.D.N.Y. 1980). Apparently because of a failure of the plaintiff-appellants to file their notice of appeal in timely fashion, on October 6, 1980, the Supreme Court dismissed the appeal for want of jurisdiction. National Coalition for Public Education and Religious Liberty v. Hufstedler, 449 U.S. __, 101 S. Ct. 55, rehearing denied, 449 U.S. __, 101 S. Ct. 601 (1980).

*Editor's Note: 444 U.S. 646, 662 (1980).

upon which it can assess the validity of the legislation it is asked to pass upon.

For example, in the case of Meek v. Pittenger, the Court struck down a Pennsylvania program. This program was not exactly modeled after Title I, but had some similarities with Title I. Under Title I the federal government gives funds to local school boards to hire its own teachers and send them to the parochial schools to provide supplemental remedial educational services. The critical issue in the Meek case was whether the presence of these publicly employed and publicly paid teachers on the premises of sectarian schools had the potential for entanglement between government and religion. As the District Court in PEARL v. Harris said, the record in Meek was totally unilluminating on this point. In fact, it had nothing in it concerning what these public school teachers did on the premises of these parochial schools and had nothing to say about how these teachers were supervised. Yet if one reads the Meek decision carefully, and the basis for the entanglement ruling, one will find that the Supreme Court simply assumed that these publicly employed teachers would be subject to pressures from the parochial school authorities, that they would be doing such things as teaching religion in their remedial reading and even their remedial math instruction.

By contrast the District Court in PEARL addressed that very question. And the basis for its decision, as distinct from Meek, was that the record before the court told the court how the program had operated for 14 years. On the basis of that record the court found that there was not a single instance of any pressure being exerted on public school teachers in the nonpublic schools to teach one way or another and that there were no conflicts between those public school teachers and nonpublic school authority.

I offer this illustration simply to make the point that the Supreme Court will come up with what I hope is a coherent and acceptable Establishment Clause theory only if the lawyers who litigate the cases and who present these issues to the Court for a final decision do their job of presenting a factual record that illuminates the issues and gives the Court a rational basis for decision.

17. The Confusion of Political Choices and Constitutional Requirements: The Perspective of a Legal Historian

Walter Berns

I would like to begin by emphasizing something that Professor Scalia suggested in his essay. The plain fact of the matter is that in Wisconsin v. Yoder, the Amish case, the Supreme Court got itself in a position where the Amish are now an established religion of the United States. If this reading of Yoder is correct, then the Amish would be immune from certain kinds of court orders. And I imagine, for example, that logically they would be exempt from supervision under the Civil Rights Act of 1964. This led me a few years ago, in an article in Harper's entitled "The Importance of Being Amish," to compose the following verse:

> Said counsel for schools suburbanish,
> "Sure, we admit that we're clannish.
> But there's no use your fussing
> for court-ordered busing,
> 'cause there's no one out here but us Amish."

I begin in a lighter vein because the rest of my comments are largely irrelevant to the discussion of constitutional considerations relating to nonpublic schools. My focus has to do with the original intent of the First Amendment, and all of us who follow the Supreme Court know that there is nothing so irrelevant to the Court's work as the original intent of a particular clause of the Constitution.

Doubts concerning the constitutionality of public programs to aid church-related schools derive from the opinion that the First Amendment requires the Congress (and the states) to be neutral between religion and irreligion. This is erroneous. The source of the error is to be found in the 1947 case, Everson v. Board of Education, involving a New Jersey statute authorizing school districts to reimburse parents for bus fares paid by their children traveling to and from schools. The Supreme Court said that the Establishment Clause of the First Amendment meant that neither Congress nor a State legislature may "pass laws which aid one religion, aid all religions, or prefer one religion over another." Nor may any tax "in any amount, large or small...be levied to support any religious activities or institutions, whatever they may be called, or whatever form they may adopt to teach or practice religion."[1] Although the Court has seen fit to ignore this principle on occasion,[2] the Everson principle of neutrality between religion and irreligion is cited time and again, and its validity is acknowledged in principle by most members of the Court. But, to repeat, it is erroneous; it does not accurately state the intent of the First Amendment.

As I pointed out in the First Amendment and the Future of American Democracy, in his opinion for the Court in Everson, Justice Black simply relied on Jefferson's metaphorical wall between church and state, which made its first appearance in an 1802 letter to the Danbury Baptists, and on Madison's "Memorial and Remonstrance," written during one stage of the Virginia disestablishment struggle. He did not even refer to the debates in the First Congress in 1789 when the Congress formally proposed the Bill of Rights, including the First Amendment. In his separate opinion in Everson, Justice Rutledge referred to the debates, but rendered a disservice to the Constitution and the country by accepting as historically accurate the account of the debates presented in briefs filed by the appellee and an amicus curiae, the American Civil Liberties Union.[3] Unfortunately, to put this in an extravagant fashion, there is no law that requires lawyers to tell the truth in the briefs they file. Or, to speak more moderately, lawyers are primarily concerned with winning the case for their client, and they understand that this can sometimes be done best by omitting some things and emphasizing other things.[4] For this reason one learns American history from legal briefs at one's peril, and we now have an official version of the First Amendment debates in the United States Reports that is not a very accurate picture of those debates. It was in this way that Everson gave birth to the legend that the First Amendment embodies in all respects the views on church and state expressed in other contexts by Jefferson and Madison.

Thus, Black found that it was the "feelings" of the Virginians which "found expression in the First Amendment," and that the First Amendment "had the same objective and was intended to provide the same protection against governmental intrusion on religious liberty as the Virginia statute." And Rutledge, who dissented because he thought the busing scheme unconstitutional, said the purpose of the Amendment "was to create a complete and permanent separation of the spheres of religious activity and civil authority by comprehensively forbidding every form of public aid or support for religion." The Virginia experience and Madison's "Memorial and Remonstrance" provided "irrefutable confirmation of the Amendment's sweeping content." In this fashion, then, in the Court's first and decisive case on aid to education, the Virginians became not merely the principal but the sole authors of the religious provisions of the First Amendment.

As the late Mark DeWolfe Howe of the Harvard Law School stated, in Everson the Justices made "the historically quite misleading assumption that the same considerations which moved Jefferson and Madison to favor separation of church and state in Virginia led the nation to demand the religious clauses of the First Amendment."[5] This, he wrote, was a "gravely distorted picture."

It was distorted because it was a partial picture. The men of
the First Congress surely wanted a separation of church and state,
but as Professor Howe showed, not all of them wanted it for
Madison's reasons. What is more, as I have shown in my volume, not
all of them wanted a complete separation. Of the Americans of his
time Madison was, with the exception of Tom Paine, the most
radical on the church-state issue. Most recognized that the
churches performed a public, or secular, service, and they favored
public support of these private institutions to enable them to
perform that public or secular service.

Some members of the First Congress wanted to avoid a
formulation of the Amendment that would forbid state laws
requiring contributions in support of ministers of religion and places
of worship. Stated otherwise, they favored public support of
ministers and places of worship. Other members sought to avoid any
formulation that might "patronize those who professed no religion at
all." Still others wanted merely to forbid laws "establishing one
religious sect or society in preference to others." What is
instructive in this context is that, collectively, the number of people
who were of this general opinion was sufficient to defeat Madison's
efforts, and Madison was forced to modify his views in order to get
an agreement on the form of the Amendment. For example, the
House debate began on the Select Committee's version of the
Amendment, which read as follows: "No religion shall be established
by law, nor shall the equal rights of conscience be infringed." The
debate was opened by Peter Sylvester of New York, who objected to
this formulation because "it might be thought to have a tendency to
abolish religion altogether." So to construe the clause seems
unnecessarily apprehensive--unless Sylvester had reason to believe
that to forbid the establishment of religion by law would be to
forbid all governmental assistance to religion, and that without this
assistance religion would languish and eventually die. What is of
interest is Madison's reply: "Mr. Madison said, he apprehended the
meaning of the words to be, that Congress should not establish a
religion, and enforce the legal observation of it by law, nor compel
men to worship God in any manner contrary to their conscience."[6]

It is on the basis of this record, rather than on the distorted
version of the record that appears in the modern Supreme Court
reports, that Joseph Story, in his great Commentaries on the
Constitution, insisted that the First Amendment was not intended to
require government to be neutral between religion and irreligion.
"An attempt to level all religions, and to make it a matter of state
policy to hold all in utter indifference, would have created universal
disapprobation, if not universal indignation."[7] Story exaggerated
if he meant to attribute this opinion to everyone, but the substance
of what he said is accurate.

The late Edward S. Corwin, one of the most respected of our
constitutional scholars, put it this way: "The historical record shows
beyond peradventure that the core idea of 'an establishment of

religion' comprises the idea of <u>preference</u>; and that any act of public authority favorable to religion in general cannot, without manifest falsification of history, be brought under the ban of that phrase."[8] Properly applied, the First Amendment forbids a national church and any preference in the aid of or recognition extended to religion. Applied to the states by way of the Fourteenth Amendment, it forbids state churches and state preferences and, therefore, sectarian state schools. Whatever else it may forbid, there is nothing in the principle of the Amendment or in the reasons for the adoption of the Amendment to forbid indirect aid that has the effect of supporting religion without raising it above the subordinate position to which the principle of separation of church and state consigns it. Understood as the First Congress understood it and as the great commentators of the past understood it, there is surely nothing in the First Amendment to forbid aid, direct or indirect, by nation or state, to nonpublic schools, including church-related schools. Whether that aid should be extended is not a constitutional question. It is a political question, and should be treated by the Congress as simply a political question.

With the First Amendment, the Founders intended to subordinate religion by consigning it to the private sphere or by relegating it to the care of private institutions; but there was a widespread recognition that these private institutions deserved public support precisely because, insofar as they provided moral education, they performed a public service. Washington made this point in his Farewell Address:

Of all the dispositions and habits which lead to political prosperity, religion and morality are indispensable supports. In vain would that man claim the tribute of patriotism who should labor to subvert these great pillars of human happiness, these firmest props of the duties of men and citizens....And let us with caution indulge the supposition that morality can be maintained without religion. Whatever may be conceded to the influence of refined education on minds of peculiar structure, reason and experience both forbid us to expect that national morality can prevail in exclusion of religious principle.

I would contend that an honest reading of the general condition of the country today would lead any fair-minded person to appreciate the importance--the <u>secular</u> importance, or what Washington would have called the political importance--of the moral education provided by church-related schools. As I put it in my recent book on the First Amendment:

No doubt there would be a problem if these schools, after the fashion of the Communist Party, taught the necessity of overthrowing constitutional government in the United

States, or, after the fashion of the Ku Klux Klan, bred hatred of Jews and Negroes. And no doubt there would be a problem if they were administered by churches that did not accept the constitutional principle of religious tolerance and all that this implies. But, assuming, as the evidence suggests we must, that nothing comparable to any of these lessons is taught in them today, the question should be asked whether it is good or bad for children to attend schools where, among other lessons, they are taught that it is right to honor their fathers and mothers and wrong to kill, commit adultery, steal, bear false witness, or covet their neighbors' possessions.[9]

In short, there are sound political reasons to support these private institutions; and, as I have indicated, there is no constitutional barrier to supporting them with tax credits or with basic grants to the children of low-income parents. In my opinion, there are also compelling political reasons for extending the same support to the private and secular colleges and universities. Their financial need is evident, and they, too, perform a public service. They do so by directly educating hundreds of thousands of young Americans, including a disproportionate number of those who go on to teach in the public institutions, and they have traditionally served these institutions by providing models of higher education. In conclusion, I would emphasize that the question whether church-related schools should be publicly supported in one way or another is a political question, not a constitutional question.

NOTES

1. Everson v. Board of Education, 330 U.S. 1, 15, 16 (1947) (Emphasis supplied).
2. In 1970, for example, the Court upheld tax exemptions granted to church properties, even properties used for worshipping purposes. Walz v. Tax Commission, 397 U.S. 664 (1970). The following year it upheld the Higher Education Facilites Act, according to which federal "brick and mortar" grants are made to church-related colleges, among others. Tilton v. Richardson, 403 U.S. 603 (1971). In 1976, a bare majority of the Court permitted Maryland to provide noncategorical grants to private colleges--"subject only to the restrictions that the funds not be used for 'sectarian purposes.'" Roemer v. Board of Public Works, 426 U.S. 736 (1976).
3. Walter Berns, The First Amendment and the Future of American Democracy (New York: Basic Books, 1976), pp. 58, 72.
4. This statement, incidentally, can be generalized, and is very germane to the whole question of an activist judiciary, for it raises a serious question concerning the adequacy of the representation

that occurs in the judicial process. See, e.g., Donald L. Horowitz, The Courts and Social Policy (Washington, D.C.: The Brookings Institution, 1976).

5. Mark DeWolfe Howe, The Garden and the Wilderness: Religion and Government in American Constitutional History (Chicago: The University of Chicago Press, 1967), p. 172.

6. "Annals of Congress," vol. 1, p. 758 (Aug. 15, 1789). See Berns, op. cit., ch. 1.

7. Joseph Story, Commentaries on the Constitution, vol. 3, sec. 1874.

8. Edward S. Corwin, A Constitution of Powers in a Secular State (Charlottesville, Va.: Michie Co., 1951), p. 116.

9. Berns, op. cit., p. 73. I say this as someone in no way involved with the church by which most of them are supported.

Discussion

SISTER RENEE OLIVER, CITIZENS FOR EDUCATIONAL FREE-
DOM (CLEVELAND, OHIO, CHAPTER): I would like to respond to
Mr. Dershowitz's query concerning what might happen to the nature
of the private school when they get federal aid. I think that the
types of aid that we are asking for and that have been the focus of
the discussion in this symposium (tuition tax credits and educational
vouchers) would have a minimum of federal control in them, and
that is one of the chief reasons why we are interested in those kinds
of assistance. It should also be noted that no particular method of
providing financial support has been wholeheartedly endorsed as yet,
because, I think, we all fear federal entanglement and restrictions
that might be placed on us. We are still leery; we are still
questioning; we still wonder in the long run how is it really going to
be implemented. Finally, I am concerned for the future of private
education because as an American I am first of all concerned about
the future of all of our freedoms, and I think that they are very
closely tied up with freedom of education.

LEE BOOTHBY, GENERAL COUNSEL, AMERICANS UNITED FOR
THE SEPARATION OF CHURCH AND STATE: My question was
brought to mind by Mr. Wilson's comment with reference to litigating the question of aid to private education from the standpoint
of presenting a record. I wonder is whether there will be a trend
and a movement towards making the private schools, the church-
related schools, less sectarian. For instance, in college aid cases,
the Supreme Court has suggested that there is no profile
establishing that church-related colleges are basically sectarian; but
the Supreme Court, in essence, has said that church-related elementary and secondary schools are pervasively sectarian. There
seems to be a trend or a desire in establishing records to demonstrate that elementary and secondary schools operated by churches
are not pervasively sectarian. My question is whether, in order to
establish this point, church-related schools will begin to diminish the
sectarian atmosphere that the Court believes to exist in these
classrooms.

PROFESSOR SCALIA: I think it surely will be a trend. And that is
basically why I disagree with the notion that the way to make progress in this field is to build better factual records—essentially
factual records showing that sectarian schools aren't sectarian

schools. That is a way to bring the war to an end by surrendering. The point is that sectarian schools should be able to remain sectarian with respect to the elements of religion that they teach in the schools without forgoing an educational subsidy for the elements of routine education which are imparted in the course of their programs. That principle cannot be established if one goes about trying to make factual cases showing that Catholic schools or Lutheran schools or Baptist schools are no different from the public schools. That is no way to solve the problem.

MR. WILSON: I believe that Mr. Boothby made reference to the profile of the sectarian schools that the Supreme Court has used in its elementary and secondary school cases. That profile is a perfect example of the question I was addressing. The profile is constructed from the allegations made in the complaint in the case of Levitt v. PEARL.* It was not based on any factual record that the schools in fact had the characteristics that the Court attributed to them. It was simply assumed to be true because the plaintiffs had alleged it to be true in their complaint. One of the elements of that profile--and I will just isolate one element to illustrate my point--is that a "pervasively sectarian" school (the type the Court believes nonpublic, church-affiliated schools are) restricts enrollment or admission on religious grounds. Mr. Boothby and I are involved on opposing sides in Title I litigation currently pending in Missouri. I can present statistics in that case to show that 55 percent of the stu-

---

*Editor's Note: The District Court in PEARL v. Levitt suggested that religiously affiliated schools in New York at that time displayed the following characteristics: They "(a) impose religious restrictions on admissions; (b) require attendance of pupils at religious activities; (c) require obedience by students to the doctrines and dogmas of a particular faith; (d) require pupils to attend instruction in the theology or doctrine of a particular faith; (e) are an integral part of the religious mission of the church sponsoring it; (f) have as a substantial purpose the inculcation of religious values; (g) impose religious restrictions on faculty appointments; and (h) impose religious restrictions on what or how the faculty may teach." 342 F. Supp. 439, 440-41 (S.D.N.Y. 1972). Despite the evidence in the record that the three intervening Catholic high schools "do not impose religious restrictions on admissions or require attendance of pupils at religious activities or obedience by students to the doctrine of a particular faith; that the schools contribute to the religious mission of the sponsoring church, but they do not impose religious restrictions on faculty appointments and they place restrictions on teaching only to the extent that it not be contrary to the tenets of the sponsoring church," Ibid. at 441, note 2, the Supreme Court adopted the profile cited above. Levitt v. PEARL, 413 U.S. 472, 476 (1973).

dents enrolled in the schools that have Title I programs on their premises in the city of St. Louis are not Catholic. That happens to be a fact. That is not an effort by the school to qualify for Title I. That happens to be the fact of inner-city Catholic schools. To the extent that fact is inconsistent with the profile, I believe that the court's decision is misguided in relying on the profile. And those facts should be called to the attention of the court.

MR. DERSHOWITZ: I'd like to make two comments. First, with respect to Mr. Wilson's suggestion about a record, there is a real problem when, as in the New York City situation, a record is set up by one side. I have very serious doubts as to whether such a "record" accurately reflects reality. For example, I find it hard to believe that church-related schools do not, in fact, restrict on the basis of religion.

My second comment deals with the concern that was raised by Sister Renee Oliver. In 1979 efforts were being made by the Internal Revenue Service to take away the tax-exempt status of private schools if they were in public school districts where there was an outstanding order for school desegregation. The concern of the IRS was with "white flight" schools, primarily in jurisdictions which, before Brown, enforced de jure segregation. But the effect of the proposed regulations was such that all of the Hebrew day schools and all of the yeshivas would have been within the scope of the regulations. This was so because most newly developing Hebrew day schools are expanding in areas where there are court orders of desegregation. The effects of the proposed IRS regulation would have been that these schools would have had to create affirmative action programs, not only to recruit minorities, but also to modify the instructional programs themselves. A yeshiva, for example, would have had to develop a black culture program in order to entice blacks. That may not have been the intent of the proposed regulation, but that was the way the regulation was drafted.

The American Jewish Congress was in a position to say, both to the Internal Revenue Service and to Congress, that the Hebrew day schools and the yeshivas do take in people on the basis of religion, do want to create a particularistic cultural and religious environment, are very proud of this environment, and are in a position to encourage this kind of a program. We could, in effect, say: "Congress and Internal Revenue Service, don't butt into our affairs." We were able to say that because there was no federal money flowing to the day schools and yeshivas.

The only way the private schools will have full control over their programs is if they do not take government largesse. I think that we're being a little bit unrealistic if we assume that we can take federal money, and still tell the government not to butt in. It's only if you don't take federal money that you can tell them, "We want to run our own programs," and "Keep federal hands off." The creeping bureaucracy is affecting everything. The only things that it is not affecting are those programs where there is no federal money involved.

RICHARD DUFFY, UNITED STATES CATHOLIC CONFERENCE: Mr. Wilson mentioned that the Court is the final arbiter of the constitutionality of any piece of legislation. And Professor Scalia mentioned that in the history of our Republic very few federal statutes have been declared unconstitutional. We have a system of government where we have a legislative department, an executive department, and a judiciary, each with a distinct responsibility, the legislature to legislate, the executive to administer, and finally the judiciary to make legal decisions. If a member of Congress introduces a piece of legislation, I do not understand why the Justice department comes in to make a constitutional determination on that piece of legislation. To say that the legislation is unconstitutional, in my view, impedes the legislative process. When the Justice Department declares legislation unconstitutional, that legislation does not proceed ahead, it is not enacted, and the Court is not given the opportunity to reach its decision on the matter. Isn't the Justice Department usurping the authority of Congress and the courts?

MR. HAMMOND: I think the answer has to be a resounding no. I do not believe that the President and the Attorney General and other Cabinet officers are impeding the proper functions of Congress or of the courts. And I do not believe that the President and the Attorney General are impeding the way our government was intended to operate. Justice Black used to have the habit of carrying around a copy of the constitution with him wherever he went, and it's a habit I ought to pick up myself. The Second Article of the Constitution says, among other things, that the President is to take care that the laws be faithfully executed. It also says that he may, if he wishes, require the opinion of any department head on any question. That is what the Office of Legal Counsel in the Department of Justice is there for. When the President wants to know whether a piece of proposed legislation is constitutional, he is expected under the Constitution to ask for the advice of his Cabinet and he is constitutionally entitled to an answer.* When he asks, the Attorney General has to give the President his best view of the law. The same thing is true of other Cabinet officers. They are often called to testify about proposed legislation that may be of importance to their department. And one of the questions that they are frequently asked is, "Do you think that this piece of legislation comports with

---

*Editor's Note: Article II, Section 2 of the United States Constitution provides: "The President...may require the Opinion, in writing, of the principal Officer in each of the Executive Departments, upon any subject relating to the Duties of their respective Offices...."

the Constitution?" Many Cabinet officers are not lawyers. A lot of them would like to have an opinion from someone who is independent and removed from the program. And those kinds of questions come to us, as they did with both the tuition tax credit and the proposed changes in the BEOG program. So when Joe Califano calls the Attorney General and says that he would like to have an independent view of whether a bill is constitutional, the Attorney General has no choice but to render his opinion. That is exactly what happened in this case, and that is what happens virtually every day that Congress is in session.

PROFESSOR BERNS: The first set of state papers of the United States were written by two famous men, Alexander Hamilton and Thomas Jefferson, in response to President Washington's query with respect to the constitutionality of the Bank of the United States. So the Office of Legal Counsel is in a long and exalted tradition when it performs that kind of service.

PROFESSOR SCALIA: I would like to add two things. First, one has to bear in mind that the President is a part of the legislative process. He, in effect, has a vote on the legislation when it is presented to him for his approval or veto. So he is entitled to get the opinion of his lawyer for that purpose, if none other. I do not think that there is any question about that.

Second, it seems to me that Mr. Dershowitz doesn't give enough weight to the distinction between a Justice Department opinion concerning proposed legislation and a Justice Department position taken in the course of litigation. I criticized the opinions concerning the tax credit proposal and the BEOG proposal as tendentious, because I do not think opinions about legislative proposals are supposed to be tendentious. But the position the Department takes in litigation is different. There the Department is operating as an advocate to uphold the constitutionality of legislation which Congress, after making its judgment that the legislation is constitutional, has passed. The Justice Department will, and should, argue vigorously in support of such legislation. (The one situation in which it does not do so is when it believes the legislation is unconstitutional as an infringement upon presidential powers; in that circumstance the Department feels it has a greater obligation to the Executive Branch.) So there is, it seems to me, no valid reason to criticize the Department for taking a somewhat different position in advisory opinions than it takes in litigation. Such differences should be expected and are, indeed, admirable.

EDD DOERR, EDITOR, CHURCH AND STATE MAGAZINE, AMERICANS UNITED FOR THE SEPARATION OF CHURCH AND STATE: First, in response to Mr. Wilson, I would like to say that the Supreme Court's profile of nonpublic schools is not based on mere allegations, but on actual evidence presented to the court in

Earley v. Di Censo,* a 1971 case in which the Supreme Court invalidated a Rhode Island program of supplementing the salaries of teachers offering courses in secular subjects in church-related elementary and secondary schools.

Another case that has not been mentioned is Norwood v. Harrison,[+] a 1973 decision in which the Supreme Court unanimously invalidated a program of lending textbooks to students in Protestant schools in Mississippi. The Court in that case said that lending the books to the students was a tangible form of aid to the institutions and that the state could not aid institutions which practice racial or other invidious discrimination. There was proof in the case that of the 40,000 students in Protestant private schools in Mississippi there was not a single black child. This is a state that's 50 percent black.

I would also like to correct the one-sided discussion of the skimming question that occurred earlier in the discussion. Every nonpublic high school in the Washington metropolitan area skims. By their own admission, they are all college preparatory schools. That means that they skim off the cream and they leave the rest for the public schools. Dr. James Michael Lee of the Department of Education at the University of Notre Dame wrote a book about a dozen years ago on Catholic schools,* in which he said that approximately half of all Catholic secondary schools skim; they select the cream of the crop. He also said that an unknown percentage of elementary Catholic schools do the same. I suppose that this would apply also to other denominational schools.

Another point that has not been dealt with adequately is the fact that none of the proposals under discussion (the Packwood-Moy-

---

*Editor's Note: Earley was a companion case to Lemon v. Kurtzman, 403 U.S. 602 (1971). In Lemon Chief Justice Burger noted that the district "court held a hearing at which extensive evidence was introduced concerning the nature of the secular instruction offered in the Roman Catholic schools whose teachers would be eligible for salary assistance under the Act. Although the court found that concern for religious values does not necessarily affect the content of secular subjects, it also found that the parochial school system was 'an integral part of the religious mission of the Catholic Church.'" Lemon v. Kurtzman, 403 U.S. 602, 609 (1971). The district court's discussion of the characteristics of the parochial school system is reported in Di Censo v. Robinson, 316 F. Supp. 112, 116-18 (D.R.I. 1970).

[+]Editor's Note: 413 U.S. 455 (1973).

*Editor's Note: James Michael Lee, Catholic Education and the Western World (Notre Dame, Ind.: University of Notre Dame Press, 1967).

nihan tuition tax credit proposal, the Moynihan baby BEOG proposal, the Coons voucher plan, the Jencks voucher plan) has in any way attempted to prohibit publicly funded schools from using religious and ideological factors in selecting faculty. This is a crucial point because the faculty in the program that you assemble determines who attends the school.

Finally, Mr. Dershowitz alluded to the IRS attempt to move in on private schools that, in its opinion, are not adequately racially balanced. Obviously a black Baptist child or a Chicano child is not terribly attracted to a yeshiva run in the traditional manner. This highlights the fact that where the administrators of a nonpublic school wish to have a program which promotes a particular faith or a particular ideology, they will do so. If they will be doing so at public expense, can we do in private schools at public expense what we are forbidden by the Constitution to do in public schools?

ROBERT DESTRO, GENERAL COUNSEL, CATHOLIC LEAGUE FOR RELIGIOUS AND CIVIL RIGHTS: My question takes off on Mr. Deorr's final comment. The Supreme Court has repeatedly focused on the ideological or value-laden content of nonpublic education. If one of the purposes of education is the transmission of fundamental values, to what extent have the courts and the Justice Department addressed the question of value transmission in the public schools? This question, it seems to me, is a very important one, especially given the recent spate of decisions which would keep voluntary religious groups off of the campus because of their value-laden content.

PROFESSOR SCALIA: I think that Mr. Destro has raised an important question. As I mentioned in my essay, the word "religion" is only used once in the First Amendment, but the problem to which Mr. Destro refers has been nicely avoided by giving the word a different meaning under the Establishment Clause than it has under the Free Exercise Clause. As applied to the Free Exercise Clause, "religion" means any deeply held, conscientious belief, whether it is theistic or not; it can be ethical humanism, secular humanism, or whatever. But as applied to the Establishment Clause, "religion" means only theistic religion. So there is no problem with establishing secular humanism or any other deeply held, conscientious belief in public schools. Only theistic religion or something very close to theistic religion (such as Transcendental Meditation) comes in for disqualification. Once you adopt that dichotomy between the two parts of the same amendment, it is easy to get where we are.

PROFESSOR BERNS: We have to recognize the fact that there are questions that arise that show the absolute impossibility of standing firm with both parts of the First Amendment. For example, Sherbert v. Verner involved a Seventh Day Adventist who refused to work on Saturday, the Sabbath as she understands it. She was required to work by her employer, a laundry owner, as I recall, on Saturday, because the laundry works on Saturday. She refused to work on Saturday, so she was discharged by the laundry. She then applied for unemployment compensation, and she was told by the unemployment compensation board that she could not have that benefit because she had failed, "without good cause," to accept the work that her employer had offered her. That case went all the way to the Supreme Court, and the Court divided, seven to two. Two of the Justices stood firm on the Establishment Clause, indicating that if South Carolina permitted this woman to get unemployment compensation, it would, in a certain sense, be recognizing Seventh Day Adventists as an established religion under the Constitution of the United States. The other Justices, standing firm on the Free Exercise clause, quite properly indicated that if the state refused to give her unemployment compensation, it would be penalizing her precisely because of her religion.

A similar dilemma of sorts arises with respect to chaplains in the armed services. If the government employs chaplains, some raise an Establishment question. If the government refuses to employ chaplains, others would say that the government is denying the free exercise of religion because it would be denying the sacraments to someone whom it put in Iceland or wherever.

FR. BLUM: First, I would like to state that I think that those of us who favor some form of public support for nonpublic schools have made a big mistake in allowing the absolute separationists to define the controversy in terms of an establishment of religion. To quote a well known phrase, "He who defines the terms of controversy has the controversy half won." So I would urge that we focus on the more basic question of parental rights in the education of their children under the First Amendment.

Second, I would like Mr. Wilson to comment on the "pervasively sectarian" character of some Protestant colleges. One Southern Baptist college that I am aware of in Arkansas, for example, receives grants from the federal government, and it requires nine hours in religion and seven chapel credit hours. A chapel credit is earned by a student, through seven of his or her eight semesters, by attending chapel one hour a week. The Supreme Court, however, has declined to adopt the view that a profile of these sorts of colleges is of any validity or relevance to constitutional analysis. It is only when it talks about elementary and secondary education that it says: "The school is sectarian." Yet in my experience, many Protestant colleges—and I do not say this critically but with commendation—are far more sectarian than Catholic elementary and secondary schools. I would like Mr. Wilson to comment on this observation.

MR. WILSON: Based on my own experience, Father, I agree with you. In fact, we represented Ouachita University; and the facts you state are correct. As a result of the Tilton case, a sharp line has been drawn between higher education and the elementary and secondary schools. And subsequent to Tilton the Court has just never questioned that line. There are any number of colleges, including those involved in the Blanton case in Tennessee, which would fit the profile of the "pervasively sectarian" college, yet aid programs benefiting those schools and the students in those schools have been held valid.* It is not a rational or logical distinction, but the distinction has been made.

PROFESSOR SCALIA: As I understand the situation, the only thing the Supreme Court has said is that statutes are facially invalid with respect to elementary and secondary schools without the necessity of a school-by-school inquiry, whereas with respect to colleges and universities, they are facially valid. That is not to say that if Mr. Dershowitz or somebody else drags a particular college into court, seeking to prove that with respect to that particular college, there is intensive religious training or whatever, the aid will not be declared unconstitutional as applied in that case.

MR. WILSON: If I may add just one point, the facts recited by Father Blum are in the record of the case in which the Court upheld an aid program. And therefore I do not think aid for church-related colleges and universities is presently a serious problem.

MR. HAMMOND: I think that it is important to observe that the distinction that the Court has drawn between colleges and elementary and secondary schools has been made on the premise that colleges are not as pervasively sectarian as church-related elementary and secondary schools. This does not mean that church-related colleges may not have a very strong religious orientation. All that this distinction means, and all the Court has said, is that it has chosen to draw the line at the college level. You can have a classroom and classes that are nonreligious in nature. A chemistry class is a chemistry class is a chemistry class at the college level. In an-

---

*Editor's Note: In Americans United for Separation of Church and State v. Blanton, 443 F. Supp. 97 (M.D. Tenn.), summarily aff'd., 434 U.S. 803 (1977), the record disclosed that "some, but not all, of the private schools whose students benefited from [a tuition assistance] program are operated for religious purposes, with religious requirements for students and faculty and are admittedly permeated with the dogma of the sponsoring religious organization." 433 F. Supp. at 100. Nevertheless, the court upheld a Tennessee program that provided tuition assistance enabling college students to attend the college of their choice. See also Smith v. Bd. of Governors, 429 F. Supp. 871 (W.D.N.C.), summarily aff'd., 434 U.S. 803 (1977).

swer to Father Blum, I would add that the fact that religion is a required course, the fact that people go to chapel every day, the fact that a good number of courses are taught by people who are affiliated with the religion, in the Supreme Court's analysis, wouldn't invalidate aid to institutions of higher education or to students attending them.

MRS. MAE DUGAN: I have a question for Mr. Hammond. How is it we who feel that we're discriminated against in the private sector because we're denied any benefits from the taxes that we pay for education cannot ask that our civil rights be defended by the Justice Department, which is so busy defending so many other types of human right violations?

MR. HAMMOND: I thought that Judge Mikva answered the question well earlier in the discussion. But let me take a little bit of a different stab at it. I imagine it's a pretty good bet that the Supreme Court is not any time soon going to hold that your freedom of choice with respect to where you send your kids to school comprehends a right to have that choice supported by the government. We really don't need to look very far back down the road to find a pretty good analogy. The Court just decided Harris v. McRae,* an abortion funding case, in which the Court, in effect, said: "We have recognized a fundamental right of a woman to control her own body and to have an abortion, if she so chooses. But we do not think the government has any duty to pay for the exercise of this right." If the Court reached this conclusion in that kind of case, I do not believe there is any doubt in the world that the Court would reach the same conclusion if the Department of Justice were to take the position in court that there is a constitutional right for you to have funding to support your right to send your child to a private school. I think we would be laughed out of court.

PROFESSOR BERNS: I wanted to make the same point that Mr. Hammond just made about the opponents to the Hyde Amendment. Their position, of course, was that for financial reasons they were being denied the exercise of a right that is protected by the Constitution. If that position were to be upheld, then since Pierce v. Society of Sisters held that one has a constitutional right to send children to private schools, it would likewise follow that one would have a constitutional right to get the funding for private education. And I am sure that the opponents of the Hyde Amendment would not like that result.

MR. DUFFY: I would like to follow up a little bit with what Mrs. Dugan just said. Since the Supreme Court has thrown prayer and Bi-

---

*Editor's Note: 448 U.S. 297 (1980).

ble reading out of the public school, I would like to know why this society cannot protect the rights of an individual Baptist, whose entire life style, concept of life, philosophy of life is absolutely 180 degrees diametrically opposed to what's being taught in public education, as fully as the rights of those who did not want to sit through a minute of prayer or five minutes of Bible reading? I would like Mr. Hammond to respond to that.

MR. HAMMOND: Well, I have tried to respond to that question. Let me try again. If what you're saying is that by not funding private education, the government is not protecting your right of religion, I think as a constitutional matter that is just not correct. Your right is one that you can freely exercise. The fact that the government has decided to have public education and to make taxpayers pay for it, whether they have children or not, and whether their children attend those schools or not, is simply a different matter.

MR. DUFFY: I don't question that everybody should pay for education. I am willing to pay my share for education for all children, even after the time when all of my children are out of school. Let's put the financing question aside for the moment. Could a Baptist, who does not believe in sex education, or who has a very strict dress code, go to court and prohibit the state educational system from teaching things that he conscientiously objects to? If the courts allowed such a person to prevail, it would absolutely destroy public education. There would be nothing that could be taught, because education cannot be value neutral, it cannot be valueless, it cannot be religiously neutral. Our contention is that the only way that society can provide for a religiously-neutral education is to allow parents with various philosophical-religious beliefs to choose where their children are going to be educated and allow them to pay for that out of the general operating budget.

MR. DESTRO: I would like to say first that I agree with Mr. Hammond and Professor Berns with respect to their analysis of the McRae case, the Hyde Amendment case, with respect to constitutional entitlements. In McRae the Supreme Court was at pains to make the point that the decision of such matters is properly a legislative judgment. While one may not have a constitutional right to an entitlement, the legislature could decide to fund the exercise of that right. There were people on both sides of the McRae case who felt very strongly about it. People opposed to the amendment felt that the amendment impeded the free exercise of their religiously ground decision to terminate a pregnancy. And people favoring the Hyde Amendment felt that they should have a religious right not to pay for abortions with public funds. Given the deference by the Court to the Congress in the face of considerable religious controvery, why would not the same kind of analysis apply to the Justice Department's analysis of one of these tuition aid bills?

MR. HAMMOND: I think that if you ask the question a little differently, if you ask whether there is anything that Congress can do to provide funds, to provide assistance for those who wish to send their children to nonpublic schools, I would say that is a productive question and I think the answer to that question may very well be yes. But I do not think that the Court can be expected to approve tuition tax credit legislation of the kind that we have seen in the last couple of years, or the proposal to amend the BEOG program to include students in elementary and secondary schools. Other proposals, such as an across-the-board voucher system, or a scholarship system for all children might fare better. Frankly, I think that the voucher proposal is a ball closer to the foul line, but it is a possibility. I think that the people who support public aid for nonpublic education make a big mistake if they think that there is still a likelihood that one of these days Congress is going to pass a tuition tax credit bill or is going to pass a baby BEOG program that is going to be upheld by the Supreme Court. I think that is just folly. It is not going to happen any time soon. And time and energy are much more productively spent pursuing these other kinds of alternatives.

PROFESSOR SCALIA: The former may not happen soon; that is, the 96th Congress will probably not pass tuition tax credits. That seems to be the case. But I still think that we do not know enough from the Court's cases to predict confidently what the Court would do with such legislation, if Congress chose to enact it. Once again, all one can really say is that the Supreme Court is not, on the basis of its prior decisions, about to uphold state tuition tax credits, the benefit of which go anywhere from 85 to 95 percent to schools operated by one religious group. To proceed from the only decisions we have on this matter to the confident conclusion that a more broadly based program enacted by the federal Congress will clearly be invalidated is, I think, a great leap of faith.

DR. JOSEPH SKEHAN, PRESIDENT, NATIONAL ASSOCIATION OF LAITY: I was somewhat amazed, I must say, with the idea expressed both in this discussion and in the earlier one that the problem of entanglement was not clear. I think it fair to say the United States Supreme Court may not be overly helpful in all of its discussion of the historical background of this issue, but I do not think that any of us sitting here could fail to understand the dangers of entanglement of the government with religion. That religion might become a glutinous thing, or less than a healthful thing in a mixed society is perfectly possible, and I think we have to realize that danger. On the other hand, our community, the Catholic community, has prospered in this country to an extraordinary degree precisely because of the concern of all Americans for preserving a distance between church and state. And I think it is a little unfair to be quite as critical of some of our major civic institutions as I think some of the remarks have been.

PROFESSOR SCALIA: I think most of those comments were addressed to me, especially the one about being critical of our major social institutions. I suppose that refers to my comments about Supreme Court opinions. To quote Little Abner: "I loves and respects the United States Supreme Court." But that doesn't mean that I have to find coherence and consistency in opinions that don't contain it. And in pointing to what I think is a pattern of incoherence and inconsistency, I am merely demanding that the Court live up to our high expectations of it.

As to entanglement, my point was not that the principle of nonentanglement is not a valid principle. Of course it is. The point I was making is that the application of that principle is not at all clear. Entanglement is an evil and should be avoided. But at what point do you reach entanglement of an unconstitutional degree? The Supreme Court opinions aren't very helpful on that question, nor does the word "entanglement" itself convey much content.

MS. PATRICIA M. LINES, STAFF ATTORNEY, LAW AND EDUCATION CENTER, EDUCATION COMMISSION OF THE STATES: The Law and Education Center was formed for the primary purpose of practicing preventive law for our constitutency. Specifically this means that we will seek to advise state policy makers--governors, legislators and educators--and local school officials of the possible legal and constitutional problems of proposed programs in education prior to implementation, with a hope that policies can be modified where there are serious constitutional and legal problems, and as a result, states will experience fewer problems with litigation following implementation of legislation. Private school aid is an area where we feel preventive law is appropriate. Although litigation seems inevitable in this area, a state could work towards reducing the volume of litigation attendent on any new private school aid program.

The Law and Education Center is in the process of studying the best ways to practice preventive law, and at this time, we have arrived at a few preliminary thoughts that we will test with time. We believe that the role of the attorney practicing preventive law, just as the role of a physician practicing preventive medicine, is partly educational. Another aspect of this special kind of law practice is that it helps remove the attorney from undue influence over the shaping of public policy. Conversely, where the legal community fails to explain the reasoning behind certain decisions as to constitutionality or unconstitutionality of a law to the non-legal community, attorneys can become gatekeepers to policy decisions, by unnecessarily frightening decisionmakers into a restricted set of choices on the false assumption that only those choices are capable of withstanding court scrutiny. Usually there is a wide range of legitimate approaches to a problem. By explaining the basis for court decisions affecting programs, lawyers enable non-lawyers to participate fully in future policymaking. The resulting public policy is more likely to reflect the product of many minds trained in many disciplines.

During this discussion, for example, Mr. Wilson and Professor Berns provided careful analysis of specific Supreme Court cases. This open-ended analysis of specific Supreme Court cases provides non-lawyers with a basis for understanding the various policy options. The attorneys do not present the single solution that they prefer, with the implicit suggestion that this is the only way to approach the problem. Rather, they are providing the listener with information, and analysis of what the Court has done, permitting non-lawyers to help invent alternative solutions. On the other hand, as much as I appreciate the presentation of Professor Scalia, I would like to provide a different perspective and make some observations about weaknesses that I suspect are in his argument.

First, I doubt that the cases involving greater deference to congressional enactments concerning aliens would have any persuasive power with the Court when dealing with public aid to nonpublic schools. The Court in the alien cases saw regulation of admission of foreigners to this country as a traditional federal role, but there is ample indication that the Court views education as a traditional state role.

Second, although the argument based on the clause giving Congress power to implement the Fourteenth Amendment appears logically correct, the Court could also logically restrict the implementation clause to equal protection and procedural due process cases, on grounds that those parts of the Bill of Rights (such as freedom of religion) that are incorporated into the Fourteenth Amendment through the due process clause can be distinguished from those rights that are explicit in the Fourteenth Amendment. This would be as logical as, for example, applying different standards of review for cases involving race, sex or age discrimination in equal protection cases.

Finally, Professor Scalia argues that a federal aid program would appear more neutral because the percentage of parochial school children nationally would be lower than it has been in states where aid programs have been attempted. On this point, one would have to examine carefully the cases that Scalia cited, for it is my impression that the Court's reliance on the proportion of parochial to secular private school children has been incidental, and that other elements of challenged programs were more critical to the decision.

I make these observations in order to balance Professor Scalia's proposal somewhat, and to remind us all that it would be foolish to assume that simply _any_ federal program would be constitutional. Also I would not give up on the effort to design aid programs at the state level. In sum, I believe that there are numerous approaches to the issue at hand that could pass constitutional muster, and that non-lawyers should be given adequate instruction in the legal principles (and I agree with Mr. Wilson and Mr. Hammond that there are coherent principles) to permit them to participate in the ultimate policy decision. The more people who do take the time to scrutinize these principles carefully, the more incentive there will be for sound proposals for future policy in this area.